The Short Oxford Hist

MW01038748

Old Regime France

The Short Oxford History of France

General Editor: William Doyle

The Short Oxford History of France

General Editor: William Doyle

Old Regime France

1648–1788

Edited by William Doyle

OXFORD
UNIVERSITY PRESS

OXFORD
UNIVERSITY PRESS

Great Clarendon Street, Oxford OX2 6DP

Oxford University Press is a department of the University of Oxford.
It furthers the University's objective of excellence in research, scholarship,
and education by publishing worldwide in

Oxford New York

Auckland Cape Town Dar es Salaam Hong Kong Karachi Kuala Lumpur
Madrid Melbourne Mexico City Nairobi New Delhi Shanghai Taipei Toronto

With offices in

Argentina Austria Brazil Chile Czech Republic France Greece
Guatemala Hungary Italy Japan Poland Portugal
Singapore South Korea Switzerland Thailand Turkey Ukraine Vietnam

Oxford is a registered trade mark of Oxford University Press
in the UK and in certain other countries

Published in the United States
by Oxford University Press Inc., New York

© Oxford University Press, 2001

Database right Oxford University Press (maker)

First published 2001

British Library Cataloguing in Publication Data

Data available

Library of Congress Cataloging in Publication Data

Data available

ISBN 978-0-19-873130-6 (hbk)
ISBN 978-0-19-873129-0 (pbk)

Typeset in Minion
by RefineCatch Limited, Bungay, Suffolk
Printed in Great Britain
on acid-free paper by
Biddles Ltd., King's Lynn, Norfolk

General Editor's Preface

During the twentieth century, French historians revolutionized the study of history itself, opening up countless new subjects, problems, and approaches to the past. Much of this imaginative energy was focused on the history of their own country—its economy, its society, its culture, its memories. In the century's later years this exciting atmosphere inspired increasing numbers of outsiders to work on French themes, so that, more than for any other country, writing the history of France has become an international enterprise.

This series seeks to reflect these developments. Each volume is coordinated by an editor widely recognised as a historian of France. Each editor in turn has brought together a group of contributors to present particular aspects of French history, identifying the major themes and features in the light of the most recent scholarship. All the teams are international, reflecting the fact that there are now probably more university historians of France outside the country than in it. Nor is the outside world neglected in the content of each volume, where French activity abroad receives special coverage. Apart from this, however, the team responsible for each volume has chosen its own priorities, presenting what it sees as the salient characteristics of its own period. Some have chosen to offer stimulating reinterpretations of established themes; others have preferred to explore long-neglected or entirely new topics which they believe now deserve emphasis. All the volumes have an introduction and conclusion by their editor, and include an outline chronology, plentiful maps, and a succinct guide to further reading in English.

Running from Clovis to Chirac, the seven volumes in the series offer a lively, concise, and authoritative guide to the history of a country and a culture which have been central to the whole development of Europe, and often widely influential in the world beyond.

William Doyle

University of Bristol

Contents

3 Culture and religion   78
David A. Bell

4 France overseas   105
Pierre H. Boulle and D. Gillian Thompson

5 The state and political culture   139
Julian Swann

List of Contributors

DAVID A. BELL is Professor of History at Johns Hopkins University, Baltimore. He is the author of *Lawyers and Citizens: The Making of a Political Elite in Old Regime France* (1994), and *The National and the Sacred: The Origins of Nationalism in Eighteenth Century France* (forthcoming, 2001). He has co-edited *Raison universelle et culture nationale au siècle des lumières* (1999), and contributed to numerous scholarly journals.

GAIL BOSSENGA is Associate Professor of History at the University of Kansas (Lawrence). She is the author *of The Politics of Privilege: Old Regime and Revolution in Lille* (1991) and is currently working on a book on the institutional origins of the French Revolution.

PIERRE H. BOULLE teaches Early Modern European History at McGill University, Montreal. He has published numerous articles on colonial issues and is currently working on a monograph on Black residents in France during the eighteenth century, as well as a series of essays on the origins of race in early modern France. He is the author of the article 'Race' in the forthcoming *Oxford Encyclopedia of the Enlightenment.*

WILLIAM DOYLE has been Professor of History at the University of Bristol since 1986, and is a Fellow of the British Academy. He is the author of *Origins of the French Revolution* (3rd edition, 1999), *The Oxford History of the French Revolution* (1989), *Venality. The Sale of Offices in Eighteenth Century France* (1996), and *Jansenism* (2000).

JOËL FÉLIX is Reader in French History at the University of Reading. He is the author of *Finances et politique au siècle des lumières: le ministère L'Averdy, 1763–1768* (1999) and, in collaboration with F. Bayard and P. Hamon, *Dictionnaire des surintendants et des contrôleurs généraux des finances du XVIe siècle à la Révolution française* (2000).

MUNRO PRICE is Senior Lecturer in Modern European History at the University of Bradford. His main research interest is the political history of late eighteenth-century and Revolutionary France. He is the author of two books, *Preserving the monarchy: the comte de Vergennes, 1774–1787* (1995) and (with John Hardman) *Louis XVI and the comte de Vergennes: correspondence, 1774–1787* (1998), as well as several articles. His next book will be a study of the French monarchy and the Revolution.

JULIAN SWANN lectures on Early Modern European History at Birkbeck College, University of London. He is the author of *Politics and the Parlement of Paris under Louis XV, 1754–1774* (1995), and is currently writing a history of the Estates General of Burgundy, 1661–1790.

D. GILLIAN THOMPSON is Professor and Chair of the Department of History at the University of New Brunswick in Canada and a specialist on the institutional history and prosopography of the Jesuit order in France and French overseas territory during the eighteenth century. She recently published a monograph on the Breton Jesuits under the suppression of 1762–1814. In preparing the sections on New France in the chapter on France overseas, she received advice from the late Louise Dechêne of McGill University.

Introduction

William Doyle

The kingdom of France was one of the longest established political entities in Europe. Over the 1,100 years since the Frankish chief Clovis became a Christian after leading his horde to colonize the ruins of Roman Gaul, the men who ruled from the Île-de-France had often wielded the dominant power in western Europe. But for much of the century after 1559 their authority had been fragile.

One king had been accidentally killed in his prime, two others assassinated. During three minorities, government was in the hands of foreign-born regent-queens, and turbulent magnate clans had jockeyed for dominance, often inviting outside assistance. Religious civil war complicated everything intermittently between 1562 and 1629. When in the 1630s a triumphant prince of the Catholic church, cardinal Richelieu, was able at last to turn his master Louis XIII's energies outwards to intervene against the Habsburgs in the Thirty Years War, the heavier taxes imposed to pay for these adventures were resisted by a wave of popular rebellion. Between 1635 and 1660 there were no less than 282 popular uprisings. And in the very depth of all this turmoil, the patience of yet another hard-pressed group snapped.

Richelieu's foreign ambitions had been paid for as much by borrowing as by weightier taxation. It took the peculiar form of venality—the sale and manipulation of royal offices. Under these arrangements, the king received money in return for granting tenure, heredity, and free disposal of their offices to his judges and other servants. Further monies could be raised by granting them new privileges, or threatening to withdraw or diminish ones already enjoyed. But this highly successful way of tapping the wealth of the king's richer subjects was stretched to the limits by a war which went on long beyond the deaths of Richelieu (1642) and Louis XIII (1643).

Louis XIV was just 5 when he became king, and for the next eighteen years royal authority was wielded for him by his mother Anne of Austria and another cardinal-minister, Mazarin. But when in 1648 they attempted to blackmail yet more cash advances from the office-holders of the judiciary, the magistrates of Paris exploded into defiance, demanding the revocation of most of the expedients by which war had been financed since the 1630s. The populace of the capital soon came onto the streets to support them; and by the end of the year the queen, the cardinal and the boy king had been driven from Paris by a revolt that would be remembered as the Fronde.

It lasted for almost five years, and developed into a civil war as magnates and their retinues re-emerged as rivals of divided and discredited royal authority. As in the previous century, some great lords were quite happy to encourage intervention by the hostile Spaniards. But the magistrates whose protests had triggered the Fronde had never dreamed or intended that their defiance should have such results. As men who had soberly invested capital and family ambitions in the acquisition of royal offices, what they sought was stability and an end to fiscal blackmail; and certainly not the complete collapse of authority. They did not welcome the disturbing sight of Paris and other great cities like Bordeaux in the grip of fickle mobs, any more than they liked the narcissistic posturings of beribboned princes who flaunted their contempt for judges 'more loaded', as Richelieu himself put it, 'with Latin than with lands', while cheerfully inviting the king's enemies to violate his dominions. Soon, therefore, the officers of the monarch were seeking to mend their fences with those who controlled his person, even if this meant the reviled and rapacious Italian adventurer Mazarin. After 1651, when Louis XIV formally reached his majority, the cardinal could be conveniently accepted as the king's chosen instrument rather than a usurper of regency powers. Conflicting ambitions and personal bickering meanwhile kept princely and noble warlords divided, while their willingness to let the Spaniards ravage frontier provinces sapped any wider support they might have hoped for. By the end of 1652 the Fronde was petering out. The king's coronation at Reims in 1654 was a symbolic celebration, as much perhaps in hope as in certainty, that this time of troubles was at last over.

The costs of the Fronde were spectacular: a ten-year prolongation of the anti-Habsburg war that seemed almost won in 1648; massive devastation of provinces north and east of Paris from Flanders down to Burgundy; huge disruptions in the economic and social life of the capital and some of the greater provincial cities. It took several generations to repair demographic ravages. Yet many provinces and towns remained relatively unaffected; and Louis XIV gained more subjects in Habsburg provinces acquired at the peace of the Pyrenees in 1659 than the upheavals of his minority had deprived him of. He and his royal successors down to 1792 would rule by far the most populous realms west of the steppes. Their main problem would be marshalling their resources to achieve their dynastic and international ambitions.

Their natural advantages included a vast and varied economy, substantial reserves of sophisticated manufacturing skills, and the seagoing population of a long coastline, well placed to exploit the promise of overseas wealth in the Americas and beyond the Cape. Much thought and energy would be devoted to building upon these assets over the next 130 years; although profound disagreements about the best approach would produce sometimes crippling inconsistencies. Consistent throughout, however, was the conviction that the State (which even then took a capital letter in French) was the best judge of economic advantage and improvement; and little would be undertaken without the assurance of government support or approval. These reflexes in turn stemmed from one of the most deep-seated instincts of French political culture: an overwhelming reverence for authority.

For the domestic upheavals of the preceding hundred years (still showing signs of continuing as aftershocks of the Fronde echoed down the late 1650s) were not so much a defiance of authority as the result of its absence. Nobody would look back with pride or nostalgia upon those generations of turbulence. Only the later years of Henri IV, the first decade of the century when a self-confident and uncontested king had promised glory and stability before a fanatical assassin struck, would be remembered as a brief golden interlude. The ritual trial and execution across the Channel of Charles I in 1649, meanwhile, was seen as a warning of what might happen if subjects usurped the right to rule. So that when the young Louis XIV, after surviving a near-fatal illness in 1658, assumed personal responsibility for government on the death of Mazarin, there would be no resistance. France sighed with relief to have once more a monarch ready and able to assume an authority that was his alone for the taking. Only two generations later would doubts begin to arise over the costs of Louis XIV's relentless pursuit of aggrandize-ment. Even then only Protestants, with nothing to lose after very popular attempts by the king to eliminate them entirely as reviled reminders of the century of disorder, would carry their discontent to the point of outright rebellion. Neither of his two successors would be confronted—at least until 1789—by anything more serious than the localized rioting which could always be expected at times of economic disruption.

It was not simply that the French liked their kings to rule as well as reign. The instruments by which monarchs would deploy their authority were now so much more powerful than those available before the wars of religion. The sale of offices, though expanded and exploited to breaking point by 1648, had at the same time harnessed the energies and investments of the socially ambitious to royal service rather than that of magnate clans. After the Fronde, office-holders were treated with more restraint and respect, and they responded loyally. The war effort since the 1630s had also led to the proliferation of intendants, executive agents with wide fiscal and administrative powers, untenured commissioners whose careers depended on results. Office-holders hated them as tyrannical rivals, and one of the first demands of the Frondeurs was for their general recall. Magnates and regional power-brokers resented them too, and in the face of such unanimity the intendants were indeed withdrawn. But even before the Fronde was over they were slipping back into quiet prov-inces, and would soon become the administrative backbone of the monarchy. Above all, perhaps, the king now could rely on the coercive power of a large standing army. When peace had finally come to Henri IV's kingdom in 1598, he disbanded all but 8,000 of his troops: after the peace of the Pyrenees, Louis XIV retained around 70,000 under arms. These soldiers were not primarily a domestic police force, but they were the ultimate safeguard against any breakdown in obedience, the last sanction of a state that was increasingly to define itself by its monopoly of legitimate violence. They also needed a numerous body of officers to command them, and Louis XIV and both his successors took care to ensure that most of these positions went to noblemen. In this way the kingdom's traditional warrior elite soon became committed, just like the holders of venal offices, to active collaboration in upholding royal authority. Not until the later eighteenth century would the confidence of all these willing collaborators in absolute monarchy begin to erode.

Military defeat would be the trigger. Although Louis XIV would make few permanent territorial gains after 1685, earlier successes, followed by the dynastic triumph of securing the Spanish Succession, left the house of Bourbon and its servants with the sense that they were the natural arbiters of Europe. Had France not been entrusted in 1648 with guaranteeing the peace of Westphalia which had brought the Thirty Years War to an end? Only forty years after the great king's death was the confidence he had bequeathed dented. But then, hoodwinked by the traditional Habsburg foe in Vienna into an alliance which precipitated the Seven Years War, Louis XV found his armies humiliated by the upstart Prussians, his navies destroyed by the British, and the makings of a worldwide overseas empire shattered. The efforts required to carry on this fruitless struggle strained the resources of the kingdom, and in its aftermath a wide-ranging inquest began in which no aspect of French culture and society, no economic or political assumption, went unchallenged. These years saw the fullest emergence of values called 'enlightened' by their adherents—rational, utilitarian, particularly hostile to the power and influence of the established Church, but critical of every established attitude and institution that could be seen as impeding the progress of human happiness and welfare. They met with bitter resistance at every level, and the result was a generation of intellectual turmoil. Institutional turmoil too: the reaction of Louis XV's and Louis XVI's ministers to the reverses of the 1750s and 1760s was to redouble their efforts to restructure the kingdom's institutions along whatever lines seemed most likely to restore its power and prestige—including 'enlightened' ones. That meant challenging the entrenched positions and privileges of the very elites on whose support absolute monarchy had established its authority in the aftermath of the Fronde. Yet when in the 1770s French diplomacy kept Europe at peace while assembling an anti-British coalition to wreak spectacular revenge for the defeats of the previous war, tried and traditional ways seemed vindicated. A generation of tinkering with change seemed like a frivolous and pointless detour. The costs of victory, however, and the efforts required to meet them, proved even more crippling than the burdens of defeat, and this time absolute monarchy and its underpinnings would fall apart under the strain.

Nobody foresaw or predicted the cataclysmic breakdown that would follow. Even those later blamed for it—declared enemies of the church like Voltaire, or critics of established society and political arrangements like Rousseau—would have been horrified by what occurred barely more than a decade after the death of both in 1778. To write the history of what later revolutionaries would call the *ancien régime* as if that future could be foreseen fatally distorts any sense of how living before it must have felt; whether it was the lost 'sweetness of living' of later aristocratic memory, or the hopeless hardship in which the majority of French people passed their lives. This volume ends, therefore, when the Revolution to come was still unsuspected, and its chapters say little to anticipate later events. It covers perhaps the longest period of calm, internally at least, in French history; a time between two ages of shocking upheaval, when Paris was widely regarded as the heart of European civilization, and the style of the French king a model to emulate. French was the language of educated Europe, even if a significant proportion of the kingdom's own inhabitants barely spoke or understood it. Nobody expected any of this to change in any fundamental way, and if the two monarchs who succeeded to Louis XIV's name and authority lacked the presence, stamina, and professional commitment that had made him so formidable, that was part of the lottery of monarchy. It cast no serious doubt on the viability of the most glittering throne in the western world. The collapse, when it came, was all the more shocking, and revolution was the trauma produced by that shock. Its sources must, of course, be sought in the world before the cataclysm. But this volume is about that world on its own terms.

1

The economy

Joël Félix

Translated by David A. Bell

For the school of classical liberal thought which arose in France in the middle of the eighteenth century, the goal of enlightened government was to substitute a rational economic order for an older, inefficient economic system. In this older system, so the liberals claimed, the dominant principles were those of the royal financiers, who, to help their sovereign slake his thirst for grandeur, were plundering their country's wealth through a multitude of unnecessary taxes, internal customs arrangements, and cumbersome regulations. In contrast, the liberals held forth the promise of a more harmonious society, and of a resolutely modern state which would be able to reform the nation's economic structures by allowing private initiative and the free play of the market to generate an endless spiral of wealth. The king would thus accomplish what he had been set on earth to do: preserve his country's health and his subjects' happiness.

Although not entirely false, this polemical contrast between two supposedly rival and incommensurate systems does not provide a completely accurate account of the economy of the old regime, or help fully to explain the crisis which overcame it in 1787. For in fact these two systems, with all their respective advantages and disadvantages, coexisted alongside one another. From Louis XIV's chief minister Colbert to Necker, his successor a century later, the economic structures of the kingdom evolved in response to changing economic conditions, resulting from the development of the state, the monetarization of the economy, and the multiplication of forms of exchange. Nor did royal ministers always act in precise accordance with prevailing economic theories, although, from 1750 onwards, successive controllers-general of finances consulted with the so-called physiocrats, who hoped to modernize the economy. And while liberal economists generally highlighted France's weaknesses and opportunities for development, the country nonetheless managed to remain one of Europe's demographic, economic, and financial superpowers.

It was this difference between theory and practice which led Louis XVI to take umbrage at a reform project written by his own controller-general, Turgot, in 1776. 'One does not have to be very learned,' the king wrote in the margins of the project, 'to judge that this report has been written ... with the purpose of condemning venerable institutions, which the author claims to be the product of centuries of ignorance and barbarism, as if the reigns of my three most recent predecessors could be equated with those of the dark ages ... Europe will hardly be persuaded that these three reigns were times of barbarism and ignorance; Europe is more likely to be persuaded these three monarchs were responsible for much of the civilisation that it presently enjoys.'[1] This exchange between a king open to reform, and the minister who symbolized the failure of liberal reform under the old regime, makes clear that such reforms as occurred in France's economic structures before 1789 owed less to the ideas of economists than to the kingdom's absolutist heritage. The reign of Louis XIV had marked the triumph of governmental practices firmly linked to a particular vision of the social and economic order, a combination which allowed the Bourbon monarchy to overcome domestic dissent and foreign challenges alike, and to establish itself as one of Europe's leading powers. The economic and financial crisis which overwhelmed the old regime was not the inevitable consequence of failure to reform a static and unchanging economy. Rather, it derived from the difficulties that arose when the French attempted to separate politics from economic and social considerations.

---

[1] Jean-Louis Soulavie, *Mémoires historiques et politiques du règne de Louis XVI, depuis son mariage jusqu'à sa mort* (6 vols., Paris, 1801), iii. 147–8.

Agricultural archaism, agricultural modernization

The most immediate concern of the majority of the king's subjects was to have enough to eat, whether by producing food themselves, or, as was increasingly the case, by earning enough to buy all or a part of their daily bread. And at the time, daily bread literally constituted the single most important part of the diet for most people—the average family of five needed more than 2 kilograms of bread per day—not because of any peculiarly French taste for carbohydrates, but because bread in these quantities was more nourishing and much less expensive than meat or fresh fish. Depending on the quality of the flour, 1.5kg of bread provided between 3,000 and 3,500 calories per day—adequate nourishment for an adult engaged in physical labour.

The tyranny of bread—which even in normal times ate up at least half of most family budgets—was not absolute, however. Diets varied according to location. On the coasts, the population had a high intake of seafood. In Brittany, buckwheat often replaced wheat, while in mountain areas chestnut trees, which were nicknamed 'bread trees', fed both humans and farm animals. Cereals were often consumed in the form of porridge, which could also contain vegetables, butter or oil, and sometimes a piece of meat or fat. This traditional meal could be complemented by cheese in cattle-raising regions, or the dried fish prescribed by the church for Fridays, not to mention fruit in season, and a swig of wine, beer, or cider, again depending on the location.

In the absence of modern machinery capable of increasing agricultural productivity, the lion's share of the economy remained agricultural by necessity. On the eve of the Revolution, 80 per cent of the population lived in the countryside and worked, to one extent or another, on the land. Nonetheless, at any one time, only 20 to 25 per cent of the kingdom's surface area was actually employed in wheat-growing. Thanks to a lack of animals, and therefore of fertilizer, cereal cultivation, which exhausted the soil, required leaving the land to lie fallow one year out of three in the north, and one year out of two in the south. On the least hospitable soils, especially in the mountains and in the hedgerow country of the west, cereal products could only be grown one or two years out of ten.

The king's subjects may have devoted most of their time to producing cereals—and also wine, which had an important nutritional and symbolic role—but they rarely owned all the land they farmed. Between a quarter and a half of all land, and a far greater proportion of the highest quality farmland, belonged to the two privileged orders: the nobility (20–25 per cent), and the clergy (6–15 per cent). The middle classes, who often enjoyed tax exemptions for their rural holdings, possessed another 20 to 30 per cent. The rest of the land, 40–45 per cent, belonged to a peasantry which also paid most of the kingdom's various forms of taxation: feudal and seigneurial rights, the church's tithe, and royal taxes.

Given these basic facts, it is easy to understand why agriculture has so often been considered the principal evidence for France's economic backwardness. Thanks to the taxes imposed on producers, not to mention the endless subdivision of peasant property and the survival of communal rights that were indispensable to the peasant's survival, the countryside seems to have been utterly incapable of increasing levels of production, or of freeing up a workforce for the cities or for raising cash crops. This image of an unchanging, traditional rural world is not entirely inaccurate, and well describes large parts of the countryside on the eve of the Revolution, especially in the poorest areas. However, the idea that the rural world as a whole was trapped in a subsistence economy, and inhabited by a peasantry hostile to all forms of innovation, that it was a world completely removed from commercial capitalism and profit maximization, is no longer sustainable. Writers from La Bruyère to Zola may have likened peasants to savage beasts, but in fact, even within the social structure of the old regime, it was possible for rural productivity to rise significantly. As long as the proper conditions were in place, the goal of the medium-scale farmer, although not of the small-scale peasant on the verge of proletarianization, was not simply to stagnate in his misery, but rather to adapt to a recalcitrant world, and to hoist himself up in the social hierarchy—even, perhaps, to rise out of the much-scorned peasantry altogether.

Cycles of growth

Growth in a rural economy depended above all on the fluctuation of prices, which in turn depended principally on the supply of and demand for bread, the first of which was highly variable. Other important factors included the government's economic and fiscal policies, and also, on occasion, the speculations undertaken by farmers and merchants. In the eighteenth century, prices fluctuated above all in relation to the harvest, the success of which could be influenced by the weather, and by diseases that attacked grain or cattle. A particularly good harvest one year could compensate for a bad one the next, thanks to stockpiling.

There were moments, however, when the weather was abnormally hot or cold, and a drought or sudden frost led to poor harvests yielding abnormally small quantities of mostly low-quality grain and other products. When the stockpiles of the previous harvest had been used up, and the new harvest had not yet been brought in, prices could rise dramatically. And if the new harvest was again poor, then prices could explode. Between May 1708 and May 1709, a year so cold that it was said Louis XIV's wine froze in the glass, the price of a *setier* of grain (roughly 200 kg) rose from 15 to 69 *livres*. Under these conditions, life became difficult, indeed almost impossible, for all those who depended on bread for their existence: the common people of the cities, and also the rural labourers who did not grow enough grain for their own needs, and in times of trouble found no one to hire them. Starved of bread, their bodies grew weak from malnutrition or from eating rotten food, and became vulnerable to epidemics which spread all the faster as groups of the wretched took to the road to beg for help—a phenomenon which also spread epidemics of fear among rural and urban populations alike.

At these moments, which historians have antiseptically labelled 'mortality crises', the drop in agricultural production threatened to become a national catastrophe. The amounts spent on bread forced families to reduce their purchases of manufactured goods (above all textiles), and in extreme cases even modified the demographic structure of the population as a whole. It has been estimated that the famine of 1693–4, caused by what historians refer to as 'the little ice age', had consequences just as deadly as the First World War, with nearly two million French dead. Such crises have often been cited as evidence that the old regime economy obeyed a Malthusian model. According to this theory, in the absence of technological progress, population growth led to a steady decline in overall agricultural productivity, since land of steadily poorer quality had to be put under the plough, until a crisis point was reached, savagely re-establishing equilibrium in the relationship between the population and the food supply. In such an economy, long-term growth would have been essentially impossible.

But in fact, widespread famines were not at all the rule. Historians have only recorded three: 1660–1, at the start of Louis XIV's reign; 1693–4, the most terrible; and finally the famine of the great winter of 1709–10, whose effects were uneven (while Normandy saw its mortality rates rise, Brittany experienced mild weather). Of course there were other periods of dearth after 1709–10, accompanied by higher mortality rates among the very poor, notably in 1739–41, at the end of the 1760s, and on the eve of the Revolution. But the French of the eighteenth century did not die in large numbers from harvest failures, and in normal years, the harvests yielded more than enough to satisfy the country's needs. As a result, the population of France, like the population throughout Europe, rose steadily throughout the century, from 21 million in 1715 to 24 million in 1760, and 28 million in 1789.

This change, passing a demographic threshold which had seemed unbreakable since the Middle Ages, obviously raises the question of whether it was caused by a modernization of the rural economy. Certain historians have claimed to see in the population increase the effects of a veritable agricultural revolution, while others attribute it more modestly to a small increase in agricultural productivity, and some think it was due to nothing more than a return to earlier levels of productivity, following abnormal lows around the time of Louis XIV's death. According to this last hypothesis, no agricultural revolution took place in France until the 1840s and the coming of the railways. This debate is important for understanding the situation of the peasants and city-dwellers who would play so important a role in the summer of 1789, and also for evaluating whether it was really possible to introduce market principles into a system where the strategic agricultural sector remained under strict state control.

In the absence of reliable statistics on agricultural productivity

THE ECONOMY | 13

itself, historians have had no choice but to study the fluctuation of agricultural prices. Using this source, they have identified long-term cycles of growth in the European economy as a whole. The period 1661–1788 divides into two parts: first a period of falling prices which lasted roughly until the death of Louis XIV in 1715, and then a rise, beginning under Louis XV, in the 1720s, and continuing until the early nineteenth century. There has been considerable debate on the causes of these price fluctuations, and their social and economic consequences. Recently, the long-standing idea that falling prices were a sign of general economic recession and misery, and rising prices the sign of general growth and prosperity, has been subjected to close scrutiny. Several regions experienced clear growth in their agricultural sectors under Louis XIV, reminding us that the old regime economy was in fact a composite of distinct, and incompletely integrated regional economies. At the same time it has become clear that the spectacular rise in grain prices after the 1760s was due to a combination of poor harvests, demand-side tensions linked to population growth, and economic reforms undertaken by the government. Therefore, while the overall shift from the seventeenth to the eighteenth century cannot be denied, it must also be recognized that it made itself felt in different ways, and that the responses of property-owners, the peasants, and the government varied considerably as well.

The hardships of the seventeenth century

At the beginning of Louis XIV's personal reign in 1661, agriculture was emerging from a long series of difficulties. The peasantry had suffered greatly from high taxes during the Thirty Years War. Revenues from the principal tax on land, the *taille*, which had ranged from 12 to 20 million *livres* a year between 1610 and 1633, had been raised brutally after France's entry into the war, reaching a high of 53 million *livres* a year in 1657. French and foreign armies alike devastated large parts of the country, and spread epidemics. The civil war of the Fronde prevented peasants, especially in the north, from taking advantage of the excellent harvests of 1651 and 1652, and the crops were partly destroyed.

It was in this dismal context that there began the long-term fall of grain prices. Although this fall is often seen as the result of mercantilist policies which favoured trade over agriculture, in fact the politics of the period benefited the rural world in several ways. Not only did the end of civil and foreign wars allow a degree of rural recovery, but Colbert (chief minister 1661–83) also took positive action in favour of the countryside by raising excise taxes, which were paid above all by city-dwellers, and by reducing direct taxes on the peasantry. Peasants also benefited from a more equitable distribution of the tax burden between the traditionally undertaxed areas with representative institutions (*pays d'états*) and those assessed by fiscal courts (*pays d'élections*). Various regulations were issued to protect farm implements and cattle against the tax-collectors' excesses.

For the king's bread-buying subjects, the first fifteen years of Colbert's ministry were marked by a reduction of fiscal pressures, a lowering of the price of bread, and the maintenance of salary levels. These 'fortunate years' were less fortunate for grain sellers, however, namely those landowners and peasants who farmed enough land to be able to sell their surpluses. 'We will die on a bed of grain,' exclaimed Mme de Sévigné, putting her finger on one of the paradoxes of the agricultural economy, namely the difficulties which could be caused by good harvests and low prices. Colbert reacted to the landowners' complaints with policies aimed at keeping up prices by loosening the laws which, in order to prevent speculation and hoarding, had limited grain trading within the kingdom. Each year he organized a flow of grain from those provinces with surpluses to those with shortages, and when the harvest was exceptionally good, he even permitted the export of surpluses abroad.

With the return of war, however, the rural world entered into another long period of crisis. After 1672 France experienced thirty-five years of almost continuous warfare against various major European powers. Steady tax increases were the result, especially after the war of the League of Augsburg of 1689–97, which added to peasant burdens that already included seigneurial dues, land rents, and the tithe. The *taille* itself remained relatively stable, but new taxes, including the capitation of 1695 (which raised 24 million *livres* a year), and special military taxes, added to the state's levies. In the tax district of Paris, the average tax burden doubled between 1670 and 1700.

This increasing tax burden was one of the principal reasons for endemic popular revolts against the tax system and its agents.

The most famous of these, directed against a new stamp tax, shook Brittany in 1675. The principal consequence of rising taxes coupled with falling prices was to compel many small peasant landowners, and also some deeply indebted yeomen farmers, to sell land and fall back into the ranks of rural labourers. Those who avoided this fate were forced to reduce the amount they worked, which in turn led to a fall in agricultural productivity. In Languedoc, for instance, where the crisis began later than in northern France, average grain yields fell from between 6 to 8 : 1 in the 1660s, to only 4 : 1 in the mid-1680s.

Under these conditions, sporadic complaints against Colbert's economic policies gave way to more reasoned criticism, especially by the magistrate Boisguilbert and the military engineer Vauban, whose writings helped inspire the Physiocrats of the 1750s. The originality of Boisguilbert's work lay in his development of a model of economic circulation, which allowed him to argue that royal financiers had interrupted the normal cycle of wealth production, thanks to their erroneous principles and poorly designed tax schemes. He offered as proof the desertion of fields, and even entire villages, by impoverished peasants. As for Vauban, he emphasized, especially in his *Project for a Royal Tithe* (1707), the terrible social effects of excise taxes, especially the *gabelle* (salt tax), which encouraged fraud. He argued that a single tax on land should replace all other taxes, that it should be collected in kind, like the ecclesiastical tithe, and that it should depend on the success of the harvest. In this way, Vauban hoped to protect the peasantry against the consequences of social inequality and the unjust distribution of the tax burden, but without harming production or depriving the state of the moneys it needed to wage war.

Possibilities for growth

The population growth of the eighteenth century suggests that the contraction experienced during Louis XIV's reign forced important changes upon the agricultural economy. In the region of Paris, for instance, the crises of the seventeenth century led to a concentration of landholding, and a subsequent increase in productivity. In other regions, the effects of falling grain prices were attenuated by the gradual introduction of new crops. In the south, for instance, wine-growing, which enjoyed relatively high profit margins, grew at the expense of wheat cultivation, while in the southwest, maize-growing areas expanded. In the eighteenth century, some of the poorest regions even turned towards potato cultivation.

In the eighteenth century, the principal factor benefiting the rural economy was the more temperate climate, although the absence of large-scale warfare between 1715 and 1740 was also important. Under Louis XIV, a typical middling peasant landowner in the Beauvaisis, north of Paris, managed to keep only 39 per cent of what he invested. His counterpart in the Vannes region of Brittany a hundred years later was left with a net profit of 53 per cent of his original crop. Meanwhile, mortality rates were improved by the end of the great epidemics (the last outbreak of the bubonic plague on French soil took place in 1720), the improvement of sanitation, and the reduction of infant deaths. These changing demographic conditions also contributed to a fundamental change in the economy. The fear of dearth was now increasingly accompanied by a desire for abundance.

This is not to say that the eighteenth century witnessed an agricultural revolution. The concept ill describes the actual nature of agricultural progress, which was very slow throughout Europe—even in England. But the concept of revolution remains useful for describing the political, economic, and social debates over agriculture in eighteenth-century France. It points to the radical change that occurred as certain prominent thinkers, besotted with reason and the prospect of human perfectibility, ceased to think of agriculture as being ultimately governed by God's will. Quesnay, the leader of the so-called physiocratic school, believed that Newtonian mechanics could be applied to agriculture, revealing the laws governing nature, and allowing men, acting in accord with reason, to take the necessary steps to ensure steady and lasting growth. The essential question is whether this movement of thought was purely an intellectual exercise, or whether it reflected the development of new agricultural practices.

While the area around Paris was certainly not all of France (as the Physiocrats themselves often seemed to think) recent research on the region does reveal slow, steady progress during the seventeenth and eighteenth centuries. The percentage of land lying fallow, which stood at 34 per cent of all cultivated land in the sixteenth and seventeenth centuries, fell to only 25 per cent under Louis XVI, and in some villages, like Dugny, north of Paris, it disappeared altogether. A better selection of seed produced heavier grains, while the use of artificial fallow, the invention of more efficient carts, and the use of urban refuse to fertilize fields all combined to increase both production levels and productivity for the farmers of the Parisian basin, who supplied the immense market of the capital city.

But can these conclusions be extended to the rest of France? In the Parisian basin, the average output was 15 quintals per hectare, but in the rest of the kingdom it stood at only 8 to 12. Grain yields (the number of plants grown from a single seed) remained very weak everywhere, with a national average of 5 to 6 : 1, and a maximum of 9 : 1 on good land even in the best years. Yet even with a yield of just 5 or 6 : 1, the village of Montigny, in one of the poorest areas of the Cambrésis in the north, managed to feed a population that tripled over the course of the eighteenth century. Part of the land in Montigny was no longer farmed in the traditional way. A portion of the fallow land was farmed, and fodder plants were grown which allowed for the feeding of more and better quality animals, which in turn aided the harvest.

Recent research has shown that increased agricultural productivity depended on a number of factors, including the local tax burden, grain prices, and especially the distance from the nearest city. But the growth of the urban population from 4 to 5 million over the course of the century, and the enrichment of the urban middle classes, also contributed, in large part because of the resulting diversification of the urban diet. An increase in meat consumption, for instance, allowed certain regions to abandon grain-growing altogether. Meanwhile, Normandy, the Limousin, and the Charolais now became secondary centres of provisioning for the capital. Finally, the improvement of roads leading to urban markets powerfully promoted rural modernization. For one thing, it encouraged agricultural specialization, such as the production of white flour for the cities and foreign markets, and brown flour for the peasantry. The overall impact of new roads was concisely summed up by the enlightened minister Malesherbes, who told Louis XVI that the first effect of a new road was a rise in prices.

The pitfalls of modernization

Agricultural progress took place in an intellectual climate which, perhaps in reaction against rapid urbanization, prized solid rustic virtue.
The number of publications devoted to agricultural matters—1,214 in
the eighteenth century, as opposed to only 130 in the seventeenth—
Louis XV's sponsorship of Quesnay's *Economic Tableau*, and the
famous story of his grandson, the future Louis XVI, being taught to
plough, all testify to the French infatuation with agriculture in the
eighteenth century. Great lords like the duke de Chaulnes, and high
officials like controller-general Bertin, supported individual reform
projects and agricultural improvement societies, and sponsored
specialized periodicals such as the *Journal of Agriculture*.

Between 1754 and 1776, the government itself contributed to the
process with a series of reforms aimed at stimulating agricultural
production. One concern was to relax the fiscal burden on ordinary
farmers. The so-called twentieth tax (*vingtième*), established in 1749,
was a 5 per cent tax levied on the net income of all landowners,
regardless of their privileges. In 1763, the government also decided to
establish a general land register that would have allowed it to assess
the *taille* and other related taxes more fairly, but the idea was never
put into practice. Royal officials also pursued inflationary policies so
as to stimulate rural investment. Among other things, the rules which
had placed the grain trade under strict state control were gradually
eliminated. In 1763, Bertin lifted all prohibitions on grain trading
within the kingdom, and his successor, L'Averdy, went even further,
lifting all bans on grain exports in July 1764.

Neither agriculture nor agricultural policies were static and moribund in the eighteenth century. On the contrary, both showed
important signs of reorienting themselves so as to address two fundamental problems: how to feed a growing population, and how to
satisfy the financial needs of the state. Government ministers, who
found it impossible to reduce royal expenditures, were particularly
seduced by the physiocratic idea of stimulating agriculture and then
taxing the resulting wealth. Because of its chronic lack of funds, not
to mention the diversity and size of the kingdom itself, and also
because of the potential political difficulties posed for fiscal reform by

the network of privileges and exemptions, the government adopted the easiest method of stimulation: releasing market forces that, in theory, would encourage modernization to take place by itself.

In making this choice, administrators hoped to lay the foundations for sustained agricultural growth, so as to put an end, once and for all, to the traditional crises in food production and distribution. The problem with this policy was that it was much more successful at raising prices than at raising actual agricultural production. While overall income from agriculture rose 140 per cent between 1739 and 1789, total production rose only 25 per cent to 40 per cent over the longer period 1709 to 1789. This discrepancy was exacerbated by population growth, which led to stagnating salaries: despite a nominal rise of 25 per cent over the century, they fell in real terms. In such a context, the opening up of the grain market inevitably provoked loud criticism. The end of price controls, which was forced upon reluctant local authorities that had traditionally overseen the grain trade in the name of public order, could only have been acceptable had there been normal harvests, and an adjustment of the tax burden. Instead, a succession of bad harvests at the end of the 1760s led to incomprehension, and even a blanket rejection of the government's policies on the part of a population which was suffering widely from the rise in grain prices. Accusations spread that royal ministers, and even the king in person, were conspiring to raise bread prices and get rich at the expense of the common people. The rumour of a so-called 'famine plot' demonstrated how much the government stood to lose in terms of public confidence when it broke the carapace of rules and regulations which accompanied the traditional image of the sovereign as the father of his subjects, and the provider for his people.

Commercial and industrial development

The old regime economy amounted to more than its admittedly vast agricultural sector. Several historians, rejecting the idea that France lagged behind England in any significant way in its economic development, have pointed out that even on the eve of the Revolution the Bourbon monarchy remained the world's leading economic power, thanks to a gross domestic product that was three to four times higher than England's (210–15 million *livres* as opposed to 65 million). Between 1701–10 and 1781–90, the increase in agricultural production (in real numbers it went from 1 to 2.5 billion *livres*) was far outpaced by the increase in trade and industry (from 385 million to 1.5 billion). If we add foreign trade to the picture (an additional 1 billion), non-agrarian activities amounted to more than half of French wealth in 1789. On the eve of the Revolution, the development of new forms of capitalist mobile wealth was therefore beginning to compete seriously with the land revenues on which the traditional system of values still rested.

There are many reasons for this emergence of a large non-agricultural sector, which was one of the most important developments in the economy before the Revolution. Aristocratic tastes had long demanded artisanal products of high quality. The real engine behind the kingdom's economy, however, was the vast internal market of consumers which grew by 7 to 8 million inhabitants during the eighteenth century and amounted to 20 per cent of the European population on the eve of the Revolution. Even the countryside was not made up solely of peasants. It also counted many artisans, who rarely made up less than 10 to 20 per cent of the rural population. Finally, industrial development was also due in part to state intervention. Whether mercantilist in inspiration, as under Louis XIV, or liberal, as would be the case a hundred years later, state intervention was a constant feature in the kingdom's economic life. The number of royal manufactures—i.e. enterprises benefiting from fiscal privileges or commercial monopolies—grew constantly. Whereas there had been only 113 such enterprises under Colbert, the number rose to 243 between 1683 and 1750. More than 1,000 official regulations governing manufacturing were issued between 1683 and 1753, and at least 500 more followed in the second half of the eighteenth century.

Far from being an obstacle to free enterprise and innovation, state intervention amounted to a critical economic stimulant, thanks to the state's growing financial resources. In the hands of a well-informed minister, the tax system did not simply impose a sterile economic burden. The exponential growth of taxes under Richelieu, for instance (1621–42), stimulated the monetarization of economic exchanges, encouraged the development of artisanal production, and encouraged migration between the cities and more remote regions. At the end of the seventeenth century, the Intendant of

Riom, d'Ormesson, estimated that the 10,000 to 12,000 who migrated every year from the Auvergne to the cities generated annual revenues of 1.5 million *livres*, or roughly 60 per cent of the amount the province was expected to raise from the *taille*. If taxes paid for the stipends of courtiers and the Court of Versailles, they also helped pay for the monarchy's military apparatus. The construction of a single warship required no less than 1,000 tonnes of iron, which suggests that if war hurt agriculture, the sums raised helped support industry and manufacturing.

The textile industry

Manufacturing and industry produced a large range of products aimed at many different markets. Paper factories, glass factories, tanneries, forges, and other such establishments, which sold principally to local and national markets, had a far from negligible output. In 1788, cast iron production alone reached 130,000 tonnes, twice the level of Great Britain. Furthermore, France was entering into a phase of rapid technical progress. The Anzin mining company, in the north, was setting up large factories equipped with steam engines, while Creusot was building coke furnaces.

Manufacturing activity, however, was still centred above all on textiles. Clothes, along with rent and heat, remained the largest sources of consumer spending after bread. In 1763, rural labourers in the Aunis spent an average of 22 *livres* a year on clothing, out of an average income of 189 *livres*. The textile industry also held a dominant position in foreign trade. In the middle of the eighteenth century, fabrics made up more than 40 per cent of French exports, scarcely less than the figure for England (45 per cent). Although spread throughout the kingdom, the textile industry was concentrated in a few important centres in peripheral provinces, above all the north-west (Normandy, Picardy, Flanders, Champagne, and Brittany) and Languedoc. In these areas, textile production was the foremost non-agricultural activity, and thousands of families made their living by turning raw materials into thread, cloth, and clothing. In Colbert's day, Amiens, with roughly 35,000 inhabitants, had as many as 500 master weavers who, depending on economic conditions, kept as many as 1,700 shops running, and employed thousands of journey-men and labourers. In Lyon, the second most populous city, and the centre of French silk production, two-thirds of the artisan population worked in the textile sector. Cloth-making also spilled out into the countryside thanks to specialized cottage industries that gave work to rural labourers who did not have enough land to survive. At Sedan, textile merchants gave work to a network of perhaps 10,000 villagers, spread out over a radius of 25 kilometres from the town.

Mercantilism and Colbertism

Like agriculture, manufacturing knew good times and bad. When Louis XIV became king, the textile sector was in the middle of a crisis, marked by falling sales, profits, and production levels, that has been attributed both to traditional difficulties (war, epidemics, high food prices) and to foreign competition. To reduce their costs, the mer-chants of Languedoc decided to transfer much or all of their cloth production into the countryside and out of the hands of trained urban artisans, even though this harmed the quality of the cloth which was produced. It was during this depression that Colbert began a series of economic initiatives which, between 1666 and 1683, involved no fewer than 150 sets of regulations on manufacturing and the textile trades. A typical example of these measures from 1670, regulating textile production in Amiens, included no less than 248 separate articles. Not surprisingly, therefore, Colbertism has often been considered a form of stifling state regulation that blocked all innovation and enterprise. Yet in fact, Colbert most often was simply complying with the demands of the commercial classes, whom he knew well since he himself was descended from a family of Reims haberdashers. He even involved them in the formulation of eco-nomic policy, by creating a royal council of commerce in 1664, which brought together ministers and delegates from the principal commercial centres, under the supervision of the king himself.

Colbertism was essentially a variety of mercantilism, which was not an exclusively French phenomenon, but rather a central aspect of European economic practices and European economic language in the seventeenth century. Mercantilism consisted of two principles:

first, that the power of a state depends on the quantity of precious metals in its possession, and secondly, that trade is the best way for countries without gold and silver mines to procure these metals. It was only in the eighteenth century that economic liberals would criticize these principles by arguing that the monetary surpluses produced by favourable trade balances are generally counteracted by exchange rate mechanisms which raise the value of the national currency, making exports less competitive.

To the extent that they followed these principles, Colbert's economic policies should not be considered innovatory. Rather, they amounted to the systematic application of a conventional wisdom that had already been codified in Antoine de Montchrestien's *Treatise of Political Economy* of 1614, and later in Cardinal Richelieu's *Political Testament*. Colbertism deserves a name to itself not because of its originality, but because its author remained in power for twenty years and had extraordinary resources at his disposal to carry out policies designed to increase the grandeur of his king.

After helping Louis XIV assume personal power in 1661, Colbert first managed, in the name of maintaining financial confidence and of enforcing strict obedience to the king, to substitute his own family network for that of his disgraced rival, Fouquet. He made particular use of a chamber of justice, originally established to put Fouquet and bankrupt financiers on trial, to maintain strict control over the officials responsible for collecting taxes. Colbert's authority was also reinforced by taking on key positions such as the supervision of royal manufactures in 1664, the controllership-general of finances and the superintendancy-general of commerce in 1665, the naval department in 1669, and finally the department of mines and quarries in 1670.

By this means, Colbert acquired the power to pursue a programme of economic development modelled on what had previously been done in the Netherlands. Through the granting of special privileges, he encouraged foreign manufacturers to settle in France, and also created new manufactures such as the Gobelins glassworks. These enterprises were designed, first of all, to decrease the need for foreign imports, and secondly to develop expertise so as to allow France to compete in foreign markets. Initially they were protected by high tariffs, and carefully regulated. Government ordinances set strict standards so as to guarantee quality, and uniformity, in French products in general. Control over the system was put in the hands of new guilds and corporations, acting under government supervision. Colbert also created new commercial companies for foreign trade and colonization in Africa, India, and America.

The building of the navy, which was originally prompted by the need to protect France's commercial interests, provides a concrete example of Colbert's methods. At the beginning, Colbert was forced to compromise his mercantilist principles by spending precious metals on second-hand Dutch vessels. He also had to hire foreign specialists to teach the arts of shipbuilding and cannon casting. But the project in the end stimulated domestic mass production very effectively. It has been estimated that the construction and maintenance of a 200-ship navy required the cutting down of more than a million trees, and the casting of more than 6,000 cannon, not to mention all the necessary anchors, nails, guns, cannon balls, rope, sail, and pitch. Colbert's family networks, and his control over tax collection, allowed him to gather the funds to establish the necessary shipyards.

Despite such successes, Colbert has been widely criticized—indeed, some detractors have credited him with nothing less than the destruction of the monarchy. Like the liberal economists of the eighteenth century, they argue that economic growth depended on the modernization of agriculture, a subject that the minister ignored in order to concentrate on commerce. They add that while commerce itself was badly in need of liberalization, Colbert suffocated it with state interference. The proof of Colbert's failure allegedly lies in the collapse of most of the enterprises he founded after his death, and in the insufficient support that the state gave to manufacturing. In 1670, out of a budget of 70 millions, only 500,000 were earmarked for economic development of this sort.

Other historians, however, have argued that Colbertism should not be measured by its immediate results, which varied from sector to sector, nor by the theoretical pronouncements of a man who was essentially pragmatic in spirit. They suggest that Colbert was in fact favourable to economic freedom—he purposely left many trades free from state interference, and planned on suppressing government aid to manufacturing as soon as the enterprises proved capable of supporting themselves. Admittedly, Colbert greatly expanded a system of privileges that could be endlessly exploited by a government desperate to pay the mounting costs of war. However, his activist policies were important for the recovery of economic sectors which had been

Some historians argue that Colbert was a failure. He didn't focus on agriculture & his enterprises collapsed after his death

Some historians argue that his policies helped a failing economy and helped France become competitive with English and Dutch.

in crisis at the accession of Louis XIV. In Languedoc, the foundation of the royal factory of Villenouvette encouraged the development of new techniques of cloth dyeing, and ultimately gave rise to high-quality products capable of capturing a portion of the foreign market and successfully competing with English and Dutch products. Nor was the collapse of Colbert's commercial companies, including the East India Company, really much of a failure. These companies survived for long enough to accomplish the crucial and difficult task of opening up trade routes, which later merchants would profitably exploit. They also laid the foundation of a colonial empire which would be one of the pillars of eighteenth-century economic growth.

However we judge Colbertism, it is undeniable that by the end of the seventeenth century the crisis in the French textile industry was nothing but a bad memory. While the agricultural sector, crushed by the tax burden and at the mercy of the climate, was plunging further into crisis, manufacturing and trade were doing well, especially after the peace of Ryswick in 1697. To be sure, economic development could still be throttled in wartime. The number of sheets of cloth produced rose from 237,500 in 1692 to 279,000 in 1708, but fell back to just 198,500 in 1716. After 1700, however, the French could also count on new markets in Spain and the Spanish empire, and they also possessed at that time the *asiento*, the exclusive privilege of supplying African slaves to Spain's American possessions.

A century of growth

In contrast to the seventeenth century's mixed economic picture, every macroeconomic analysis suggests that between the stabilization of the *livre tournois* in 1726, and the eve of the Revolution, France experienced rapid economic growth. The rate has been estimated at an average of 1.9 per cent a year for the industrial sector, and 0.6 per cent a year for the agricultural sector, for the years between 1701 and 1790. The expansion of the domestic market, above all thanks to urban population growth, goes a long way towards explaining the quadrupling of cast iron production, and the expansion of the various textile sectors by as much as a factor of five. Growth was also facilitated by improved transport. The Crozat canal, linking the Oise and Somme rivers, was finished in 1738, and around this date, the controller-general Orry introduced forced labour for road building. The school of bridges and roads, founded in 1749, trained engineers skilled in low-cost road construction, which helped the government to lay the basis of a national road system linking Paris to the major provincial capitals, as well as of a secondary system (not yet complete in 1789), linking the capitals to each other. Rivers and canals, which remained indispensable for heavy cargo, supplemented the road system. Thanks to these developments, the cost of transport fell, leading to an expansion of trade. The number of vehicles paying river Rhône tolls at Valence tripled in the second half of the eighteenth century.

The most dynamic sector of all, however, was foreign trade, which expanded fivefold in real terms between 1716–20 and 1784–8. Colonial trade, above all with the Caribbean, brought untold wealth to the ports of Bordeaux, Marseille, Nantes, Rouen, and Le Havre. The volume of merchandise imported from Saint-Domingue and Martinique—above all sugar, indigo, tobacco, and coffee—went from 4.4 million *livres* in 1716 to 77 million in 1754. Far exceeding the demands of the French market, these colonial products were mostly re-exported to the Netherlands and Germany, thus greatly increasing trade with Northern Europe.

This growth in trade with the Caribbean colonies was essential to the economy. The colonial population, which grew significantly in both numbers and wealth over the course of the eighteenth century, especially because of the importation of thousands of slaves from Africa, became an important market for manufactured items which the colonies were legally obliged to obtain from French ports, according to the principle known as the 'exclusive'. Colonial trade, meanwhile, had an impact far beyond the port cities and their immediate hinterlands. It stimulated the economy as a whole by increasing demand in the sectors of shipbuilding, fishing, and agriculture. It prompted the building of sugar refineries and other such manufactures, and above all it proved a tremendous stimulus for the textile industry, which could export its products both to the French islands, and from there to the vast markets of Spanish America.

Prosperity and economic liberalism

This economic growth led to an enrichment of the population as a whole. To be sure, the profits from trade did not significantly influence the shape of the social pyramid, even in great commercial centres like Bordeaux. Except for a relatively few merchants and their sons who made their way into the privileged classes by purchasing ennobling offices, the top of the pyramid in 1789 was still occupied by large landholders and legal office-holders from the traditional nobility. But economic growth did help create a much larger middle class composed of merchants, small businessmen, and artisans, who enjoyed unprecedented prosperity. At Rennes, for instance, the number of artisans and shopkeepers who paid more than 20 *livres* a year in capitation taxes almost doubled over the course of the eighteenth century.

This enrichment of the mercantile bourgeoisie gave birth to what some historians have characterized as the birth of a consumer society. The evidence from Parisian households shows that the value of linens and clothing possessed by the average family went up by a factor of 3.5 over the course of the century: from 1,800 *livres* in 1700 to 6,000 in 1789. Nor was this growth limited to the social elites—it was shared by every important urban social group. Even in the poorest sectors of the Parisian population, the value of cloth possessions rose from an average of 42 *livres* to 115. By contrast, the rural population did much less well. In the Perche, in Normandy, the only group to join consumer society to any extent were the well-off sailmakers, who had commercial contacts with the cities. During the eighteenth century, tapestries appeared on their walls and porcelain supplanted pewter in their cabinets, while coffee-pots and new styles of cloth and clothing were also adopted. These new patterns of consumption in turn gave rise to new systems of production which competed with the traditional world of the trades, in which work had been done by a specialized master artisan, helped by two or three journeymen or apprentices. The luxury trades, which required a highly trained and specialized labour force, were not particularly affected by the changes. However, the enthusiasm of the public for new products, in particular cotton ('Indian') fabrics, which were cheaper, sturdier, and more colourful than their traditional competitors, led to a crisis in the world of work.

Even in the second half of the eighteenth century, most of the trades remained in thrall to venerable regulations, mostly devised under Colbert and reinforced in the 1730s by the neo-Colbertist Orry, who, like his idol, wanted to ensure the production of superior quality merchandise. The system was not flexible enough to allow the trades to adapt easily to increasingly volatile patterns of demand, and especially the increasing demand for cotton, which remained theoretically illegal to import and refine. Since cotton cloth was a highly popular product in Europe, and one that required sophisticated machinery to produce, the prohibition deprived industrialists of a flourishing source of income, and threatened to put France at a technological disadvantage vis-à-vis England. This last problem was overcome in the 1760s thanks to spies who smuggled machinery back from England, and by the hiring of English specialists like John Holker, who were ready to help introduce new techniques. In addition, the prohibition on cotton was partially bypassed by the establishment of new factories which were not bound by the traditional regulations.

In some great textile centres such as Valenciennes and Clermont-de-Lodève, the slowing—and in some cases the collapse—of traditional textile production was all the more upsetting to the population because it took place in a period of overall growth. The guilds blamed the crisis on the loosening of regulations by the government, and argued for the reinforcement of the traditional system of production, which had allowed as many people as possible to obtain their fair share of work. From their point of view, the success once enjoyed by the system justified the maintenance of an unchanging economic order, characterized by the absence of competition. Government inspectors, who were charged with enforcing the traditional rules, were also divided between liberals, and supporters of Colbertism, which had made particular regions into textile centres that were threatened by new products they did not yet have the ability to produce.

At the same time, the guilds themselves were increasingly the target of government ministers who hoped to end commercial monopolies, thereby lowering the costs of production and stimulating consumption. Under the influence of liberal economists, and especially the

THE ECONOMY | 29

THE ECONOMY | 29

physiocrat Gournay, author of the phrase *laissez-passer, laissez-faire*, guild monopolies were increasingly bypassed so as to allow market forces to take their course. It became more and more difficult to issue regulations for trades influenced by rapidly changing fashions, and by the desire of bourgeois to use consumption as a means of distinguishing themselves from other social groups. In 1759, controller-general Silhouette decided to lift all prohibitions on coloured fabrics. Three years later, country-dwellers were authorized to produce finished cloth as long as they obeyed existing regulations. Finally, in 1776, Turgot decided to suppress the guilds altogether. The economic interests threatened by this measure were so vast, however, that they combined to help force his resignation, and to have his measures repealed.

Some historians have argued that the Physiocrats' critique of the guilds was not always justified. The trades were not closed to all but the sons of masters. Nor did the guilds themselves necessarily obstruct economic growth. The creation of a particular product often required the cooperation of different trades, with the result that no single trade could dominate the production process. Furthermore, the guilds themselves often attempted to adapt to the demands of fashion. In Lyon, silk merchants tried to profit from the birth of an heir to the throne by marketing a new colour of silk, which was nicknamed *caca dauphin* (literally, 'dauphin's shit'). Finally, the guilds did not necessarily impede the development of manufacturing. The printed fabric factory at Jouy-en-Josas, near Paris, employed nearly 4,000 workers, while in Lyon twelve master artisans employed 1,600.

The general growth of the eighteenth century thus affected the different sectors of the economy in different ways. Indeed, it had very uneven effects even within the same sector. In Lyon, the average wealth of master artisans went up 31 per cent in real terms, while that of silkworkers increased only 7 per cent, and stagnating wages for workers seem to have been the rule. Yet some workers still managed to rise out of the ranks of apprentices and journeymen and acquire masterships themselves. Income growth depended on changes in both the structures of production and consumption. And beyond these factors, and the general economic policies of the government, the system of state finance must also be taken into consideration.

The economy and state finances

The state was at once a producer, consumer, and distributor of wealth. Until 1661, the system of state finances had traditionally been managed by the superintendent of finances. But Fouquet's fall from power in 1661 was followed by a reorganization, in which the superintendency passed to the king himself, assisted by a royal council of finances. Then, in 1665, a new position was created, that of controller-general of finances, whose department would henceforth oversee the economic and financial affairs of the kingdom. Not only did the controller-general therefore have tremendous powers, he also had the rare privilege of having one-on-one working sessions with the king, whose views he was expected to follow. Successive controllers-general also participated in meetings of the council of state, which discussed overall royal policy, especially in military and diplomatic affairs.

Despite these vast powers, in reality the controller-general's influence depended on the technical and human resources available to him, and for years these resources remained extremely limited. Colbert managed with only a handful of assistants, although by the end of the old regime his successors in Paris and Versailles oversaw a staff of more than 350 persons. By then the minister had also acquired the help of a powerful official, the first clerk of finances, as well as a dozen other senior clerks and several principal secretaries directing bureaux. The controller-general also had six intendants of finances at his disposal, recruited from a small number of families prominent in the robe and finances, such as the d'Ormessons and the Trudaines.

The financial administration collected information from provincial administrations, and especially from the royal intendants. These officers were themselves assisted by a secretary, numerous clerks, and reliable agents, including the subdelegates. This administrative structure, whose foundations had been laid in the sixteenth century, expanded under Richelieu, and systematized in 1661, was the government's central nervous system. Its efficiency, however, depended to a large extent on the smooth working of the controller-general's personal network of clients.

The need to gain ever more information about the kingdom's

wealth and needs, however, also sometimes required bypassing the intendants. For this reason, the government also established new administrations such as the department of bridges and roads of 1663, and the school of mines of 1749. Tax collectors, and particularly the 100,000 agents of the 'general farm', were responsible for collecting economic data as well, and in fact provided the best information on the general direction of the economy. Finally, the ministry also oversaw a central bureau of trade that collected information from merchants, and provincial chambers of commerce, which multiplied rapidly during the eighteenth century in principal ports and manufacturing centres.

Finances and war

The controller-general's basic role was to pay the state's bills, and to find sufficient funds to do so. These funds could come in on a permanent or temporary basis, and could derive from taxes (direct or indirect), from the proceeds of lands owned directly by the crown, or from borrowing. The management and control of revenues and expenditures required the minister to act as both accountant and judge. He was also frequently called on to implement economic policies aimed at increasing the country's wealth. Although they could draw on impressive resources, controllers-general nonetheless faced real limits on their powers. Even Colbert, so his critics have argued, was never capable of controlling fluctuations in the economy. They were regularly frustrated by the resistance of various pressure groups, and by the tendency of their ministerial colleagues, particularly from the departments of war, the navy, and foreign affairs, to spend freely without first asking permission. Finally, it must be remembered that the controllers-general were creatures of their age, above all in their respect for those keystones of the social system, the sanctity of fiscal privileges and the supreme prestige of landed property.

The state spent the most heavily on war. From the rise of Colbert to the Revolution, France was at war for 54 years, or almost one year out of every two. War meant a sudden, large, and lasting increase in state expenditures. For instance, the Seven Years War of 1756 to 1763, which cost a total of 1.2 billion *livres*, led the state to spend an extra 171 million *livres* a year, or 60 per cent more than in the previous years of peace. Moreover, since wars were preceded by extensive military preparations, and since armistices were generally followed by the reconstruction of the army and the paying-off of debts, the state was in effect on a permanent war footing, and the budget was above all a military budget. In 1694, a year of war, military expenditures amounted to 125 million *livres*, or 75 per cent of the total budget. A century later, in 1788, a year of peace, civil and military expenditures were roughly equal (145 million *livres* versus 164 million), with each part representing roughly a quarter of the budget (610 million *livres* altogether). But the rest of the budget, 310 million *livres*, or more than half the total, went towards payments on the debt, which is to say, interest on sums borrowed during previous periods of war.

Constant high rates of spending were therefore one of the fundamental characteristics of the economy. Yet even so, thanks to the ubiquity of fiscal privileges, the total level of taxation remained small by modern standards. In the eighteenth century, even in wartime, the monarchy's budget never amounted to more than 17 per cent of domestic product, and in peacetime the sum barely reached 10 per cent. If war made the state one of the principal actors in the economy, it was more because of the effects of fiscal inequality, because of wartime disruptions in trade, and because of the effects of taxation on private savings.

Paradoxically, while war placed a heavy burden on non-privileged taxpayers, it was only partly financed by taxation. The reason was that total tax revenues could only be raised or lowered very slowly, thanks to the slow and tortuous process of tax collection itself, and the fact that the wealthiest groups in society were largely exempt from taxes altogether. Nor was it possible to raise taxes very far on those who did not enjoy exemptions, given how little disposable income they generally possessed (10–20 per cent of taxpayers in fact lived in a state of indigence). Overtaxing the countryside raised the risk of revolts, of driving peasants from their villages, or of forcing them to stop farming fields which had ceased to be profitable. As for excise taxes, above a certain level raising them simply encouraged fraud and reduced levels of consumption.

But neither was it practical to start levying taxes on the privileged classes. If they were richer than their taxpaying fellow subjects, they were also far less numerous. It has been estimated that if the state had wished to pay for the Seven Years War only by taxing those persons then paying the modest twentieth tax on their income, it would have had to raise not three-twentieths, at it did by 1760, but fourteen: that is, to raise the tax rate on landowners to a confiscatory 70 per cent. To the extent that even preparing for war required raising state revenues by 10 to 20 per cent, and since no one could predict how long conflicts would last, the controller-general had to look elsewhere. He had to find ways of rapidly finding sums that had no relation to ordinary needs. He had to be able to make up the difference between spending and revenue so as to preserve the state from bankruptcy, and maintain its credit—its ability to borrow money as cheaply as possible.

Forms of state credit

To make the rich pay tax, the government resorted to numerous financial expedients, known by the name of 'extraordinary affairs', carried out by several different groups of financiers, brokers, and bankers. 'Financier' was the generic name given to people with the responsibility for collecting royal revenues, including especially the farmers-general, who specialized in excise taxes (on tobacco, salt, alcohol, postage, etc.), and the receivers-general, who took in the direct taxes levied on individuals (the *taille*, the capitation or poll tax, the tax of a tenth on income, etc.).

The so-called tax farms—essentially, the right to collect particular forms of taxation—were publicly auctioned off to private persons. A lease was signed between the government and the tax farmer, who agreed to pay an advance and a regular annual sum to the government but also to pay all costs involved in actually collecting the taxes and various expenses on behalf of the state, especially the interest on loans. He could keep, as a profit, whatever additional tax sums he managed to collect on the price of the lease and received the interest on his advance. In 1661, when Colbert joined the government, the collection of excise taxes was divided among many different farms, which increased expenses and made it difficult for state officials to oversee operations. Colbert combined several different leases and gave them to a private company of financiers, dubbed the general farm. The monarchy thus created a powerful association which, by the eve of the Revolution, was collecting over half the annual revenues of the state, paying half of its revenues and also using its credit to lend money to the government. The general farm issued its own paper notes, which could be cashed in for future tax revenues, and which therefore amounted to an important form of state credit. The farm, which formed a veritable state within the state, was widely hated on account of the inquisitorial powers wielded by its officials, and on account of its often exorbitant profits, which were indeed particularly high in the first half of the eighteenth century. Ministers like Turgot and Necker, who cared strongly about reducing the deficit, attempted to reduce the farm's profits by transferring the collection of certain taxes to other, less expensive companies which were more efficiently controlled.

By contrast, the receivers-general who operated in each generality purchased their offices from the state, and were effectively impossible to dismiss. In terms of state credit they resembled the farmers-general, particularly in their ability to issue notes exchangeable against future tax revenues. According to the needs of the treasury, these bills were either used by the royal treasurers to pay state expenses, or sold to individuals. Thus the state was provided with credit, while the financiers could attract private investors, who could count on recouping their investments from future tax revenues. The ministry, in turn, sometimes insisted on these investments being put into state manufactures. For the system to function properly, however, the ministry needed to maintain strict control over the treasurers. Otherwise, it risked the receivers-general abusing their position by mixing their own business with state business, not to mention the government ruining its credit by borrowing too hastily against several years of anticipated tax revenues. Yet maintaining political control was a delicate matter, because the exigencies of war always ended up creating new privileges for the financiers, and put the government at their mercy.

While borrowing against future tax revenues provided the ministry with a way of covering ordinary state deficits, even this expedient fell short when it came to paying the expenses of warfare. During wartime, the government therefore also took advantage of the ingenuity of various private individuals, known as *traitants* or *partisans*, who proposed various schemes for bringing in revenues. If the proposals were accepted, contracts were drawn up between the state and the *traitants,* in which the latter promised to provide certain sums. These financiers played a particularly important role under Louis XIV, providing 371 million *livres,* or a third of net state revenues, during the war of the League of Augsburg.

Important additional revenue came from the creation and sale of government offices. Sold by the thousands to all comers, offices were often extremely profitable investments. Not only did many purchasers receive annual interest payments, they also obtained revenues from the office itself, and various fiscal, commercial, and honorific privileges, of which the most highly prized was ennoblement. The creation of new offices often amounted to a form of forced loan. Guild members were frequently obliged collectively to buy up new offices in their corporations, or to purchase new privileges or an increase in the wages they received. Thus the state obtained large sums, albeit at the cost of greater annual payments to its office-holders. Ministers also devised many other, similar devices for obliging individuals to hand over capital sums, in return for the promise of different forms of annuities.

The state also took out loans from bankers, who had access to large sums thanks to their role in currency trading and handling letters of credit from merchants and traders. By the middle of the eighteenth century, the financiers on whom Colbert had relied so heavily were losing ground to bankers whose activities were rapidly expanding, thanks to general economic growth. The transition was particularly evident during the Seven Years War, when Jean Pâris de Monmartel was obliged to surrender his position as Court banker to Jean-Joseph de Laborde, whose business with Spain and the Americas had put him at the centre of the market in precious metals. The nomination in 1776 to the ministry of Necker, a Genevan banker of modest origins whose talents had propelled him to the top of one of the most powerful European banks, sealed this transformation in the structure of state credit.

Borrowing grew in importance throughout the eighteenth century. As early as the 1730s, for instance, Orry decided to raise new funds above all by creating a new form of state borrowing, called *rentes viagères*—life annuities purchased by individuals from the state. They had the advantage of ending the state's interest payments upon the purchaser's death, but the disadvantage of carrying extremely high

interest rates (from 6.66 to 12 per cent)—much more than the traditional *rentes perpétuelles*, which paid only 5 per cent. This overall
shift in borrowing had terrible consequences for the monarchy's
credit. A succession of ministers, incapable of achieving serious fiscal
reforms, found themselves torn between the eagerness of French,
Swiss, and Dutch investors to loan money to a prosperous country,
and the accumulation of a mammoth state debt, the interest payments on which exceeded annual economic growth. Eventually,
ministers would have to balance the revenues from financial capital
on the one hand, against the needs of the overtaxed countryside
and an industrial sector starved of investment by the high returns
available on state loans on the other.

Peace and the repayment of state debts

If Louis XIV's ministers and their successors often displayed particular ingenuity in paying armies, their efforts did not stop after the
signing of peace treaties. War made it possible to take advantage
of patriotic sentiment to raise taxes and unilaterally to abrogate
long-standing privileges. In 1695, for instance, the creation of the
capitation for the first time introduced the principle of universal
taxation. All, even princes of the blood, were obliged to pay. Fifteen
years later, military reversals forced controller-general Desmaretz,
Colbert's nephew, to create another new tax, the *dixième* or 'tenth'
tax of all incomes. This wartime tax required all taxpayers to
declare the amount of their incomes to the state, leading the duke de
Saint-Simon to make a famous protest against fiscal 'despotism'.

At the return of peace, the government consistently found itself
needing to pay only 'ordinary' expenses (as opposed to 'extraordinary', wartime ones), but at the same time could draw only on 'ordinary' revenues. Furthermore, these revenues were often non-existent,
because the money had already been spent in advance. And the state
still needed to pay interest on sums borrowed during the war, and to
diminish its considerable debt. For example, at Louis XIV's death in
1715, ordinary revenues stood at 165 million *livres* a year, while interest
on *rentes* cost 86 million, the annual deficit stood at 77 million, and
overdue payments on the debt, including as yet unpaid wartime

expenses, totalled not less than 700 million. In 1763, following the end of the Seven Years War, the situation was apparently marginally less catastrophic. The total debt was roughly the same as in 1715—2 billion *livres*—but ordinary revenues had increased to 309 million. The increased reliance on *rentes viagères,* however, had swollen interest payments to 120 million a year, or 40 per cent of the total budget. On top of this, the state also had overdue payments of at least 500 million *livres.*

Peacetime ministers, therefore, just like wartime ones, faced a daunting array of problems: how to balance the budget with reduced revenues; how to pay off the debt without worrying lenders, whose credit the state still needed to meet the deficit, and all this without stirring up protests from long-suffering taxpayers, and without ruining merchants and manufacturers who had invested heavily in the debt, and whose bankruptcies might paralyse the economy's return to a peacetime footing. To pay its debts and bring the budget back into balance, the monarchy had long resorted to authoritarian methods which consisted of threatening to try financiers before a chamber of justice unless they returned a portion of the 'undue' sums they had supposedly collected. In truth, many financiers had indeed profited unduly from the state's desperate need for wartime revenues, and from the exhaustion of the treasury. In the last years of a war, when money was becoming more and more scarce, it was not uncommon for interest rates to rise to 25 per cent, or even higher. The last two chambers of justice, established by Colbert in 1661 and the duke de Noailles in 1716, were designed to re-establish political control over the financiers and to satisfy the public's desire for vengeance against certain individuals who had found money for the state in particularly unsavoury ways. This measure, when reinforced by the imposition of stricter controls over moneys received and spent, as well as by a forced reduction in the interest paid on annuities, a better distribution of the tax burden, and by the proceeds from the growing economy, generally allowed the state to achieve a balanced budget within a few years. And if by any chance the peace lasted, as under Colbert, the controller-general was in a strong position to introduce basic reforms aimed at reducing the costs of tax collection, state spending, and borrowing.

When Louis XIV died, Noailles decided to follow Colbert's example. However, the financial recovery proceeded so slowly, and the size of the debt remained so imposing that the regent for the infant Louis XV, Philippe d'Orléans, adopted a new, original plan devised by the Scottish adventurer John Law. While the royal ministers had been struggling to reduce the debt without losing the confidence of the state's creditors, Law proposed, by contrast, to put the debt to work. His idea was to transform it into shares in two new institutions: a General Bank (1716), and an overseas monopoly trading company, the Company of the West (1717). By multiplying commercial activity, and by reaping a profit from colonial possessions in Louisiana they would promote economic growth, while consolidating the debt itself. Driven by intense speculation, Law's system was initially marked by a huge rise in the price of the shares, and of paper currency, issued by the bank, that temporarily took the place of coin. But the successes of 1719, which enriched many speculators, were followed a year later by a bankruptcy which ruined countless families. In the short term, the episode allowed the government quickly to re-establish financial equilibrium, while many private individuals found themselves able to pay off their own debts with almost worthless paper notes. But in the long term, the system led to a damaging hostility towards the establishment of a state bank, although this was proposed during every subsequent economic crisis as something which modern states need in order to regulate the amount of money in circulation and to set the cost of government borrowing.

A different system for paying down the debt was established by controller-general Machault d'Arnouville in 1749, inspired by reforms enacted after Law's disgrace. It centred on a new financial institution, the sinking fund (*caisse d'amortissement*) which would henceforth serve as a central clearing house for paying off the debt. This new system had at least two advantages. By forcing the state to make regular payments on the debt, it justified the maintenance of a high level of taxation even during peacetime, and also the adjustment of tax collection to patterns of wealth in the country. Machault's first goal was to replace the wartime tax of a tenth on income with a permanent twentieth, to be levied on the net income of all landowners, regardless of privilege. By reducing budgetary tensions, the revenues from the sinking fund gave the government the means of reducing the cost of borrowing, and of promoting economic growth. This policy was immediately sabotaged by the conflicts between the parlements and the clergy which both took advantage of the fiscal problems of the government to try to resolve their religious quarrels, and above all by the Seven Years War, which forced the sinking fund to suspend repayments altogether. However, Machault's ideas were revived and improved after the peace treaty of 1763. The new sinking fund gave the government the ability to justify the principle of the taxation of *rentes* and also to reduce the legal rate of interest from 5 to 4.5 per cent. Yet once again, this promising reform was cut short, this time because the burden of debt proved too great and because the economic crisis that raged after 1767 limited the expected benefits from the introduction of free trade in grain. In 1770, the new controller-general Terray reversed course altogether. To balance the budget, he resorted to a partial bankruptcy, defaulting on the state's debt. To bring in additional funds, he raised interest rates again, and returned to Colbert's repertoire of financial expedients.

Less than twenty years before the Revolution, in other words, the monarchy attempted to introduce significant reforms to banish the spectre of bankruptcy, and to direct private savings towards the agricultural and manufacturing sectors by reducing the state's own debts (which had acted as a magnet for private investment), by reducing the cost of borrowing and by opening up markets. But the reforms failed. At the end of the experiment, nothing remained but a slight redistribution of the tax burden away from the countryside and towards the elites, whose privileges were now openly challenged by the government.

The American war, economic crisis, and the end of the old regime

Although it has often been attributed to the reckless policies of Necker or the public spending of Calonne, the financial crisis which sounded the old regime's death knell in 1787 was actually the result of a series of crises which reinforced each other in disastrous ways. A traditional agricultural crisis, marked by a succession of poor grain and wine harvests after 1786, was only one factor at work. The resulting rise in bread prices might still have proved tolerable—except for the employment crisis. It was here that the demographic growth of the eighteenth century, by greatly multiplying the number of urban and rural wage-earners, had made the entire economy hostage to the demand for agricultural and manufacturing labour. And this demand, in turn, was greatly affected by the failure of financial reform, and by the state's long-standing inability to work out coherent economic policies.

Trade and manufacturing also had a large role in the crisis. The American war, like the Seven Years War, was in large part a naval conflict, and therefore had a large impact on an economy dependent on colonial trade. After the peace of 1783, merchants attempted to profit as quickly as possible from the resumption of international exchange, and therefore imported huge quantities of colonial produce, whose prices collapsed as a result. At the same time, France had been growing increasingly dependent on revenues from textile exports. After the Seven Years War, Spain, her most important foreign market, had greatly reduced its imports. In Nîmes, a Spanish ban on silk stockings led to a reduction in the number of silk workshops from 5,000 to 2,500, and a 55 per cent fall in overall production. Trade with the Ottoman empire, an essential market for Languedoc's textiles, was harmed by its war with Russia. This closing of markets had nothing to do with technological backwardness, even though the textiles in question were produced by workshops operating in the traditional fashion, in what remained an essentially Colbertian system. The difficulties were often eventually overcome by a reorientation of production, and by the opening up of new markets. Nonetheless, in the short term, at the end of both wars, unemployment haunted the towns and countryside alike. On the eve of the Revolution, the depression in the manufacturing sector was further aggravated by the Franco-British commercial treaty of 1786, which opened the French market to British textiles.

The problem of the state's debts put the final touch on the looming economic catastrophe. In times of crisis, merchants and manufacturers who owned portions of the debt were obliged to sell them at a loss, leading to a general loss of confidence. A poor harvest, by worsening the deficit, then forced the government to borrow even more heavily, keeping interest rates high and undercutting all attempts at paying off the debt, at reducing its cost, or at stimulating economic growth. To break this vicious circle, the government had only three possible solutions: suppress barriers to production and trade so as to open markets and increase their flexibility; increase the profitability of landed investments by reforming the tax system; and continue to nibble away at fiscal privilege as much as possible without provoking large-scale protests from the elites.

To put an end to the deficit, the debt, and the economic crisis all at once, Calonne finally convinced Louis XVI to accelerate the modernization of the monarchy and to enact, once and for all, the various reforms which his predecessors Machault, Bertin, L'Averdy, Turgot, and Necker had failed fully to implement. Calonne aimed mainly to replace the twentieth by a land tax levied in kind (*subvention territoriale*), to replace the *corvée* by a tax on landowners, to standardize the salt tax, to free the grain trade from regulations, to suppress internal customs, and to create a state bank. But previous experiences had shown that any large-scale attempt at permanent reform in a traditional and only partly unified economy risked provoking fratricidal debates between the supporters of a 'moral economy' in which market forces remained under strict state control, and advocates of economic liberalism who aimed at breaking the old-established structures of privilege which benefited the privileged and stifled growth. By convoking an Assembly of Notables, Calonne acknowledged the need to develop a true consensus for reform. However, by demanding agreement on complex reforms which would modify the essential principles of the monarchy's social and economic organization, he effectively confronted them with a choice between obedience or obstruction. From that point on, the economic and financial crises inescapably expanded to involve the political foundations of the state itself.

2

Society

Gail Bossenga

When Louis XIV began his personal rule in 1661 he envisioned restoring order to a society suffering from civil strife, international war, and periodic waves of disease and famine. The society over which Louis XIV cast his gaze was a traditional, preindustrial one, characterized by minute distinctions of status, extremes of wealth and poverty, poor communication networks, low life expectancy, and close economic ties to the land. Legally it was a society characterized by privilege, that is, by an acute consciousness of rank and the practice whereby some groups enjoyed particular rights—tax exemptions, economic monopolies, or favoured access to occupations—denied to others.

Over the course of the eighteenth century, France retained most of its traditional, preindustrial characteristics; no dramatic economic 'take-off' or sudden spurt of industrial activity transformed French life. Nonetheless, many men and women experienced a variety of improvements within their everyday lives. Periodic food shortages continued, but they no longer triggered detectable surges in mortality. Between 1700 and 1789, the population gradually increased from approximately 21,500,000 to 28,000,000 inhabitants. Internal trade quadrupled, and trade with the colonies rose tenfold. In the fifty years before the Revolution, over 25,000 kilometres of roads were constructed, an advance that allowed specialized consumer goods to move more quickly and cheaply from one region to another. Life became more comfortable. Larger numbers of people, including servants and artisans, were able to buy new clothes, watches, mirrors, pottery, and books, items that earlier had been associated with elite status. A mini-hygienic revolution was launched when individuals began to change their linen undergarments on a regular basis, even though people still bathed only occasionally.

The gains associated with the economic growth and social refinements of the eighteenth century, however, were not enjoyed equally by all social groups. Renters were squeezed by high rents in the decades before the Revolution, and many peasants found themselves facing lords who collected seigneurial dues with more rigour than ever. The booming colonial trade after 1700 was fed by the forcible enslavement of 955,500 Africans. Meanwhile, the royal government was helping to raise the population's consciousness of the inequities of the old regime by repeatedly trying to reform perceived abuses without success. In the end, all the aristocratic titles, guild monopolies, tax exemptions, seigneurial dues, provincial customs, and other privileges that had characterized the old regime were swept away in a tide of revolution. Yet, on the eve of the Revolution, few would have predicted this dramatic course of events in a country where the aristocracy and privilege had for so long reigned supreme. The story of society in the old regime, therefore, is one of startling contrasts in life experiences culminating in an outcome that took Europe by surprise.

Social stratification: class and status

Most people in the old regime did not think of society as the product of autonomous, self-interested individuals. Instead, society was commonly regarded as a series of hierarchically ordered groups, all of whom were expected to fulfil particular roles in order to maintain social harmony. It was these groups that gave an individual his or her identity and set the general scope for life opportunities. Individuals were bound by their place in the family, by the negative or positive obligations imposed by rank, by the rights ascribed to particular localities and professions, and by the dictates of religion. Such institutional constraints did not obliterate individuality, but they did markedly shape the possibilities for individual expression by perpetuating norms for proper conduct, by shaping the distribution of resources, and by imposing sanctions on deviant behaviour.

The most basic hierarchical division of society was that of the three orders or three estates. The clergy, mediators between God and man, constituted the first estate; the nobility, reputedly descendants

of valiant medieval warriors, comprised the second estate; and commoners, who performed the labour to sustain the superior estates,
formed the third estate. Each order, in turn, could be subdivided into
other groups ranked according to more subtle gradations of honour
and dignity. Individuals in the old regime were intensely concerned
with questions of status and rank. As the Parisian lawyer Target stated
in his *Lettres d'un homme* of 1771, 'The French are all ranked, and each
have their own occupations; they have a corporate spirit and hardly
any other.'[1]

Historians have waged vigorous debates over the nature of the
social hierarchy in the old regime. Some have claimed that the formal
system of ranks was superficial and that the 'real' social structure
could be traced back to wealth or to class. Class, as it is used in this
context, referred to a group's place in society based upon shared
economic position or level of wealth. From this perspective the pre-
eminent place of the clergy and nobility in the old regime could be
attributed to their vast control of material resources. Other historians
argued that the old regime was a society of orders in which members
were ranked 'in accordance with the social esteem, honour, and dignity attached by society to different social functions, without there
being any direct link between this and the production of material
goods'.[2] The venerable attributes associated with the clergy and nobility as a whole—their spiritual calling, heroic deeds on the battlefield,
service to the king, and pure blood—entitled all members of these
groups to honour regardless of the economic standing of any individual member. Technically, the latter view was correct, for wide vari-
ations in economic standing could often be found inside orders and
corporate groups. For this reason, orders and corporate groups may
best be considered status groups, where status is defined as ranked
positions in society based upon shared perceptions of social honour.

That said, our understanding of the old regime will remain rather
static unless we look at status as a dynamic form of social identity and
ask how the forces of wealth and honour intersected. There has often
been an implicit tendency to treat rank, dignity, and honour merely
as a set of prescriptive ideals, a kind of 'mind' of the old regime, that

---

[1] Cited by David Bell, *Lawyers and Citizens: The Making of a Political Elite in Old Regime France* (Oxford, 1994), 142.

[2] R. Mousnier, *The Institutions of France under the Absolute Monarchy, 1598–1789* (Chicago, 1979), i. 6.

did not influence economic behaviour. Yet norms governing notions of honour and reputation cannot so easily be separated from actual decision-making. Throughout the eighteenth century concern for reputation and status continued to exert a strong influence on the use of wealth. Individuals were not free to choose just any occupation, spouse, education, or investment opportunity if they wished to maintain their rank in society. In fact, the acquisition and maintenance of social rank could well require the outlay of large sums of money. In 1786 the count de Saulx-Tavanes, for example, spent 25,000 *livres* to have his lands elevated into a duchy, an honour that undoubtedly cost far more monetarily than it reaped. It would not be difficult to cite other instances in the old regime where individuals made economically 'irrational' choices, because they followed codes of conduct that supported status distinctions rather than a profit motive. To a striking degree, then, status was able to co-opt wealth by establishing standards for the acceptable use of money.

Because the eighteenth century was a period of rising prosperity and continuous social mobility, some historians have suggested that the old regime was evolving from a society of orders based in honour to one of classes based in wealth. This assessment appears problematic. In fact, from the old regime to the early nineteenth century, the class structure of France underwent little change: it remained a country of wealthy landlords; small, impoverished peasant proprietors; and dispersed protoindustrial activity. What the Revolution changed in France was not class structure defined by wealth, but a system of legal status relations. The Revolution redefined the cultural values signifying social prestige, and overturned the juridical system that had upheld status distinctions in the old regime. In place of legalized status hierarchies arose the principle of citizenship, an ideal which upheld merit as the foundation of the social hierarchy and equality before the law as the basis of membership in the state.

Law has often been ignored as a constitutive element of social organization, but it plays an important part in the definition of social roles and distribution of resources. In the old regime, law codified all important status relations and channelled resources to those holding honourable rank. The status system of the old regime that underpinned the society of orders, therefore, consisted of two elements: the first, hierarchical position in society based upon publicly shared ideas of honour and esteem; and the second, position in society based upon legal entitlement. Status thus consisted of subjective and objective components, cultural ideals, and legal rights. Both of these elements were shaped by wealth, but both of them, in turn, influenced how material resources were perceived and used. From this interplay came many of the characteristic features of society in the old regime.

Honour and rank

Honour was essentially an aristocratic notion whose origins could be found in the medieval, knightly code of physical prowess, self-sacrifice, and service to the king. In the early modern period, however, honour was also used more globally to describe the distinctive, ranked positions of groups in society. Montesquieu called honour 'the prejudice of every person and rank', while the widely-read German jurist Pufendorf stated that 'honour properly so called is the indication of our judgement of another's superiority.'[3] Honour was a source of both social solidarity and distinction. It united those of the same station by providing codes of conduct appropriate to members of that group; at the same time it furnished the terms by which lesser groups were excluded. Although all groups in society might claim some sort of honour, the expression of honour varied by rank. A noble defended his honour through duelling, but also emphasized his superiority by refusing to duel with commoners. A journeyman felt insulted if his master did not let him eat at the master's table. The distinctions between ranks could be subtle and even trivial, but that often only served to make the participants more jealous of their prerogatives. In some judicial courts in the early eighteenth century, attorneys had to kneel while university-educated advocates pleaded at the bar.

Although social esteem could be acquired by an individual by practising an honourable lifestyle and profession, honour was never a purely individual affair; it remained closely associated with institutional roles and family pedigree. In the old regime, distinguished

---

[3] *De l'esprit des lois*, bk. III, ch. 7; *On the Duties of Man and Citizen According to Natural Law* (Cambridge, 1991), 164.

birth (*naissance*) was a synonym for nobility and conferred honour automatically. According to the entry *naissance* in the *Encyclopédie*, it was with good reason that birth conferred 'a great ascendancy over the members of a state who are of less elevated extraction'. Birth acquired even greater lustre the further back in time it could be traced. As the seventeenth-century jurist Loyseau remarked, 'Simple nobility affects the blood and passes it on to posterity in such a way that the more ancient it is, the more honourable'.[4] Birth was also considered a source of quasi-moral attributes and inherent aptitude for certain functions. According to Furetière's *Dictionnaire universel* of 1723, birth was 'the good or bad qualities with which one is born'. Because it was commonly believed that birth predisposed some individuals to positions of authority over others, social opportunities were strongly conditioned by this quality. A minor, but illustrative, example may be found in the Daughters of the Childhood of Jesus Christ of Toulouse who established an uncloistered congregation for young women who wished to devote their lives to prayer and acts of charity. They divided their organization into three groups: those from noble families who served as administrators, those from 'good' families who were instructors, and those of 'low extraction' who had to work as servants.

Like birth, profession and lifestyle were associated with intrinsically honourable or dishonourable qualities. The article *profession* in the *Encyclopédie* arranged professions into three categories: 'glorious,' 'honest', and 'base'. Because honour was a quality that had to be displayed and lived out, men and women concerned with maintaining their honour could only accept employment suited to their station in life. Service as an army officer, which demonstrated power of command and heroic sacrifice, was regarded as the quintessential noble occupation. 'There is nothing that honour prescribes more for the nobility', observed Montesquieu, 'than to serve the prince in war.'[5] Positions as magistrates in the sovereign courts were also suited to nobility, because, as Loyseau observed, magistrates represented the Majesty of the king. The professions that required a liberal arts degree from a university, including medical doctors, lawyers, and professors, had favourable connotations of independence, for the word *liberal* in

---

[4] *A Treatise of Orders and Plain Dignities*, trans. Howell A. Lloyd (Cambridge, 1994), 81.
[5] *De l'esprit des lois*, bk. IV, ch. 2.

this context meant 'worthy of a free man'. Such employment offered
enough leisure and time for self-cultivation that these professions
were considered compatible with nobility, even if most of the prac-
tioners were well-to-do commoners, those usually referred to in this
period as the bourgeoisie.

The bourgeoisie were those who lacked the great honour associated with nobility, but enjoyed a lesser prestige that came from being
educated, having enough wealth to engage in conspicuous consumption, and avoiding manual labour. Of all the professions linked to the
bourgeoisie—those of lawyer, doctor, office-holder, and rentier—
that of the merchant was the most suspect. From an aristocratic
viewpoint, the profession of merchant was tainted, because it was
associated with profit-seeking and self-interest. As a note sent to the
government stated in 1701, merchants could not aspire to true honour,
because 'the wealth which is created by their efforts enriches them
first'.[6] Even though the wealth and status of merchants was rising
throughout the eighteenth century, it proved hard to shake the traditional prejudice against business activities, and the desired lifestyle
for the bourgeoisie remained a cultured, aristocratic one that
revolved around consumption and leisure rather than production
and exchange. In the 1780s Restif de la Bretonne still placed the bourgeois 'living nobly', that is, the bourgeois who lived off inherited
wealth or investments, above wealthy international merchants (négo-
ciants) in terms of prestige: 'the occupation of merchant is very
important and should be placed before the man of means [rentier] in
the hierarchy of conditions, but I have held to the old prejudice that
says that the bourgeois living nobly on his revenues holds the first
rank after the nobility'.[7] The inclination to favour the idle rentier
over the merchant was suited to a preindustrial society in which the
economies of cities were frequently directed toward consumption
and the provision of services to nobles, magistrates, lesser officials,
and professionals. Even in the great commercial and manufacturing
centre of Lyon in 1788, 13.2 per cent of the population on the capitation roll was listed as rentiers (nobles and bourgeois), compared to
only 6 per cent as merchants. It is not surprising that in the second

[6] Cited by R.B. Grassby, 'Social Status and Commercial Enterprise under Louis
XIV', *Economic History Review*, 13 (1960), 31.
[7] *Les Contemporaines par gradation* (Paris, 1783–5), 7:243, cited by Yves Durand, *Les
Fermiers généraux au xviii*^e *siècle* (Paris, 1971), 208.

half of the eighteenth century, Paris and provincial capitals became centres of a refined, elite sociability based in reading clubs, academies, masonic lodges, and cafés. The leisure, genteel wealth, and consumption associated with an urban *rentier* lifestyle provided the basis for the great intellectual flowering known as the Enlightenment.

Toward the bottom of the social scale were occupations, like those of artisans and peasants, that required manual labour and/or that obliged a person to cater to the demands of others, such as shopkeepers. The order of advocates in Rennes actually barred those whose fathers had been involved in 'mechanical crafts' from admission to their ranks. Nonetheless, within their own circles, members of these groups retained a concern for rank, honour, and reputation that could be expressed in a variety of ways, for example, by becoming a member of a guild or village assembly, by guaranteeing the quality of their wares, by maintaining the self-sufficiency of their farms and enterprises, or by keeping up the appearance of their shop or house. The Parisian guild of sausage-makers (*charcutiers*), for example, fined a member 30 *livres* for having employed someone of bad morals. At the bottom of society, the most marginal groups possessed no property, autonomy, or corporate affiliation at all—day labourers, landless peasants, the poor and beggars. The ambiguous nature of honour as one descended the social hierarchy was captured in a court case in 1782 pitting a master against a female servant: 'although in the most obscure rank, a man has an honour that belongs to him, which it would be as unjust to deprive him of as life, nevertheless, that which brings dishonour in a superior class is scarcely noted in an inferior'.[8] Men and women of a lesser condition might stake out a claim to honour, but those above them did not feel bound to acknowledge it.

Gender and family roles further conditioned status within the various levels of the social hierarchy. In general, owing to the perceived inferiority of the 'second sex', women were barred from professions conferring authority and the highest honours in society: they could not serve as bishops, priests, army officers, or magistrates.[9] It

---

[8] Document in Yves Castan, *Honnêteté et relations sociales en Languedoc (1715–1780)* (Paris, 1974), 588.

[9] Jean Domat refers to women as the 'second sex' in *Les Loix civiles dans leur ordre naturel, le droit public et legum delectus* (Paris, 1723), vii.

was the lot of women to hold status mediated by family relationships that were subject to change over the course of the female life cycle. Under the authority first of a father, and then of a husband, a woman could achieve her greatest degree of independence as a widow who inherited her deceased husband's authority as head of household. Yet widowhood could also mean economic disaster among the lower classes where the labour of both husband and wife was essential for survival. Few opportunities existed for unmarried women, and those that did provide a respectable existence often had the character of a substitute family: sisters in convents, households composed of unmarried brothers and sisters, or servants living in their masters' homes. Virtually the only jobs available to single women involved retail sales or manual labour, both of marginal status in the world of work. Usually such female employment was an extension of household tasks—domestic servants, hairdressers, linen drapers, seamstresses, herbalists, and petty retailers of fruit, eggs and butter. Although examples of successful businesswomen in the old regime can be found, their success usually began by working through husbands who had the proper formal credentials, even if the women were the ones who made the actual decisions.

The derivative quality of female status was starkly illustrated by the patrilineal transmission of nobility. Legally, a wife took on the status of her husband while she was married, even if she was noble by birth and her husband a commoner. Likewise, the status of the father determined that of the offspring; the children of a noble-woman who married a commoner would not be noble. Owing to these rules, hypergamy, the marriage of a wealthy woman of lesser status to a man of superior status was not uncommon in the old regime. Nobles of illustrious lines could 'manure their fields' with the dowry of a rich non-noble heiress but not jeopardize their lineage. The jurist Jean Domat offered a good summary of the principle at work: 'the husband and the wife are only as it were one and the same person, so that the wife derives from her husband all that can go to her sex.'[10]

The power of status was expressed routinely through ceremonies of deference. The writing of a letter, the passing of someone on the street, the wearing of an article of clothing, the seating arrangement

---

[10] *Les Loix civiles*, 578.

at a dinner or play, the selective use of the familiar *tu* and the formal
vous—all these, and many more, were opportunities to confirm and
make visible the lines of status. The system took its power, in part, by
the active participation, and preferably voluntary acquiescence, of
inferiors in acts of deference to superiors. This provides the reason
for such a rash of seemingly ridiculous battles over things like
hats, displays of swords, and placement in ceremonial processions.
Through these symbolic rituals, individuals were continually obliged
to reaffirm their place in the social hierarchy and were forced to
compare the relative worth of their existence to that of others. For a
man to remove his hat in another man's presence, for example, indicated his respect for the other person, as well as a recognition of his
inferior position. The so-called *affaire du bonnet*, fought over whether
magistrates in the parlement of Paris had to remove their hats when
addressing the peers of the realm in court, occupied nearly twenty
years of Louis XIV's reign. The sun king himself wisely refrained
from issuing a verdict. Not unsurprisingly, the old regime also ended
with a brouhaha over hats. On 5 May 1789, at a royal session of the
estates general at Versailles, Louis XVI gave his nobles permission to
put their hats back on. Some members of the third estate, however,
decided that they would no longer remain bareheaded in the presence
of the king, and, like the nobles, covered themselves. In the ensuing
confusion, everyone in the room, king, nobles and commoners alike,
ended up removing their hats, and the meeting continued on a note
of sartorial equality. Of course, the etiquette of the hat was not
limited to skirmishes in the upper reaches of the social hierarchy. Nor
was 1789 the first time that commoners had decided to keep on their
hats in the presence of superiors. The chronicler of a bread riot in
Arles in 1752, for example, was outraged that members of the crowd,
mere day labourers, had the impudence to meet with the archbishop
himself while wearing their hats. The crowd's action illuminated a
long-standing belief of the lower orders: rank carried responsibility,
and authorities who failed in their duties to the poor forfeited their
right to respect.

Legal status: the importance of privilege

Perhaps the most important difference between social organization in the old regime and society after the Revolution was the role played by law. In the old regime, a person's status in society was not only shaped by public attitudes concerning honour; it was also governed by legal opportunities and restrictions. The special legal rights accorded to particular groups were known as privileges, whose Latin root literally meant private laws. The use of the word privilege in the old regime should not be confused with its modern connotation of a wealthy, pampered existence, though many privileged individuals were rich and coddled. Privilege before 1789 referred to legal entitlement. Such entitlements extended deep into society and created a whole series of ranked subjects with unequal rights in the state.

It would be misleading to try to describe the system of privilege in this period in an overly logical and coherent manner, for many privileges had been acquired in the past, and as conditions evolved, some privileges had lost their original justification. Yet it would be equally misleading to say that privilege represented a completely irrational juridical organization of society, a vestigial remnant of the Middle Ages that would naturally fade away as the modern forces of the state and capitalism grew. The network of privileges was as much, or perhaps even more, a construction of the early modern period as the medieval. Its vast increase in the sixteenth and seventeenth centuries and its routinization in the eighteenth occurred in tandem with the growth of the state and the economy. The proliferation of privileges in the early modern period was a sign that society was moving from an oral to a written culture, achieving greater legal sophistication, and acquiring a greater degree of institutional differentiation. In France, privilege also signalled the development of the monarchical state, for by the time of Louis XIV, the king had become able to enforce his claim to be the fount of privilege and the supreme arbiter of legal status. The far-reaching network of privilege by 1661, therefore, was a testimony to both the rise of the monarchical state and a host of interests that clamoured for recognition and protection.

Privilege served a variety of purposes, but three were fundamental. First, privilege helped to secure the political right of a social group to regulate its own affairs; second, privilege offered protection for the economic interests of particular groups; and third, privilege served as a marker of honour and distinction. Law in the old regime thus had a function different from that in modern society. Whereas a central goal of law in democratic societies is to ensure equality of opportunity and uniformity of rights across the nation, in the old regime the purpose of law was to shore up the social hierarchy and preserve pockets of special, local rights. These legal entitlements were not of trivial importance; they formed a valuable part of opportunities for income and social advance in the old regime. In fact, it is a testimony of their resilience and significance that it took a revolution to destroy them.

Although privileges existed at many levels of society, and even peasants occasionally benefited from them, it would be inaccurate to view privileges as neutral entities. Privilege continually remained tied into the status system of the old regime: its rewards were most lucrative at the top of the hierarchy. As the *Encyclopédie* stated in the article *privilège*: 'Birth has its privileges. There is no dignity that does not have its [privileges]; each has the privilege of its type and nature'. Some privileges were purely honorific, that is, they allowed a group to demonstrate publicly their superior qualities for all to admire. Whenever the magistrates of the parlement of Paris, the highest judicial court in the land, walked past a military post, the guards were ordered to present arms while drummers beat their drums. Other privileges were useful and entailed monetary advantages, such as tax exemptions. In some ways, however, it is not really helpful to distinguish 'useful' privileges conferring economic advantages from purely 'honourific' ones, because financial benefits, pensions, and occupational entitlements were all considered testimonies to superior status. As the clergy of Normandy stated in 1634, 'The most significant mark of honour which places the church of this province above the common people is exemption from the *taille* which is common to it with the nobility.'[11] A central function of privilege, then, was to serve as the legal mechanism for transforming perceptions of superior status into material advantage. The most extensive privileges were enjoyed by the nobility and clergy, but guilds, municipalities, professional bodies like

---

[11] Quoted by Edmond Esmonin, *La Taille en Normandie au temps de Colbert, 1661–1683* (Paris, 1913), 196.

those of magistracies, and provinces also had their own prerogatives. In addition, not all members of the clergy and nobility enjoyed identical rights. Privilege thus never created a society of unified classes: it was perpetually concerned with establishing subtle gradations not only between the orders but also within the orders themselves.

The clergy in a confessional state

In 1788 the church was composed of perhaps 130,000 ecclesiastics, less than 1 per cent of the total population, but it owned between 6 and 10 per cent of the land. The church not only derived a substantial income from the rents, fees, and produce of its lands, but, in addition, had the privilege of collecting the tithe (*dîme*), a tax levied on grains, wine, and other 'fruits of the earth'. Despite its name, the incidence of the tithe varied widely by region, ranging from as little as one-thirtieth to as much as one-seventh. Originally created to support the costs of services of worship, in many regions the tithe had fallen into the hands of third-party tithe owners (*gros décimateurs*) who pocketed its substantial revenues and left the parish priests with only a meagre salary known as the *portion congrue*. Estimates of the total ecclesiastical income of the clergy range anywhere from 60,000,000 *livres* to 180,000,000 *livres* per year. Owing to extensive tax exemptions, justified on the grounds that clerical property was a sacred trust from God, the church paid few taxes on its vast riches. Overall before the Revolution, the clergy turned over a mere 3–5 per cent of its revenues to the government in the form of gifts or clerical taxes.

At its upper reaches, the clergy was completely entwined with the aristocratic status system. Over half of the approximately 1,000 abbeys were held *in commendam*, a practice by which an absentee abbot from outside the house performed no functions, but could appropriate over a half of its income. The church also supported approximately 15,000 to 18,000 canons of cathedrals and other priests without cure of souls, a group of benefices that were invariably reserved for younger sons of distinguished families. Although one benefice might only provide a modest income, perhaps between 1,000 and 2,000 *livres*, it was possible to accumulate them and live a quite comfortable life. Extra daughters were sent off to live in respectable refinement at convents, so that the family would not have to dower them as lavishly and divide the family patrimony. At the top of the clerical pyramid were 136 bishops and archbishops, whose income in the most important ecclesiastical sees could exceed 100,000 *livres*. From 1682 to 1700 just 8 per cent of the bishops came from non-noble families, but in the period 1774–90 this meagre showing was reduced even further, to a mere 1 per cent. In the mid-eighteenth century, approximately 60 per cent of the bishops had at least 200 years of nobility behind them.

At the base of the Catholic church were approximately 50,000 parish priests (*curés*) and their assistants, the curates. These men baptized, married, absolved, and buried their parishioners. They supervised village schools, sat on hospital boards, arbitrated local disputes, and were called on by the king periodically to publicize important edicts issued in Paris. In general, priests were recruited from the literate, financially secure sector of their communities. The church required that clerics provide proof of a yearly income sufficient to live on until they received their first benefice, a practice that effectively closed off the profession to the poor. A noticeable decline in recruitment was observable after 1760, perhaps a sign of the waning of religious ardour in general. The average priest in the eighteenth century, however, was more learned, committed, and professionalized than in any century before. The reform movement of the Catholic Counter-Reformation had succeeded in setting codes of conduct that separated priests more clearly from the laity and enforced higher standards of morality.

A second branch of the clerical hierarchy was composed of nuns and monks who were members of the regular religious orders. In the late sixteenth and seventeenth centuries, the Catholic Counter-Reformation had inspired a profound revival of spirituality. A host of new religious orders and lay confraternities were founded to preach, teach, tend the sick, and care for the poor. Although the vibrancy of baroque Catholicism gradually declined in the eighteenth century, evidence of religious commitment could still be found. In the eighteenth century, the 800 schools of the Christian Brothers instructed more than 30,000 children from non-elite families. Women were particularly drawn to the new piety, so much so that writers of the period began labelling them 'the devout sex'.[12] Although women

[12] Cited in Wendy Gibson, *Women in Seventeenth-Century France* (New York, 1989), 209.

could not be priests or bishops, convents and sisterhoods provided professional opportunities to women in a society where few respectable professional outlets existed.

Within the framework of the Christian society of orders, social bonds were also religious bonds, for God was considered the author of society. The church marked the entrance of individuals into the world with baptism, it sanctioned reproduction through vows of holy marriage, it offered forgiveness and reconciliation for social wrongs through penance and holy communion, and it prepared the dying for glory by administering extreme unction. Those who refused to receive the sacraments of the Catholic church, many believed, could be in harmony neither with God nor their neighbours. Within this vision of society, it was difficult to conceptualize a generalized freedom of worship, though the right to worship might be permitted to non-Catholics by special dispensation. The edict of Nantes of 1598 had granted toleration to French Calvinists; in 1685, however, Louis XIV revoked this edict. Henceforth only Catholics could legally hold services of worship, be married and baptized, enter French universities, obtain masterships in guilds, or serve in any public capacity, including even minor posts like those of notary, bailiff or attorney. The religiously diverse province of Alsace, annexed to France in 1648, offered one exception to this intolerance. There religious rights continued to be governed by international law, the treaty of Westphalia. Under its provisions, the king was permitted to establish a state religion, but he could neither persecute nor expel Alsatian Calvinists and Lutherans. Although not officially tolerated, a handful of Alsatian Anabaptists also received protection from local lords who welcomed them as honest workers. After the revocation of the edict of Nantes, it is estimated that between 140,000 and 160,000 Protestants fled France from 1685 to 1689, but a sizeable number, perhaps as many as 200,000, remained in southern France where an underground church perpetuated itself in the 'desert' of the Cévennes. For the rest of the old regime, until civil status was granted to Protestants in 1787, to be fully French was to be Catholic.

Jews were the second group of religious outsiders in Catholic France. Jews as a whole had been banished from France in 1394, but several Jewish groups had eventually re-established themselves within special juridical niches so typical of the old regime. Bordeaux and the suburbs of Bayonne were home to Sephardic Jews, descendants of *marranos* or 'New Christians' from the Iberian peninsula who had fled Spanish persecution and often retained crypto-Judaic practices under a veneer of Catholic conformity. These New Christians were allowed to live and trade in France under the status of privileged foreigners. In Eastern France, the French kings who had acquired Alsace and Lorraine from the Holy Roman Empire continued to honour pre-existing legal arrangements from those regions. This situation allowed Ashkenazic Jews to bargain with local and royal officials for limited rights of residence. No Jew was allowed to own land or hold office, a legal predicament which forced them to remain in commerce. In general Sephardic Jews, who participated in the booming international trade of Bordeaux, were far more wealthy and cultured than their Ashkenazic counterparts, who were limited to a menial existence eked out of petty usury, peddling, smuggling, the old-clothes trade, and other precarious retailing ventures. Commercial jealousy reinforced religious hostility against Jews among French merchants, but the royal government allowed pockets of Judaism to persist. Jews were needed to provide taxes and loans, supply armies on the eastern front, and keep prices down for consumers by offering competition.

A divided nobility

The nobility formed just a tiny fragment of French society, but they controlled the lion's share of social resources. Estimates of the number of nobles range anywhere from 120,000 to 350,000 individuals, or between 0.75 and 1.25 per cent of the population, but they owned perhaps one-quarter to one-third of the land. A wide variety of privileges demonstrated the honour of this estate. Symbolic prerogatives included the right to carry swords, an age-old token of their warrior status, and to be beheaded, rather than hanged, for capital crimes. In regions where the humiliating *taille* was levied on persons, nobles were exempt, although in areas of the *taille réelle*, mainly in southern France, tax exemptions followed the status of the land, not the person, so that nobles paid the *taille* when they held non-noble land. Nobles also enjoyed exemption from or reductions on a variety of indirect taxes, including the salt tax and excise on wine. They could not be forced to perform labour services (*corvée*), were given preference in eminent civil and military positions, and had the right to have their judicial cases heard directly in higher level courts of appeal. Nobles were also the greatest beneficiaries of the seigneurial system, which allowed them to collect a wide variety of dues and services from dependent peasants. In provincial estates and the estates general (which last met in 1614), both they and the clergy were able to vote in separate chambers as orders, a policy which ensured them a degree of political power far beyond their numbers.

Although nobles shared a common legal status, they were profoundly divided by wealth, lineage, profession, and institutional affiliation. The greatest fortunes in France belonged to nobles; that was true even in bustling commercial cities where banking and commerce were thriving. Not all nobles, however, were wealthy. At the summit of the entire kingdom stood *les grands*, the great Court nobles of ancient feudal lineage who owned extensive land in the provinces and enjoyed extravagant annual incomes ranging between 50,000 to 250,000 *livres*. Although these nobles set the tone for the aristocratic lifestyle, they represented only between 1 and 2 per cent of all nobles. Rich nobles who lived in grand style in the provinces formed the next 13 per cent. Another quarter of the provincial nobility lived in comfortable circumstances that allowed them to entertain and keep servants. The majority of nobles, however, led existences that could be described as modest at best. About 40 per cent were able to live decently if they were frugal and avoided outward show. The last 20 per cent faced actual poverty, some of them even destitution. According to one estimate, at least one third of the rural nobles living in upper Normandy and nearly one-third in the lower Auvergne could be considered poor.

In addition to sheer wealth, professional affiliation created marked subgroups within the second estate, often referred to as the nobilities of the Court, finance, sword, and robe. By the eighteenth century, nearly all of *les grands* had become Court nobles best known for their opulent and sometimes dissolute lifestyle. The idle existence of the great aristocratic courtier is the source of the myth that all nobles were useless parasites who had traded away their political power and functions for the pensions and prestige found at Versailles. The courtier's exchange of political power for status was largely a product of Louis XIV's strategy. In the sixteenth and seventeenth century, feudal grandees, who controlled large patron–client networks, had believed that their status freed them from the obligation to submit to the law of the king, and they were notorious for their constant scheming and even outright rebellion. After the Fronde, Louis XIV brought these obstreperous princes, dukes, counts, and others to Versailles in order to begin the process of divorcing aristocratic status from claims to political power. Status at Versailles, with its intricate rituals and ceremonies, became a reflection of the glory of the king. Feudal prestige, tamed at Court, was gradually stripped of its inherent tendency toward political insubordination and reoriented to pleasure-seeking and conspicuous consumption.

By the mid-eighteenth century, the rigid etiquette at Court was being replaced by a more open sociability oriented around the aristocratic salons in Paris where *le monde*—great nobles, distinguished parlementaires, clever intellectuals, and wealthy financiers—rubbed shoulders together. Nonetheless, the continued importance of formal Court connections for gaining access to the highest perquisites of state—army commissions, pensions, ecclesiastical sinecures, and rake-offs (*croupes*) from tax farming contracts—should not be forgotten. The Court at Versailles put a premium on ancestry, though the king made sure the status system revolved ultimately around his own good pleasure. According to a regulation of 17 April 1760, formal presentation at the Court of Versailles required ancestry going back to 1400, or the king's special dispensation. By this regulation, only 'presented' nobles could be promoted past the grade of colonel, so that all the top army posts of commanders and generals tended to be monopolized by families of ancient extraction who enjoyed the king's favour. It has been estimated that at the end of the old regime perhaps 4,000 noble families had been presented at Court.

A second group of nobles who wielded great influence at Versailles were the financiers, men of great wealth and relatively fresh ennoblement, who served as bankers to the king. These men were central to the operation of what has been called 'Court capitalism,' a pre-modern form of capitalism that was nourished by aristocratic connections, speculation, state loans, and tax revenues skimmed from the lower orders. This capitalism was not to be confused with more modern kinds of manufacturing or industry in which technological advances, organizational innovation, or investment yielded profits to businessmen. Court capitalism was wed to state finance and drew upon an aristocratic pool of investors, including the royal family, which was able to use its proximity to power to reap fabulous rewards. The quickest route to riches in the old regime was not through mere investment in business, but through the well-connected, patron-laden route of tax collection consortiums and high-interest government loans. Financiers were the moneyed underside of Versailles and its gilded aristocracy. Despite their enormous wealth, and even the marriage of their daughters into noble dynasties of illustrious extraction, the status of financiers was never the equal of that of the Court nobility itself, and the rest of society commonly regarded them as bloodsuckers and parasites.

Serving as an army officer was considered the most honourable and aristocratic occupation, and at the end of the old regime 90 per cent of army officers were noble. Inside the army, however, nobles were deeply divided, because private wealth and court connections were needed to advance an army career. Not only did the presented nobility monopolize the top grades in the army, officers in the most prestigious military units, the royal household and the calvary, had to purchase their positions for sums far beyond the means of a poor provincial noble. Until reforms of 1762, moreover, army officers were expected to purchase their own uniforms and replace horses and equipment lost in battle, an obligation which could be prohibitively expensive for a noble of modest means. As a result of such policies, the system favoured those nobles who had the money to support the costs of an army career, and these were often the sons of wealthy new nobles who were more concerned with the status attached to an army career than with actually fighting. The frustrations of the poor provincial nobles was one factor leading to to the famous Ségur law of 1781, which required four quarterings of nobility in order to become an officer. This law was an interesting mixture of professionalism and status consciousness. It spoke to professional concerns, because army reformers were convinced that wealthy new nobles who had experienced a soft and indolent upbringing were unsuited for the rigours and sacrifice of military life. It revealed a concern for status distinctions because reformers took for granted that there was a natural fit between being an officer and a *gentilhomme*, that is, a noble of ancient lineage.

The nobility of the 'robe' formed another important sector of the second estate. These were nobles, so-called for the robes they wore, who owned judicial offices, particularly in the parlements, the thirteen sovereign courts of appeal established by the king in the provinces. Virtually all judicial offices in the old regime were venal, that is, a candidate for office had to purchase the office he wished to fill. Although forms of venality of offices had existed since the late Middle Ages, in 1604 the system became formally institutionalized through the creation of the *droit annuel* or *Paulette*, a fee paid to the royal government that allowed office-holders to bequeath or sell their offices at will and that turned offices, for all practical purposes, into their patrimony. Because members of the royal judicial courts owned their offices, the king could not dismiss them unless he reimbursed them the purchase price for their offices. The price of an office usually was a sizeable sum; in 1750 a magistracy in the Parisian parlement cost about 50,000 *livres*. The royal government thus found itself unable to reform the judiciary, unless it chose to do so by trampling on nobles' property rights and exercising 'despotic' powers. The sale of offices also facilitated the formation of powerful dynasties at the centre of the many parlements, and prevented advocates who worked in these courts, no matter how brilliant and hard-working, from being promoted to a magistracy on the basis of merit alone. In the sixteenth and seventeenth centuries, nobles of the robe had frequently been characterized as upstarts and even 'bourgeois', only ennobled by virtue of possessing high administrative and judicial office. By the eighteenth century, many parlementary nobles controlled vast landed estates and boasted well-established aristocratic pedigrees. In the century before the Revolution, only 19 per cent of those entering the French parlements were non-nobles; 50 per cent could flaunt four or more generations of nobility.

The purchase of ennobling offices in the judiciary continued to be the main source of legal social mobility down to the Revolution. These offices were found not only in the parlements, but also in other sovereign courts such as the chambers of accounts, courts of aids, and bureaux of finances, as well as the chancelleries attached to sovereign courts and a smattering of municipal offices. It has been estimated that in the period 1774 to 1789, a total of 2,477 men were ennobled, and the numbers, if anything, were rising slightly directly before the Revolution. The easiest route to ennoblement, at least for the very wealthy, was the purchase of an office of 'king's secretary', an office which sounded important but really had no administrative functions at all: its purpose was to confer nobility and tax privileges on wealthy non-nobles and to generate a variety of revenues for the royal government. These extravagantly expensive offices, which cost approximately 120,000 *livres* on the eve of Revolution, were particularly attractive because it was possible for a businessman to continue to run his business affairs while he held the office, and because the office conferred first-degree, that is, hereditary or transmissible, nobility on the office-holder and his posterity after twenty years of service or death in office. Other, less prestigious ennobling offices required two generations to serve in office before conferring transmissible nobility. There is little question that venality was the central reason behind the bloated, cumbersome nature of the French judiciary throughout the old regime. The fiscal interests of the royal government and the proprietary interests of the office-holders were too tightly rooted in the system, however, to permit any kind of substantial reorganization. Established nobles feared that the constant influx of new members into their estate diluted their status and undermined their claims to social superiority by associating noble status too directly with money rather than with the heroic deeds of ancestors. In 1789 half of the *cahiers* of the nobility demanded the end to ennoblement through venal offices. In his article on 'Political Economy' in the *Encyclopédie*, Jean-Jacques Rousseau issued this scathing critique of the system:

finally, venality pushed to such excess that consideration is counted with pennies and virtues themselves are sold for money: such are the most obvious causes of opulence and misery, of the substitution of particular interest for the public interest, of mutual hate between citizens, of the indifference for the common cause and the weakening of all the resources of government.

For Rousseau, venality represented the antithesis of citizenship.

Peasants, seigneurialism, and rural communities

In some respects the most honourable lifestyle for a noble involved no work at all, but demanded that one practise genteel idleness, or what was known as 'living nobly'. To live nobly meant living a refined, but essentially non-productive, life of cultivated leisure made possible by inherited wealth and *rentes*, that is, money from investments, pensions, dues, and rent paid by tenants. A person in this situation, it was assumed, did not demean his status by 'earning' money. He was able to amass wealth by rightfully collecting what was owed to him by virtue of his property and station in life. In his famous revolutionary pamphlet of 1788, *What is the Third Estate?*, the abbé Sieyès lamented the great respect granted this parasitic existence: 'What kind of society is it where work causes a loss of status (*fait déroger*)? Where it is honourable to consume and humiliating to produce?'[13]

The seigneurial system was intimately bound up with the ideal of living nobly: it was designed to let seigneurs consume what peasants produced. Peasants who fell under seigneurial jurisdiction, which included the vast majority, were legally obliged to pay to their lords an assortment of dues, which not only were a source of income for the lord but a sign of the peasants' servile status. The lesser personal status of the peasant was expressed through the incomplete and inferior nature of his property. Peasants 'owned' approximately 33 per cent of the land in France, that is, peasants could sell their plots or bequeath them to heirs. Nonetheless, a lord always retained rights over these plots, although the nature of these rights varied by region. In general, the lord received fees when land was sold, had priority in buying land when it came onto the market, could require tenants to use his mills and winepress for a fee, and was entitled to a portion of the harvest, whether paid in kind or in money. The right of the lord and the royal government to exact labour services from peasants further attested to the peasants' inferior position. The lord, meanwhile, had the right to set up seigneurial courts to judge in the first instance civil and criminal cases falling within their jurisdiction. His rank was put on constant display by means of a variety of honorific privileges: lords enjoyed a monopoly over hunting, could set up dovecotes, erect weather vanes on their roofs, and, if they had rights of high justice, set up gallows on their lawns. Although most lordships were owned by nobles, it was possible for non-nobles to purchase them, and enjoy the associated

---

[13] *Qu'est-ce que le Tiers État?* (1789; reprint, with an introduction by Roberto Zapperi, Geneva, 1970), 164.

legal prerogatives, so long as they paid a special fee (*franc-fief*) to the royal government.

Historians disagree over how effective the seigneurial system was at extracting surplus from peasants. The number of seigneurial courts in operation and the frequency of their sessions did appear to decline over the course of the eighteenth century, but active courts could still be found on the eve of the Revolution. It has been argued that seigneurial courts were probably not particularly effective in ensuring the collection of seigneurial dues, because the cost of maintaining a courtroom and jail exceeded the gains derived from enforcing payment of dues. Not all enforcement of dues, however, was accomplished through prison sentences, because lords could also issue liens against the property of delinquent peasants and encumber the transfer of those properties. It has also been noted that seigneurial courts did not solely serve the interests of lords, because peasants relied on these courts to protect their own property rights by punishing trespassing and theft, settling inheritance disputes, establishing wards for orphans, and so forth. The peasant grievances voiced in 1789 point to both the utility and abuse of these courts, for peasants wished to have some sort of local court to serve their needs, but also wanted these courts to be administered in a more fair and impartial manner.

It is difficult to make generalizations about the weight of seigneurial dues, because they varied so greatly by region. In general, the burdens were heavier in less economically developed areas and lighter in regions where capitalism had penetrated more fully and where regional customs had curbed lordly rights. In 1789, lords might extract as little as 2 per cent of the peasant's total harvest through dues in the Cambrésis, a bustling region where protoindustrial activity flourished, or as much as 33 per cent in the more remote and backward Limousin. Nonetheless, it cannot be concluded that the growth of capitalism always eroded seigneurial exactions. On the contrary, the privileges of lords could produce powerful market monopolies that became more vexing as the economy grew and regions became increasingly dependent on the market for goods. Seigneurial dues, for example, formed less than 10 per cent of the income of lords in the economically developed region of Pont-Saint-Pierre in Normandy overall, but lords fortunate to have mills that gave them a monopoly over grinding grain stood to earn substantially more. One mill in this region brought in half of the income of that particular estate. In Picardy where seigneurial dues were also minimal, seigneurs used their privileges to lease out logging rights in forests at a time when wood prices were skyrocketing. Around Toulouse and Bordeaux, lords used their option rights (*droit de retraite*) to force individuals who had recently acquired land to resell it to the lords. Seigneurial rights thus allowed these lords in these regions to corner the lucrative market in land. As these examples suggest, evaluating the weight of seigneurial rights by looking solely at exactions on peasants is misleading: seigneurial privileges also created legal arbitrariness and significant market distortions within an emerging system of commercial capitalism.

Another issue relating to the weight of seigneurialism is that of the so-called 'seigneurial reaction'. This term refers to the attempt by lords to hire professional *feudistes* to comb the original charters regulating peasant obligations in the hopes of finding old dues that had lapsed and resurrecting them. Historians disagree whether enough dues were revived to constitute a discernible trend and whether this practice was characteristic solely of the eighteenth century or was part of a longer trend. In some regions, however, it appears that the term was warranted and that lords were aggressively attempting to reclaim forgotten rights. It seems likely that both professionalization and commercial capitalism contributed to this trend. The recovery of neglected dues was a kind of rationalization of the business side of the fief, while the growth of the economy made seigneurial market monopolies that had earlier been of little value suddenly worth looking into. The lack of a statute of limitations that would prevent lords from dredging up obsolete claims, finally, provided the legal mechanism that made possible this sort of juridical capriciousness.

Beside the economic and legal issues at stake in seigneurialism, there were questions of dignity and respect. In Burgundy, for example, there was an increasing use of the humiliating term 'vassal' to refer to peasants. In some regions, there is also evidence that peasants were more willing to combat seigneurial pretensions in court. In both the Sarladais and Languedoc, a substantial number of lawsuits brought by peasants against nobles in the eighteenth century involved issues of honour, including insults, ceremonial distinctions, and the like. Peasants protested against the enormous size of the bench a lord had installed in the church, or challenged the lord's right to march in the front of a procession with his wife and children, an innovation which broke the old custom by which all the men followed the lord while women and children followed his wife. The changing role of both the lord and the state may have fed the growing self-assertiveness of the peasant. During the eighteenth century, lords tended to leave their ancestral châteaux, become absentees, and migrate to cities to enjoy the amenities of urban life. The lord abandoned his traditional role as the patron of his community, but was still intent on enjoying all the economic perquisites and honourable distinctions customarily afforded him. Inevitably peasants would resent seigneurial burdens more the less they were justified. Meanwhile, the presence of the royal government at the local level had expanded. Communities came to realize that the king's officials, the intendants, might help them settle their disputes or plead their cause to distant royal ministers in Paris. In the Franco-Spanish border region of the Pyrenees after 1720, villagers on both sides of the border began to petition their royal governments for help in maintaining their communal rights from usurpation by foreign villages. In the seventeenth century, by contrast, these disputes had been regulated by the communities themselves.

In the eighteenth century, there appears to have been a growing, although wary, acceptance of the state by the peasantry. The seventeenth century had witnessed numerous peasant revolts directed largely against the fiscal exactions and bureaucratic intrusion of the state into local communities. After 1675 large-scale peasant upheavals ceased. The government restructured the tax base to place greater emphasis on indirect taxes (duties, tariffs, excise taxes, and state-owned monopolies over sales of salt and tobacco) rather than on the peasant-based *taille*. Although the government still utilized repression, state officials also took on more of a protective role to shield communities from the unjust exactions of seigneurs and creditors.

Nonetheless, although full-scale popular uprisings ended under Louis XIV, there were important undercurrents of popular protest throughout the eighteenth century. A nationwide data base recording 4,495 incidents of collective violence from 1661 to 1789 reveals the following trends. First, riots became secular in nature: by the end of the eighteenth century religion played virtually no role in popular violence. Second, anti-fiscal incidents still occurred, but they increased only slightly over this period and were falling when considered as a percentage of all events. Third, anti-seigneurial activity was rising. There were only 44 cases in 1690–1720, but 145 in 1760–89. Despite the growing hostility toward lords, the number of anti-seigneurial events still lagged behind anti-fiscal actions and was far below the anti-seigneurial explosion that was to develop as the Revolution unfolded. Fourth, the most striking change in collective action was the steep rise in food riots: 182 in 1690–1720, but 652 in 1760–89. The food riot had become the classic form of popular protest of the eighteenth century.

The ability of peasants to engage in collective action and court cases was aided by corporate forms of village organization. Besides the seigneurie, the community of inhabitants and parish structured village life. The community of inhabitants was a form of village self-government by which peasant communities could own and sell communal property, borrow funds, hire schoolmasters, initiate law-suits, choose syndics to represent their interests, and organize tax collection at the local level. Interestingly, the royal government was primarily responsible for solidifying this kind of village administration, because the monarchy realized that a higher degree of village organization would allow the government to extract labour and taxes from the countryside more easily. In the war-torn fourteenth century, Charles V made communities elect their own tax collectors and made all members of the community responsible collectively for the payment of the *taille*. In some regions lords retained some control over the community by appointing its officers or giving the village permission to hold assemblies, but many other villagers enjoyed the right to choose their own syndics and related representatives independently. There were cases where membership in the village assemblies was open to all heads of households, including women; but it was more common for only property owners or those who paid a minimum tax to be eligible. The government's reform of 1787 strengthened the oligarchic tendencies of village communities by limiting membership to those paying at least 10 *livres* in direct taxes.

The parish provided an additional basis for village solidarity. Villagers played an essential role in the upkeep of the local church and its property, which was handled by churchwardens on the parish council (*fabrique*). In many areas, the parish council and the official village assembly blurred together, and sometimes the churchwardens and syndics of the village were the same people. The importance of the church as a centre for peasant solidarity is revealed in patterns of collective action. A majority of rural protests in the old regime began on Sunday after mass when peasants had an opportunity to discuss their grievances and plan appropriate action. The role played by peasant communities and parishes in facilitating protest can also be illustrated in the strike against the tithe begun in 1777 in Gascony. Although the tithe was usually one-twelfth or one-fourteenth of an individual's harvest, in Gascony it was unusually high, one-eighth. Several villages contested the payment by taking their case to the parlement, and other villages followed suit by convoking general assemblies, naming syndics to represent their interests, and refusing to pay the full amount. At the height of the controversy, as many as 400 parishes were federated together to contest unfair tithe assessments.

While villages were united against outside enemies, they also suffered from internal tensions, resulting primarily from inequalities of wealth. Most peasants lived a precarious existence at a subsistence level, but a few acquired substantial means. In one village in Picardy, for example, 68 per cent of the households had 5 hectares or less of land, while 3 per cent owned 50–100 hectares. If the threshhold of independence is measured at 5 hectares, it is clear that the majority of the peasants could not survive from their land alone. Men combined agriculture with seasonal migrant work, charcoal burning, woodcutting, and peddling, while women took up wet-nursing, spinning, and weaving. In a pinch, illicit expedients like poaching, smuggling, and begging made up the difference between survival and starvation. The economic divisions between the wealthiest peasants and the rest could be exacerbated when seigneurs employed prosperous cultivators as their estate managers. Many absentee lords leased out their personal lands and the right to collect dues to rich tenant farmers. As a result, poor peasants might find themselves paying their dues to a wealthy peasant, and never see the lord at all. In fact, in some regions during the early Revolution, peasant violence was directed against these agents, rather than against the seigneurs themselves.

cities could be exempt from taille

Urban groups and privileges

Urban dwellers formed approximately 17 per cent of the total population in 1700, a figure which had risen to 22 per cent by 1789. Culturally and juridically, cities were always associated with special rights and liberties. In the dictionaries of the period, cities were typically defined less by their size than by their walls, which set them apart from the countryside, and by their privileges, such as the right to elect a city council, to be free from the *taille,* and to collect separate urban tolls and excise taxes (*octrois*). It is not clear, however, that fiscal and political privileges were of great benefit to cities by 1789, for even though the crown had retained their form, it had denuded and altered their content. It is true that most cities were exempt from the *taille,* but the crown tended to make up for this loss by raiding urban treasuries. By 1781, most cities were required to impose a hefty surcharge of 50 per cent on their excise taxes and tolls, all of which went to the royal government. As for urban elections, royal officials like the provincial governor or intendant exercised tight control over the nomination and selection of candidates. Under royal tutelage, many urban governments ended up as narrow, self-perpetuating oligarchies.

A variety of urban groups enjoyed economic protection through special tariff situations, monopolies over the sale and production of goods, bans on imports or exports, subsidies to businessmen, and the like. Traditionally, the largest cities had benefited the most from economic protectionism. Lille, for example, enjoyed the exclusive right to produce long-stapled woollens; the countryside was legally limited to producing yarn and lesser quality cloth. Marseille, the key port in the Mediterranean, wielded a virtual monopoly over imports from the Levant, because tariff policy dictated that all merchandise from the Near East had to go through Marseille or pay a sizeable 20 per cent surtax. Lyon, too, was protected by favourable internal tariffs. In 1540, Francis I had ordered that all silk cloth coming into France would go through Lyon and pay a fee of 5 per cent. The city, in return, loaned the king money secured by this tax. In 1756 Lyon's privilege was suppressed, but it was resurrected only two years later when Lyon advanced the royal government more money.

As these examples suggest, commercial capitalism had not developed in opposition to privilege; rather the biggest cities expected urban hinterlands and smaller cities to perform a function similar to that which colonies performed for their mother countries. The countryside was to be the supplier of raw materials and goods of lesser quality; the city was to produce goods subject to more stringent regulations, perform expensive finishing processes, and control import and export markets. By the mid-eighteenth century, the rapid spread of protoindustrial activity in the countryside and the great expansion of internal trade was calling into question the traditional arrangements whereby the merchants of privileged cities dominated their surrounding regions. New brokerage networks and upstart middlemen from small towns threatened the mastery of old mercantile elites over the market. Of course, merchants from large cities had helped to create their own competition. They had promoted manufacturing in the countryside because it was less expensive than production through artisanal labour in the cities. Soon, however, these merchants realized to their chagrin that rural cloth manufacturers were expanding their enterprises and attempting to market their cloth on their own. Rural manufacturers had become threats not just to artisans in privileged cities, but to the control of merchants over their markets as well.

The rise of commercial capitalism, then, did not so much pit the nobility against the bourgeoisie; rather it set rapidly growing hinterlands and small cities against the market monopolies of large cities. Although a number of these market monopolies were reduced or repealed by the royal government after mid-century, the victory of rural merchants was far from complete. Urban governments and established merchants continued to battle to retain their privileged economic position. In 1759 the city government of Lille required rural textile workers who subcontracted out work to other labourers to sell their cloth to brokers licensed by the city and regulated by Lille's chamber of commerce. The goal was to keep rural manufacturers dependent upon Lille's merchants for outlets for their goods. In Rouen, the merchants in the guild of mercer-drapers, who included some of the wealthiest traders in the region, relied on offices of cloth inspectors that they purchased in the early 1700s to require that all cloth produced in the countryside be measured and sold at Rouen's cloth hall. This policy both constrained the ability of weavers to sell cloth independently of the city's merchants and ensured a certain degree of quality necessary for success on international markets. Grain merchants in Paris benefited from licences issued by the city government and in the 1690s were able to nip in the bud a challenge from rural interlopers who wanted to set up their own brokers to sell grain directly in the city. The Parisian grain merchants crushed incipient rural competition by buying up every possible bit of grain in the countryside and driving the new brokers out of business. After that rural merchants had no alternative but to sell through the brokerage system that Parisians controlled.

It is true that much economic activity escaped legal controls; the value of legal monopolies in the face of continual non-compliance is difficult to calculate. The worth to cities of port privileges, tariff protections, urban inspectorships, and related controls, however, should not be dismissed out of hand. An interesting case in point is the port of Bayonne, whose fortune was in great decline over the eighteenth century owing in part to high sand that blocked access to Adour River. Nonetheless, when the city obtained the privileged tariff status of a free port in 1784, goods arriving from abroad at Bayonne rose by 60 per cent.

Guilds, organizations holding a legal monopoly over the production and sale of specific goods, are perhaps the most familiar form of economic protection. The importance of guilds, however, was not limited to their economic roles, for guilds, like many privileged institutions in the old regime, performed multiple functions. They served at times as units of political representation, sponsored charitable activities through associated confraternities, were fiscal intermediaries who played a role in tax assessments and loaned money to the king, and gave members legal standing in their community. Guild masters could be wealthy merchants, such as those of the *six corps* of Paris, who dominated the luxury trades in gold, silk, dry-goods, and furs, or poor artisans and retailers who had trouble making ends meet. Recent scholarship has emphasized the viability of these institutions. From 1776 to 1788, for example, an average of 1550 new masters were received each year in the Parisian guilds, and in 1785–7 the receptions were at nearly the same level as in 1700.

Many guild regulations and privileges were designed to protect independent artisanal status, that is, to guarantee each master a modest but secure livelihood, appropriate to his station in life. To this end, many (but not all) guilds limited the number of apprentices coming into the trade, restricted the number of looms or other types of equipment permitted to each master, and prohibited masters from working for other masters. In return for this favourable environment, guilds were to contribute to the public good by guaranteeing the quality of their goods through careful supervision. In fact, the image of the guild master as a sheltered, independent artisan producing goods for the local market was true only in some cases. Economic growth and the spread of commercial capitalism had led to a great deal of diversity and stress within guild organization. At one end of the spectrum were the specialized and small crafts catering to the local market, such as goldsmiths or the provisioning trades. There a master might use family labour and a small number of apprentices or journeymen who could expect to become masters themselves one day. Because regulations restricted the number of new masters admitted to the guild, artisans in these kinds of guilds were more likely to be protected from competition and enjoy economic security. At the other end were guilds which produced a large volume of goods like hats or cloth for international markets and were embedded in commercial capitalist networks. Here some masters had become virtual entrepreneurs and employed large numbers of journeymen who could never hope to become masters. Sometimes these successful masters put out work to other impoverished masters in the guild, a situation that might well be illegal according to guild regulations. Labour strife was far more likely in manufactures penetrated by capitalism, because wealthy masters employed other masters, journeymen, or waged workers with little chance for advance. In general, guild masters enjoyed greater security and a higher standard of living than other workers in cities. There were masters, however, particularly in depressed textile industries, whose material situation was no better than a common day labourer. Nonetheless, even the most destitute guild master had a socially recognized position that conferred a degree of honour and standing in his community, something a mere labourer lacked.

Many urban labourers were not integrated into the guild system, which never encompassed the majority of the workforce. Large numbers of workers spent their lives eking out a living by doing subcontracted work, selling second-hand goods, working in small trades, mending clothes, hiring themselves out as day labourers, or producing goods illegally in garrets removed from the watchful eye of officials. Servants formed a substantial portion of the labouring classes, ranging anywhere from 4 per cent of the total population in a port city like Marseille to as much as 16 per cent in a refined, aristocratic town like Aix-en-Provence. They had their own hierarchies: male servants were generally a sign of status in aristocratic households and were paid relatively well; female servants made do with lower wages and might have to worry about unwanted sexual advances by their masters. At the very bottom of the urban world was a floating population of the truly indigent formed of the sick, the unemployed, beggars, and prostitutes. The underdeveloped technical and economic conditions of the period meant that this latter group might grow or shrink in response to economic conditions, but it never disappeared.

Given the poor medical conditions of the period, all groups, even those in the elite, faced the threat of disease and death, but the lower classes suffered disportionately more. In a sample compiled from the city of Lyon, only 6 per cent of the nobles and bourgeois died between the ages of 20 and 40, whereas 30 per cent of the domestics and day labourers did. The reasons for the discrepancy are not hard to find. Disease spread more easily in the cramped quarters in which the poor lived. It was not uncommon for individuals to have to share a bed with several others, regardless of their health. Occupational hazards abounded. Metal workers, hatters, potters, and glaziers were exposed to the poisonous vapours of mercury, copper, and lead, and porters, sometimes obliged to carry loads weighing several hundred kilograms, suffered from strokes and internal injuries. Open burial pits in the middle of cities and the practice of emptying chamber pots into the street created a nauseating stench and spread disease. The poorer classes also suffered from debilitating malnutrition. Bread, supplemented perhaps by some cheese or a few vegetables, was the mainstay of the diet of the people, though the destitute might be reduced to eating watery gruel or porridge. Because so many people lived on the brink of subsistence, any crisis, such as the death of a spouse or loss of a job, could plunge them from a state of bare survival into destitution. In times of economic depression, the number of individuals seeking poor relief ballooned to include a substantial percentage of the labouring population, and the likelihood of food riots increased.

It may appear puzzling that food riots characterized the eighteenth century rather than the seventeenth. Except in the most backward regions of France, the eighteenth century witnessed the end of crises of subsistence that left significant numbers of people dead from malnutrition and disease. The introduction of highly productive crops, like maize, more favourable climatic conditions, better coordination among governmental authorities, and the expansion of roads all contributed to the end of these crises. Paradoxically, the growth of food riots may have been a symptom, in part, of economic development itself. The economy was able to support more consumers who did not produce their own grain and had to buy food on the market, but it did so in a highly volatile and uneven manner. As cities grew, more urban dwellers depended on grain flowing in from the countryside to supply their needs. Some of the worst food riots of the eighteenth century followed a potent combination of actual dearth and political disturbances in the market. The food shortages of 1740 were exacerbated by currency manipulations by the government, while those in 1770 and 1786 occurred in tandem with experiments to free the grain trade from traditional regulations governing its sale.

Grain riots occurred both in towns and in the countryside, especially in rural areas like the highly productive Parisian basin where impoverished peasants and protoindustrial workers had to purchase most of their food on the market. In towns, crowds often broke into the shops of bakers or seized bags of flour and sold it for a 'just' price. In the countryside, the export of grain out of a grain producing region was likely to stimulate rural crowds into forcibly trying to prevent wagons carrying grain from leaving. The activity of crowds, however, was more than a mechanical response to rising prices. The moral fury of the crowd was based in its claim to enforce the cause of justice when authorities and elites neglected their duty or actively harmed the community. Crowds demanded the punishment of elites who had violated communal norms and allowed harmful practices such as the imposition of new taxes, the hoarding of food, or the erosion of corporate regulations protecting workers. Violence was directed specifically at these wrongdoers: the crowd burned the images of social transgressors in effigy or ransacked their homes, while others were left unscathed. Members of the crowd who sold grain for a 'just' price took on the role of governmental officials and enforced the law themselves, where law was defined as the customary rights of the people, not the changeable will of the king.

The close connection between perceptions of justice and food riots is illustrated by the activity of a crowd in the small market town of Beaumont-sur-Oise in 1770. There a riot erupted when a merchant charged 32 *livres* for a measure of grain that had sold for 26 *livres* only five days earlier, even though the market appeared to be amply supplied. Rioters reacted by dunking the hapless merchant in a fountain twice and then demanding justice from the local lieutenant general of police. He refused to set the price of grain in accordance with old traditions and declared instead that 'the sale of grain was free at all times.'[14] Far from satisfied by this response, the rioters returned to the market, set their own price of grain at 12 *livres* per measure, and ransacked the stalls of the merchants.

Members of crowds were generally not rootless individuals. Crowds tended to mobilize individuals from a particular village or neighbourhood, a strategy that meant most members of a crowd knew one another. Large crowds were formed by joining these smaller units together. Although the violence of crowds often had only ephemeral direct effects, such as a temporary lowering of food prices, the chronic threat of crowd activity helped to make food supply in large cities like Paris an ongoing concern of officials that was not taken lightly.

Conclusion: stresses in society in the old regime

In 1789 the old regime fell. Historians have debated at length the reasons for its demise, and have perhaps been more successful in refuting theories explaining this fall than in advancing new explanations. The old regime fell because the government went bankrupt, despite an expanding economy and population, because the elite was divided and at odds with the government, and because the system of privilege no longer worked. Several reasons for the division of the

---

[14] Cited in Cynthia A. Bouton, *The Flour War: Gender, Class, and Community in Late Ancien Régime French Society* (University Park, Pa. 1993), 83.

elite and the failure of the system of privilege may be suggested. The problems were predominantly institutional and legal in nature, that is, they stemmed from the way in which the laws and institutions of the old regime extracted the wealth from an increasingly capitalist economy that was becoming more dependent on the market. The crux of the issue was not that privilege blocked the growth of the economy, as has sometimes been suggested. Nor was commercial capitalism successfully whittling away privilege, although a degree of economic erosion did occur. Rather the dilemma of the old regime was that its legal system was so favourable to the commercialization of privilege. The old regime was continually converting into negotiable property things that modern society regards as outside of the domain of the market altogether. A glance at what could be sold in the old regime reveals that a central problem of this society was not so much the lack of property rights, but a surfeit of property rights. In the old regime it was legally possible to purchase such things as: status (titles of nobility), rights of jurisdiction (fiefs and judicial offices), rights of employment (military ranks and guild masterships), rights of political representation (in certain provincial estates), and other human beings (slaves).

The legal system of the old regime had its roots in a far more personal and paternalistic society that failed to distinguish explicitly between personal status, political rule, and rights of property. As society became more impersonal and dependent on the market, the honorific marks and rights attached to these personal relationships did not disappear, they were exploited through the mechanism of the market. The result was a monetization of social relationships, but not exactly in the way we think of social classes today, because the domain of money encompassed aspects of personal status, political rule, and rights that have been put off limits to modern commercial transactions. The outcome of this situation was a divided elite which was dependent upon money for survival and whose claims to legitimacy based in honour and service rang increasingly hollow.

The state played its role, too. It exploited the sale of titles and offices for its own benefit and became in the process the supreme legal arbiter of social mobility. The growth of the state did not consistently bring about a greater differentiation between the private and public spheres, that is, between private property and public authority. Instead, it mixed the two spheres together by making status and jurisdictional rights subject to purchase, and it never succeeded in disentangling itself from this confusion. In fact, from an institutional perspective, it may be asked whether 'state' and 'society' existed as distinct entities in the old regime, for political and social roles were not yet fully differentiated and institutions performed several functions simultaneously. The judicial system provides a striking example of the embeddedness of social functions in political institutions. Judicial courts tried civil and criminal cases, but they also were the main channel for legal social mobility, a source of emergency loans to the government, and an important type of private economic investment.

What the Revolution did, ultimately, was to change the rules by which institutions in the old regime operated. The Revolution made 'society', in the way in which we think of it, possible through legal transformation and institutional differentiation. Equality before the law, the separation of property from public service, freedom of markets, the end to religious tests for social membership, and the divorce of legal status from concrete social attributes (at least in theory): these kind of revolutionary changes signalled the end of the old regime and the emergence of a new kind of society and politics.

3

Culture and religion

David A. Bell

To many of the eighteenth-century intellectuals known as the *philosophes*, the story of their age was a story of epic conflict. On the one side stood the defenders of faith and tradition. These, in the story, were the forces of darkness: fanatical, superstitious, irrational, and arbitrary. On the other side stood the *philosophes* themselves, and like-minded allies. They were the forces of light, or, as they liked to say, of Enlightenment: advocates of science, reason, utility, and freedom. The defenders of faith had the full apparatus of the French state at their disposal, and legions of priests promising eternal damnation to the heterodox. The forces of Enlightenment, so the story continued, had on their side only the rightness of their cause, the support of a few high-placed friends, and that staunch servant of freedom of thought, the printing press. Nonetheless, they would inevitably prevail.

The story remains a compelling one, especially to those who consider themselves, in one way or another, modern heirs of the Enlightenment. And it is by no means wholly inaccurate. Not only were there armies of censors and police to suppress anything deemed contrary to religion, the state, and public morality; dissenters could be treated with remarkable savagery. The 19-year-old François-Jean de La Barre learned this lesson in the 1760s, when he was arrested for the adolescent prank of mutilating a wooden crucifix. The court sentenced him to have his tongue cut out, his head cut off, and his body publicly burned, in a case that stirred continent-wide revulsion. Nor was La Barre by any means the only victim of what one enlightened reformer called 'the bloody shoals of our criminal jurisprudence'.[1]

---

[1] [C. M. J. B. Dupaty], *Mémoire justicatif pour trois hommes condamnés à la roue* (Paris, 1786), 240.

Nonetheless, the story is also terribly misleading. It obscures the extent to which the most supposedly orthodox sectors of society generated some of the century's most innovative and radical thinking, and also the extent to which the *philosophes* themselves quickly gained comfortable elite acceptance. It portrays as monolithic camps what were in fact fractured, shifting constellations of institutions and personalities. Finally, it ignores the way in which important cultural changes moved through society as a whole, affecting the 'traditional' and the 'radical' alike. There was indeed a great, overriding issue at stake in eighteenth-century French culture, but it was not the issue of how Enlightenment could overcome obscurantism. It was the issue, faced by priests and *philosophes* alike, of how to act in a world from which God had seemingly withdrawn, leaving mankind to its own devices.

The two Romes

All through the period from 1660 to 1789, French culture was Janus-faced, but with a twist: both faces looked towards a place called Rome. On the one side was the Rome of the Roman Catholic church, on the other the Rome of classical antiquity.

It is hard to overstate the extent to which Roman Catholicism permeated early modern French life. For the century between Louis XIV's expulsion of the Protestants in 1685 and Louis XVI's edict of toleration in 1787, Catholicism was the sole permissible religion, exception being made only for the Protestants of Alsace and small pockets of Jews. Catholic sacraments marked each stage of a person's life: baptism, confirmation, marriage, and death. Church festivals, and the weekly ritual of the mass, structured the calendar, while religious confraternities provided one of the principal forms of sociability outside the family. In the countryside that was home to over 85 per cent of the population, the parish church was the village's principal link with the outside world. Agents of the central state might come calling on occasion, mostly to collect taxes, but it was the priest who could be counted on to relay news, to deliver teachings about the heavenly and terrestrial cities alike, and even, in those areas where the common people spoke a language other than French, to translate news and official documents into the local dialect. Until the middle of the eighteenth century, the majority of all books published were religious in nature. And until the expulsion of the Jesuits in the early 1760s, the church controlled virtually all educational institutions, from village schoolhouses to university faculties. While patterns of belief changed greatly, even in 1789 France remained by modern standards a tremendously devout country.

The church's cultural influence was underwritten, of course, by its enormous economic and political power. It owned, outright, at least 6 per cent of the land (much more in some regions), and collected a hefty tithe on virtually all agricultural produce. Churches and convents dominated cityscapes, with over twenty churches crammed into Paris's small, central island, the Île de la Cité, alone. In most representative assemblies, including the estates general whose convocation in 1789 marked the start of the Revolution, the church had one chamber to itself, out of three. The church provided the crown with crucial revenues in the form of 'free gifts' voted by the assembly of the clergy, and cardinals and archbishops such as Mazarin, Fleury, and Loménie de Brienne often held the highest position in the royal ministry. The church possessed its own system of justice and could condemn books it judged irreligious. Until the middle of the eighteenth century, it remained the source of most charitable aid given to France's armies of the destitute and travelling poor. It also provided careers for the surplus children of the wealthy and well-connected, and a principal avenue of social mobility for the children of the poor and middle classes. In short, the common phrase 'outside the church, no salvation' resonated not only in people's inner consciences, but in virtually every aspect of their daily lives.

This broad blanket of Christian faith did not, however, stifle the infatuation of the elites with pagan, classical antiquity. Between 1660 and 1789, the Latin language, and the Latin literary classics, remained the basis of secondary education. As the educational reformer La Chalotais remarked in the 1760s, 'a foreigner to whom one explained the details of our education would imagine that France's principal goal was to populate Latin seminaries, cloisters and colonies'.[2] Only those capable of understanding, and recognizing Latin quotations

<hr>

[2] Quoted in Ferdinand Brunot, *Histoire de la langue française* (13 vols., Paris, 1905–53), vii. 95.

could pass as truly learned, and few authors could resist scattering them liberally through their own writings. Serious literature might no longer be written in Latin (as had been the case as recently as the sixteenth century), but the language remained critical in the professions of medicine and law, and of course in the church as well. Schoolchildren knew the history of Rome (and to a lesser extent, Greece) as well as that of France itself, perhaps better. Painters of all styles and schools, from the most playful and sensual rococo to the most severely neoclassical, routinely took their subjects from classical mythology and history. Sculptors and architects modelled their work heavily after classical examples. Nowhere did these classical influences appear more forcefully than at the royal Court of Versailles, where overtly Christian imagery was relatively scarce, while representations of Apollo, Minerva, and Hercules, many of them based on the poetry of Ovid, proliferated.

The classics had a profound presence not only in the high culture, but in the inner lives of educated persons. The great rulers and writers of antiquity were not dusty monuments to them, but living examples. The terms in which the moralist Vauvenargues described his youthful encounter with Plutarch were typical: 'I cried with joy when I read those lives. I never spent a night without talking to Alcibiades, Agesilas, and others. I visited the Roman Forum to harangue with the Gracchi, to defend Cato when they threw rocks at him'.[3] When, at the beginning of the Revolution, the deputies to the National Assembly took a solemn oath to continue meeting until they had provided France with a new constitution, they raised their arms in a self-consciously Roman gesture, like that in Jacques-Louis David's great 1784 neoclassical Roman history painting *The Oath of the Horatii*.

The demands of Christian piety could and did come into conflict with the enchantments of antiquity. The *philosophes*, in particular, frequently held up Greek and Roman examples as a counterpoint to Catholic teachings. Yet most educated people managed to reconcile the two heritages without difficulty, much as their ancestors (and centuries' worth of Christian philosophers) had done before them. Louis XIV went through no great existential crisis to reconcile posing one moment as Apollo, god of the sun, and the next as the 'most

[3] Quoted in Peter Gay, *The Enlightenment: An Interpretation* (2 vols., New York, 1966), i. 47.

Christian King'. The fundamental cultural tensions and conflicts came from elsewhere.

A widening cultural gap

One of these tensions involved a widening cultural gap between the common people—peasants in the countryside, artisans and servants in the towns—and the noble, clerical and bourgeois elites. To be sure, these elites had always possessed their own learned culture, which was off limits to the common people. But as late as the sixteenth century, the elites had participated quite fully in popular cultural practices as well. They collected and read popular proverbs, attended popular festivals and theatricals, and took part in civic and religious processions with people from various ranks of society. Even before 1660, however, this participation had begun to drop off, and between 1660 and 1789 it did so in such dramatic fashion that from some perspectives it seemed as if France had split into separate and mutually incomprehensible cultural spheres. The great *Encyclopédie* of Denis Diderot and Jean d'Alembert testified to this cultural gap when it commented, in reference to peasants, that 'many [educated] people see little difference between this class of men and the animals they use to farm our lands'.

One important measure of the widening gap can be seen in the very language people used for daily communication. Throughout the early modern period, relatively few people spoke standard French. Around the periphery of the kingdom, the spoken languages included German, Italian, Dutch, Catalan, Basque, and Breton. In roughly the southern third of the country, the common people spoke dialects of Occitan, a Romance language distinct from French. French itself had many distinct dialects, and the story went that when a hungry crowd in Picardy, barely 80 kilometres north of the capital, harangued Louis XIV, he could not understand what they were saying. Until the mid-seventeenth century, bourgeois and nobles in many regions used the local tongue among themselves, and even wrote literary works in them. Toulouse's Pèire Godolin was one of seventeenth-century France's notable poets, but he wrote his masterpiece, *Le Ramelet Mondin*, in Occitan, not French. But after 1650, such traditions died nCULTURE AND RELIGION | 83

out, and the educated elites increasingly spoke and wrote little but standard, Parisian French. Local languages were now derided as 'patois', a pejorative term deriving from *patte* (an animal's paw).

Another measure can be found in the period's major literary works. A great sixteenth-century author like Rabelais gloried in the language and love of the common people, which he knew intimately. By contrast, late seventeenth- and eighteenth-century works of serious literature were written using a precise, educated, remarkably restrained vocabulary, and employed 'bourgeois' or 'peasant' words mostly for farcical or satirical effect, as in the stiletto-tipped comedies of Molière which skewered every sort of pretentiousness and hypocrisy. Dramatic works, including Molière's and the profound tragedies of Racine, obeyed rigid classical conventions (particularly the 'three unities' of time, space, and action), and reflected the speech and values of the royal Court. They became the chief showpieces of a culture that was increasingly seen to radiate out from Paris and Versailles alone.

In keeping with this idea, and in a cultural parallel to the ongoing processes of political centralization, the elites increasingly oriented themselves to the capital. By the middle of the reign of Louis XIV, the high nobility spent much of its time at the court, and sent its sons to top Parisian schools like the collège Louis-le-Grand. Instead of the king routinely travelling around his kingdom, the elites now travelled to him, to observe the minutely choreographed spectacle of Court life, and to see the latest fashions and customs. From the Court, nobles and ambitious bourgeois alike learnt increasingly complex codes of politeness and etiquette, thereby setting themselves further apart from peasants and artisans. True, no ordinary noble or bourgeois household could live up to the obsessive standards of etiquette set at Versailles (for the king and queen, the very act of getting dressed in the morning was a precise ritual in which a string of nobles handed them their different items of clothing). Still, instructional manuals like the 1714 tome *French Civility*, proliferated among the anxiously socially mobile, prescribing new rules for daily life, and advising their readers on how not to be taken for members of the lower classes:

Do not keep your knife always in your hand, as village people do, but take it only when you need it . . .

It is against propriety to give people meat to smell, and you should under no circumstances put meat back into the common dish if you have smelled it yourself . . .

You should not throw bones or eggshells or the skin of any fruit onto the floor . . .[4]

Through such works, we can trace the development of modern forms of politeness and table manners.

For entertainment and edification, the upper strata of society spent less and less time in the streets of their towns and villages, and more in exclusive activities common to people of their social standing throughout the kingdom. For instance, by the middle of the eighteenth century, most major towns had acquired theatre companies, whose repertoires were based on a standard French canon. The reading of novels proliferated, especially among women, and the most popular (for instance the works of Samuel Richardson, in translation) went through scores of editions, feeding a rising tide of print. Book reading in general expanded remarkably. Fewer than 1000 books a year were published in France in 1715; more than 4,000 in 1789. News reading expanded even more. In 1700, there were three newspapers, all published by the government, but by 1750 more than twenty were circulating, including several published illegally or abroad. In 1785, the number had risen to over eighty. Other new venues for elite cultural exchange could be found in literary societies, and learned academies, modelled after the French Academy in Paris. All these activities, however, were limited to the well-educated and well-off. Books and newspapers, for instance, remained expensive for all but the wealthiest peasants and artisans, thanks in large part to the cost of paper, which was still made by hand, from rags.

The rest of the population did not remain entirely untouched by these changes. Particularly in the northern cities, literacy was the rule, not the exception (in Paris, by the end of the old regime, over 90 per cent of men and 80 per cent of women could read). True, only one quarter of Parisians actually seem to have owned books in the late eighteenth century, but others probably had access through that great eighteenth-century invention, the lending library, or through church or family, leading the writer Mercier confidently to assert that 'people certainly are reading ten times more in Paris than they did a hundred years ago'.[5] In the rowdy pit of Parisian theatres, where spectators

---

[4] Quoted in Norbert Elias, *The History of Manners: The Civilizing Process* (2 vols., New York, 1978), i. 94–5.

[5] Quoted in Daniel Roche, *La France des lumières* (Paris, 1993), 600.

stood throughout performances, better-off artisans and servants literally rubbed shoulders with nobles and bourgeois. Even in the countryside, where literacy rates trailed badly (especially in the south), peasants had some access to books, principally the inexpensive volumes, bound in blue paper, that made up the so-called *bibliothèque bleue*. Winter evening gatherings could bring together several peasant families, and there it was common for these books to be read out loud.

Yet the *bibliothèque bleue* consisted in large part of almanacs, and devotional and fabulous works that dated from the seventeenth, or even sixteenth, century. Nor did the occasional glance at a newspaper amount to the same thing as a regular subscription (prohibitively expensive for most). Outside north central France, language itself posed a formidable obstacle between poorer subjects and the culture of the salons and the academies. In short, the social tensions that would manifest themselves so violently during the death spasms of the old regime were reinforced, and aggravated, by a growing mutual cultural incomprehension between elites and the common people.

A militant and divided church

A closely related set of tensions existed within the religious sphere, where they derived above all from the Catholic church's continuing attempts to deal with the aftershocks of the Protestant Reformation. To be sure, Protestantism itself, with adherents among scarcely five per cent of the population in 1660, was no longer a major force. Louis XIV's persecutions, culminating in the revocation of the edict of Nantes in 1685, further decimated Protestant ranks. Yet the spectre of religious schism, which had drenched the country in blood within recent memory and led to the assassination of successive kings, remained a terrifying one long after the reality had passed, and the authorities in church and state devoted much energy to trying to banish it forever.

At the parish level, the fear of schism ensured that the church remained a militant one, committed to the policies of Catholic reform first promulgated by the council of Trent. Perceiving the peasantry as an ignorant and superstitious mass whose Christianity remained a thin veneer (and who were therefore susceptible to heresy and error), many priests saw it as their mission to wage undying war on popular customs and beliefs, while tirelessly instructing their flocks in the catechism and proper morality. A 1752 manual for priests in Languedoc, for instance, suggested the following: 'Winter evening gatherings, which can be occasions of such debauchery in the countryside, can be made holy by the zeal of a priest, who can assign a catechist to read aloud in each of these nocturnal gatherings, and then question the children'.[6] The priests were reinforced by bands of self-described missionaries, who bore the gospel to villages much as other members of their orders were bearing it to the Chinese and to American Indians. At the same time, vigilant bishops policed the priesthood itself, ensuring that members of the clergy received a proper education, lived in chastity, and maintained a proper social distance from their parishioners.

By the middle of the eighteenth century, these policies had succeeded in fashioning a priesthood that was more learned and disciplined than ever before, and in substantially raising the level of religious knowledge among the general population. Yet they also created a formidable gap between the priests and the people they ministered to. 'Let us regard ourselves,' a Breton priest wrote to a colleague in 1731, 'you and I, in these cantons, as if we were in China or in Turkey, even though we are in the middle of Christianity, where one sees practically nought but pagans'.[7] The 'pagans' themselves did not appreciate being treated in this condescending manner, and their resentment helps account for a striking decline in overt Christian observance that can be traced from the middle of the eighteenth century: the dying left less and less money to pay for masses for their souls in Purgatory; local elites abandoned religious confraternities in favour of masonic lodges; priestly vocations declined; the use of primitive contraception increased, as did the rate of illegitimate births.

While many Catholic countries experienced these changes in religious life, France did so most dramatically, and the reason has

---

[6] Bibliothèque Municipale de Toulouse, MS 892: 'Catéchisme dogmatique et moral traduit en langue vulgaire de Toulouse' (1752), 459.

[7] Quoted in Roger Chartier, *The Cultural Origins of the French Revolution* (Durham, NC, 1991), 104.

much to do with the strength of the Catholic movement called Jansenism. Named after a Flemish bishop Cornelius Jansen, who had died in 1638, the Jansenists believed with particular fervour in reforming popular religious practices, and in holding the faithful to high standards when it came to confession and absolution. Moreover, the Jansenists advocated a form of Catholicism that was far more austere, demanding, and difficult to understand than that advocated by most leaders of the church. In reaction against the Calvinist doctrine of predestination of souls, some theologians of the 'Catholic Reformation', particularly in the Jesuit order, had stressed the ability of all believers to gain salvation through good works, and the intervention of the clergy. The Jansenists, by contrast, stressed the utter depravity and sinfulness of humanity, and claimed that salvation could only come about through God's 'efficacious grace', bestowed on a predestined elect. The most fervent Jansenists opted for a life of severe self-denial and constant prayer, in retreat from the world. They argued that holy communion should be given as sparingly as possible, advocated a direct relationship between believers and God grounded in intense individual study of scripture, and sought to diminish the importance of the priesthood. 'One can be damned for following the advice of one's confessor,' wrote the Jansenist popularizer Quesnel.[8] The great success of this gloomy and demanding strain of Catholicism among the parish clergy (particularly in north central France) exacerbated the split between priests and ordinary believers.

At the same time, Jansenism created another large and fateful split, within the Catholic church itself, which further harmed the church's stature in France. Despite the difficult, indeed esoteric nature of Jansenist ideas, which effectively limited its influence to the clergy and the educated classes, Jansenism terrified both the church and the state (cardinal Richelieu had written early on that one of Jansen's French allies was 'more dangerous than six armies'). They saw it as Calvinism in disguise, feared the effects of a new schism, and worried that Jansenist teachings about individual believers and the priesthood could dissolve the bonds of obedience to secular and religious authorities alike. As a result, they repeatedly solicited papal bulls

---

[8] Quoted in Catherine Maire, *Les Convulsionnaires de Saint-Médard: miracles, convulsions et prophéties à Paris au XVIII*e *siècle* (Paris, 1981), 33.

condemning Jansenist works, and persecuted priests who refused formally to accept the condemnations.

The struggles over Jansenism dominated eighteenth-century religious life. In 1709, soldiers expelled Jansenist nuns and priests from their stronghold, the abbey of Port-Royal, which they destroyed. Four years later, Pope Clement XI issued the bull *Unigenitus*, which condemned 101 propositions taken from a book of Quesnel's. The determination of both the religious and political authorities to force acceptance of the bull on the clergy not only led to controversies with the parlement of Paris, but ripped the church asunder. In 1717, thousands of clergy signed a so-called 'appeal' for the convocation of a general council of the church to overrule the pope. This movement in turn stirred democratic tendencies within the clergy, and throughout the century dissident priests pressed for ordinary parish clergy to exercise more power in an institution controlled mostly by noble-born bishops.

The history of Jansenism in Paris produced some particularly dramatic scenes. In 1727, a popular, ostentatiously pious, and obsessively self-mortifying Jansenist deacon, François de Pâris, died. Soon afterwards, pilgrims to his tomb in the cemetery of Saint-Médard started going into convulsions, speaking in tongues, and claiming miraculous cures from illness. The authorities quickly closed the cemetery, leading to a notable piece of graffiti pinned to the gate:

| De par le Roi, défense à Dieu | God take note, by royal command |
| De faire miracle en ce lieu | Miracles in this place banned |

However, groups of so-called 'convulsionaries' continued to meet in secret throughout the century, practising painful rituals (such as the literal carving of stigmata on each others' bodies), and treating the ongoing political struggles as a re-enactment of biblical persecutions. In another episode, the militantly anti-Jansenist archbishop of Paris, Christophe de Beaumont, insisted in the late 1740s that no one could receive the last rites without a note (*billet de confession*) certifying that he or she had received absolution from a priest who had accepted *Unigenitus*. The subsequent refusal of the sacraments (and therefore, in theory, of salvation) to several Jansenists not only sparked tremendous political unrest, but led to religious unrest that shook the city—at precisely the moment usually seen as the heyday of the French

Enlightenment. The persecution of the Jansenists finally subsided in the 1760s, after the expulsion of their great enemy, the Jesuit order. By this point, however, the struggles had distracted the church from its supposed mission of evangelization, provided an unedifying spectacle for even sympathetic onlookers, and ammunition for the growing number of its enemies (Voltaire mocked the combatants as insects swarming over the bodies of dead theologians). The Parisian lawyer Barbier wrote in his diary in 1731: 'The only problem I see in these disputes, which are very amusing for witty folk . . . is that they will take away the common people's submission and subordination to the Church'.[9]

The hidden God and the terrestrial city

The *philosophes* may have scorned the Jansenists, but they had more in common with them than they liked to admit. In fact, the two groups can be seen as two sides of a single great intellectual shift.

The Jansenists frequently spoke of God as 'hidden'. He had, they said, withdrawn himself from the corrupt world of mankind, to the point that his intentions were no longer discernible to human observation. This sense of divine abandonment could lead to the sort of despairing, tragic vision that informs many of Racine's great dramatic works. Yet a world where God did *not* intervene regularly (for instance, stopping the sun in its course as he did for Joshua in the Old Testament) was a world where natural phenomena obeyed inflexible laws that human observation could make knowable, and where humans could exploit nature for their benefit. In this sense, the Jansenist view of the world was in fact surprisingly compatible with the development of modern scientific knowledge, and of a sceptical philosophical outlook that questioned the extent of a supernatural presence in daily life. Not coincidentally, the greatest French thinker influenced by Jansenism was also a great mathematician and scientist: Blaise Pascal.

Already in the early seventeenth century, the works of the

---

[9] Edmond-Jean-François Barbier, *Chronique de la Régence et du règne de Louis XV* (8 vols., Paris, 1885), ii. 148.

philosopher Descartes had helped to ignite the so-called Scientific Revolution, and the rise of sceptical philosophy. In the late seventeenth and eighteenth centuries, France remained central to these fronts of European learning. Louis XIV founded the Royal Academy of Sciences, which encouraged the work of individual scientists, and also sponsored ambitious projects such as a 1735 international expedition to Peru to determine the precise shape of the earth. The *philosophes* set science on a particularly high pedestal. In Voltaire's famous fable *Candide*, the utopian Latin American society of El Dorado contains no prisons, but does possess a massive palace of sciences. The *philosophes* particularly embraced the works of Isaac Newton, which suggested that secular, scientific explanations existed for all physical phenomena, and the empiricist philosophy of John Locke, who insisted that knowledge can be derived only from actual observation with the senses.

The *philosophes* claimed as their own French forefathers men like the sceptical, empiricist writer Pierre Bayle, a Protestant who fled Louis XIV's persecutions. Making use of mordant wit, precise reasoning, and the periodical press, Bayle both articulated at length a case for religious toleration, and waged undying war on the certainties of his readers. For instance, he challenged the received notion that comets (observable natural phenomena) were auguries of disaster, carefully taking apart the supposed historical evidence on the subject, and pointing out that even if millions of people had repeated a story, that did not make it true. Bayle today is considered one of the fathers of modern historical science. Other, contemporaneous sceptical writers applied their unsparing lenses not only to popular tradition, but even to holy scripture, risking ecclesiastical censure by judging the Bible itself a corrupt text, full of repetitions and contradictions.

The perception of God's withdrawal from the world, and the rise of a sceptical, scientific method, all raised the possibility that just as Newton seemed to have discovered the fundamental laws governing the behaviour of physical bodies, so it might be possible to discover natural laws governing human society as well. It was, in fact, precisely at the turn of the eighteenth century that the French began using the word 'society' in its modern sense, i.e. an autonomous arena of human activity (separate from the natural and divine realms alike), and possessing its own knowable laws. To the extent that there existed a single great project of the French Enlightenment, it was arguably to achieve a scientific understanding of society and its underlying laws, the better to improve it. Before turning to this project, however, we need to consider the social and cultural conditions in which the Enlightenment emerged.

From the Court to the city

Under Louis XIV, cultural life revolved in close orbit around the sun king and his Court. Not only did the educated classes look to Versailles for instruction in manners, fashion, and the arts; most of the great artistic achievements of the day, such as the painting of Le Brun and the landscape architecture of Le Nôtre, had a close association with the crown—indeed explicitly celebrated the king's glory. But at the king's death in 1715, the regent, Philippe d'Orléans, moved the Court back from Versailles to Paris, and while Louis XV later made Versailles the royal residence once again, the kingdom's cultural centre of gravity had returned to the capital city for good.

This shift had major consequences. At Court, rank and royal favour counted, if not quite for everything, then for more than anything else. In the city, they had to compete with other influences. For instance, money. Great financiers built and decorated sumptuous, expensive Parisian mansions, and became major patrons of the arts, challenging the influence of the Court. The new prosperity and the increasing commercial nature of urban life allowed some writers to live from their pens, without dependence on royal or noble pensions, and also increased the influence of publishers. By the end of the eighteenth century, a publishing tycoon like Panckoucke (who printed the second edition of the *Encyclopédie*) wielded more cultural power than any noble patron. In the city, anyone with enough money had easy access to all the most recent books, newspapers, plays, and exhibitions. In sum, a new sort of cultural market was taking shape, with different priorities from those found at the Court.

The city also fostered new sorts of cultural institutions. One of these was the periodical press, which, as we have seen, expanded dramatically over the course of the eighteenth century. The periodicals not only provided news, but also reviews and critical discussion of new books. Another institution was the café, which gave people a place to meet and discuss matters of common interest, and also to read the newspapers. The Café Procope, founded in 1694 (and still in existence today), served as a rendezvous for many of the *philosophes*, and by the middle of the century had scores of competitors. Diderot set one of his greatest works, *Rameau's Nephew*, in a Paris café. Academies also contributed to the new urban milieu, as did the first French masonic lodges, which were founded in the 1720s and proved remarkably popular. Yet another important institution was the biennial exhibit of paintings in the Louvre which began in 1737, and which allowed interested onlookers to peruse and discuss the newest works chosen for display by the Royal Academy of Painting and Sculpture. This institution, called the salon, in turn provoked commentary in the press, thereby giving birth to a new genre of writing: art criticism.

Just as significant was a different institution also going by the name of salon, which consisted of gatherings at the house of a wealthy sponsor (usually a noblewoman) for the purposes of structured discussion. This sort of salon had existed long before the eighteenth century. But until then it had served primarily as a school of aristocratic manners, a way for *parvenus* to learn how to behave in Court society. During the regency and afterwards, it turned increasingly into a serious literary and intellectual forum, where writers presented new work, and had a place to meet the wealthy and the well-connected. In a salon, children of provincial artisans like Diderot could rub shoulders with members of the oldest aristocratic houses. The greatest of the *salonnières* governed their gatherings with remarkable skill and finesse, not only pleasing the participants but stimulating the emergence of new ideas. As one *philosophe* wrote of Mlle de Lespinasse, her guests 'found themselves in harmony like the strings of an instrument . . . Following this comparison, I could say that she played this instrument with an art that resembled genius'.[10]

Although the salons cannot be said to have given birth to the Enlightenment, in the person of Mme de Tencin they came close. This remarkable woman, whose career would probably have fizzled nastily at the Court of Louis XIV, exemplified many of the new possi-

---

[10] Marmontel, quoted in Dena Goodman, *The Republic of Letters: A Cultural History of the French Enlightenment* (Ithaca, NY, 1994), 100.

bilities opened up by the regency. Her father, a noble magistrate in Grenoble, sent her, against her wishes, to become a nun. After his death, she successfully sued to win release from her vows, and went to Paris, where she quickly became a subject of scandal for carrying on affairs with many of the leading figures in the government, including prime minister Dubois and the regent himself (in some cases, the liaisons served principally to advance the career of her brother in the church; he eventually became a cardinal). She went on to host one of the regency's most important salons, and became a patroness of the early Enlightenment (among her frequent guests were Fontenelle and Montesquieu). She also gave birth, in 1717, to an illegitimate son: Jean Le Rond d'Alembert, one of the most important of the *philosophes*.

The periodical press, cafés, and artistic and literary salons all helped bring into being a new phenomenon to which the French gave the name public opinion. By this, they meant not the opinions of the entire population, but rather the considered judgement of those people who had sufficient income, education, and leisure to read the newspapers, visit the cafés and salons (and academies and the theatre), and engage in rational discussion of what they saw, heard, and read. A fundamental feature associated with public opinion was equality: in this forum, the voice of a marquis counted for no more than that of an illegitimate noble like d'Alembert, a commoner like Diderot, or even a foreign (Swiss) commoner like Jean-Jacques Rousseau. What mattered, in theory, were talent and wit alone. In practice, of course, the new public behaved rather less rationally than its eulogists claimed. Money, favour, rank and connections still mattered in determining who had access to the salons and the press. Nonetheless, in this new intellectual environment associated with public opinion, writers and artists could appeal to a unprecedentedly large, varied, and impersonal audience, and engage in a new sort of interchange, based on the idea of rational, unrestrained criticism of matters literary and artistic—and ultimately political and religious as well. It was in this environment, inseparable from the city of Paris itself, that the Enlightenment could take form, and pursue its reflections on human society.

The Enlightenment

While the term 'the Enlightenment' only appeared after the fact, its leading figures, the *philosophes*, were recognized by the 1740s as forming, if not an organized movement, then at least a sort of family (of course like many families, they had their share of bitter quarrels, and the occasional divorce). Certainly, their enemies in the church perceived them as an organized 'philosophical party', and predicted disaster on an apocalyptic scale if their works were not suppressed. It is no coincidence that the single greatest monument of the French Enlightenment is not any single book, but a collaborative venture: the *Encyclopédie* edited by Diderot and d'Alembert, and published from 1751 to 1772.

The *Encyclopédie*, and the story of its composition, reveal a great deal about the character of the Enlightenment as a whole. First, while it was not the oldest encyclopedia (in fact, it started out as a translation of an English encyclopedia), at the time it was the largest and most ambitious ever undertaken. Not only did it involve a team of publishers and over 140 contributors eventually producing no less than 35 folio volumes; it aimed at nothing less than the wholesale reshaping and reorientation of human knowledge. In this way, it reflects both the *philosophes'* boundless optimism, and their considerable ambition. Second, Diderot and d'Alembert chose their contributors from many different social backgrounds, including clerics, members of the high nobility, and the sons of artisans. The Enlightenment as a whole was similarly the ideological property of no single social group, but amounted to a current moving through the educated classes as a whole.

Third, the *Encyclopédie* was an enterprise that lay on the shifting and uncertain borders of legality. Although initially approved by the royal authorities, the council of state suppressed a number of volumes, and in 1759 halted publication entirely for a time, after protests from the church. Similarly, nearly all the major *philosophes*, despite enjoying the support of high-placed patrons (including Frederick the Great of Prussia and Catherine the Great of Russia), for a long time had run-ins with the authorities. Voltaire, despite gaining renown as the greatest living French playwright while still in his twenties, endured a long stay in the Bastille, a thorough beating by an offended nobleman's lackeys, and several periods of exile. He ended up spending most of his career close to the Swiss border, bitterly describing France to Diderot as 'the land of monkeys transformed into tigers'.[11] Many of the *philosophes'* works were either published illegally, or were suppressed after publication.

The *Encyclopédie* also exemplified the general philosophy of the French Enlightenment. That is to say, it did not construct any grand philosophical system, but it did express a systematic outlook: empiricist, sceptical and resolutely practical. In a detailed diagram of human knowledge that they prepared for the work, Diderot and d'Alembert gave the most space to 'knowledge of nature', followed by 'knowledge of man'. They exiled 'knowledge of God' and 'general metaphysics' to a distant corner, accompanied by 'divination' and 'black magic'.[12] The intellectual method that they adopted was not Cartesian deduction from abstract first principles, but induction, based on careful, scientific observation. Their chief criterion for measuring value was utility, defined in terms of what produced the most material benefits and the most spiritual comforts for the most people. In keeping with this perspective, the *Encyclopédie* included, along with articles on such topics as 'genius', 'reason', and 'knowledge,' long and learned disquisitions on clock-making, metalworking, agricultural techniques, weaving, artillery, printing, electricity and much else, all illustrated by volumes of sumptuously detailed engravings. As Rousseau remarked in *Emile*, in a line that might have served as the *Encyclopédie's* epigraph, 'it is not a question of knowing what is, but only what is useful'.

A different side of the Enlightenment is revealed by a short, anonymous fable written in the mid-eighteenth century. It tells of a man who hated humanity, to the point that he withdrew from society and went to live in a remote cave. Yet not even solitude satisfied him, and he brooded long and hard about how he might do positive harm to the largest number of people. After contemplating many dreadful acts, he finally decided on a course of action. He left his cave, went to the nearest town, and called all the people to listen to him. And then,

---

[11] Quoted in Goodman, *The Republic of Letters*, 43.

[12] Reproduced in Robert Darnton, *The Great Cat Massacre and Other Episodes in French Cultural History* (New York, 1984), 210–11.

when they had all assembled, he announced to them the existence of God.

This fable, which still has the power to shock, most obviously expresses the *philosophes'* abhorrence of organized, revealed religion, which they considered a source of superstition, error and persecution (for obvious reasons, this point of view made it only obliquely into the legally-published *Encyclopédie*). Few *philosophes* followed Diderot and d'Holbach into outright atheism, but many more abandoned Christianity for deism, a belief system that considered God the creator, but not the active ruler, of the universe, and prescribed no tenets other than the natural religious sentiments supposedly present in every person from birth.

In addition, the fable was not only irreverent, but deliberately offensive, and the great figures of the Enlightenment liked nothing more than violently to upset their compatriots' established beliefs. Montesquieu, for instance, wrote a satirical epistolary novel called *Persian Letters*, which purported to recount the reactions of two Persians travelling through France, and showed, among other things, how strange even the most revered aspects of French life might appear through alien eyes (one of the Persians referred to the king as 'a great magician', and continued: 'there is another magician, even stronger than him ... called the *pope*').[13] Rousseau, in his great autobiographical *Confessions*, explained with bizarre pride how he had taken each of his newborn children, and left them on the steps of an orphanage.

It is also characteristic of much of the Enlightenment that the point was made through the telling of a story. The authors of the Enlightenment loved accessible fiction far more than dense treatises. Voltaire is best known for his fable *Candide*, about the adventures of a young and naive German, which touts the virtues of an empirical, broadly utilitarian approach to life. One character in the fable, a metaphysician named Dr Pangloss (based on the German philosopher Leibniz), hangs onto his unempirical belief in the pre-established harmony of the universe, even after catching syphilis, losing an eye and an ear, nearly dying in an earthquake, nearly getting hanged, getting cut into by a surgeon, getting flogged almost to death,

[13] Charles Louis de Secondat, baron de Montesquieu, *Lettres persanes* (Paris, 1964 edn.), 56.

and being forced to row in the Turkish galleys. Diderot, after the *Encyclopédie*, is remembered for unconventional fictional works like *Rameau's Nephew*, *Jacques the Fatalist*, and *The Indiscreet Jewels* (an especially provocative text: the jewels in question are women's genitalia with the capacity for speech). Montesquieu first burst on the scene with *Persian Letters*, and as for Rousseau, in the eighteenth century his reputation rested less on his works of political theory, than on his wildly popular epistolary novel, *La Nouvelle Héloïse*. Clearly, the *philosophes* were not aiming to persuade a small, scholarly, and princely elite through abstract reasoning, but rather to reach out and grab hearts and minds on a large scale.

In all these ways, the Enlightenment represented the culmination of the social and intellectual trends described above. In the wake of the perceived withdrawal of God from the world, and the rise of sceptical, scientific thought, the philosophes addressed themselves resolutely, and in a spirit of scientific practicality, to the problems of human society. And as children of an urban, commercial culture in which the phenomenon of public opinion had ever-increasing importance, they aimed to accomplish their goals not simply by demonstrating the justice of their views to a small audience of their peers, or even by persuading princes and prelates, but by making converts on a large scale.

Yet did the *philosophes* produce a coherent programme of social and political reform? The answer is no. Their explicit political views in particular varied widely. Voltaire's first major work, *Philosophical Letters*, a series of observations on England, praised the English parliament for checking the power of the king, and ridiculed the prejudices of the French nobility. Yet by the end of his career, Voltaire had evolved into a defender of royal authority, and even wrote pamphlets in favour of chancellor Maupeou. Montesquieu, by contrast, served for many years as a member of the parlement of Bordeaux, and never entirely abandoned the parlementaire point of view. Both *Persian Letters*, and also his masterpiece *The Spirit of the Laws*, warned vividly against the dangers of despotism (the latter also heaped praise upon the mixed constitution of England). Rousseau made little direct comment on French politics, but his work inspired the most radical pamphleteers of the end of the old regime, as well as the radical revolutionaries who followed.

The two most ambitious Enlightenment attempts to establish

a science of society and politics—*The Spirit of the Laws*, and Rousseau's *Second Discourse* and *Social Contract*—themselves point in strikingly different directions. Montesquieu's huge and eccentrically organized work strove for a scientifically impartial tone, and presented its conclusions as induced from the raw data of (copiously cited) history and travel literature about societies from the Americas to east Asia. He attempted to find governing principles for different sorts of political systems, and to relate them to the character and climate of the nations in question. Rousseau, by contrast, cast his work as a speculative, and moralizing account of society in general. In his *Second Discourse* he asserted that mankind had evolved from a state of nature, in which individuals lived in almost total isolation from one another, into a primitive but admirable condition of savagery. Then, however, they had degenerated into the modern condition where egotism in its many forms prevailed, leaving most persons miserable slaves to each other and to their own unslaked passions. This contrarian view of human history not only amounted to a bold critique of much Enlightenment thought (the *philosophes* tended to see history as a story of continuous progress, with themselves in the vanguard), but led many of Rousseau's former colleagues to break angrily with him. In his *Social Contract*, Rousseau then went further and suggested that mankind could create conditions of harmony and justice if citizens engaged in a radical renunciation of individual rights to the benefit of the collective 'general will'. In this way, Rousseau proposed, political action could transform human nature itself. It was a promise which would help beget two centuries of revolutionary thinking and action.

Most of the *philosophes* shied away from Rousseau's implicitly democratic prescriptions (many blenched at the idea even of educating, let alone empowering, the common people). The French Enlightenment really spoke with a single voice on only two political causes: establishing religious toleration and reforming the system of criminal justice. In both these cases, the principal weapon it used was the judicial *cause célèbre* that dramatically highlighted an individual case of persecution and injustice before the 'tribunal of public opinion'. Most famously, in the 1760s, Voltaire led the way in fighting for the posthumous rehabilitation of Jean Calas, a Toulouse Protestant falsely accused of murdering his son and gruesomely executed after a trial tainted by bigotry. The poor chevalier de La Barre subsequently joined Calas in the ranks of the Enlightenment's martyrs. The *philosophes* used any and every means to bring these cases widespread attention, including pamphlets, newspapers, and judicial briefs filed by sympathetic lawyers. Their successes led directly to the granting of limited emancipation to Protestants in 1787, and also to the partial reform of criminal procedure (particularly the abolition of officially sanctioned torture).

The broader connections between the *philosophes* and the breakdown of the old regime, however, are more subtle, and complex. They amounted less to a battle between self-conscious, organized parties, than to changes that cut across social and ideological lines.

Les enfants de la patrie

In one sense, far from plotting to overthrow the old regime, the *philosophes* became part of it. After the decades of official hostility and persecution, there followed a period of largely peaceful, even complacent coexistence. Those members of the philosophical 'family' with good connections benefited from lucrative posts and pensions. The most important cultural institutions fell under their control (d'Alembert even became permanent secretary of the French Academy). Previously censored works circulated more freely. Two men associated with the *philosophes*, Turgot and Necker, became leading ministers, and pursued reform programmes pleasing to large sections of enlightened public opinion. In the most dramatic symbol of the change, Voltaire, in 1778, staged a triumphant return to Paris. At an adulatory ceremony at the Comédie française , his bust was crowned with laurel leaves before a performance of his last play, *Irénée*. His death shortly afterwards occasioned louder public grief than that of Louis XV four years earlier. It was the virulent clerical critics of the *philosophes* who now seemed voices crying in the wilderness.

The very success of the *philosophes*, however, provoked strong reactions. Rousseau, for instance, poured scorn on those supposedly corrupt and complacent colleagues who were growing fat from official patronage, and preached the virtues of living like Diogenes: poor and solitary, but honest. Similar criticism issued forth from the many would-be *philosophes* who had flocked to Paris in the hopes of

becoming the next Voltaire, only to find the gates of what one historian has dubbed the 'High Enlightenment' slammed in their faces.
Many of them ended up as hired hacks, making ends meet by writing
pornography, or libellous lampoons of Court figures (including the
queen, whose supposedly unslakable lust for sexual partners of both
sexes they chronicled in detail). They poured their resentment of the
society which had rejected them into these illicit works, which dif-
fered from previous examples of 'underground' literature in being
able to draw on the language of the Enlightenment itself to portray
corruption in high places not only as deplorable, but as the inevitable
product of a system of unjust privilege and hierarchy.

Even those *philosophes* who revelled in their success sometimes
harboured doubts about the cult of reason and science whose triumph was coming to seem inevitable. Diderot, most notably,
expressed these doubts in his eccentric masterpiece *Rameau's
Nephew*, which he never dared publish in his lifetime (it only came to
light in the nineteenth century). The book consists of a dialogue
between characters labelled 'Me'and 'Him', the first initially identified with Diderot himself, the second with Jean-François Rameau, the
nephew of France's most famous composer (later, the question of
their identity becomes more tangled). While 'Me' is a wise, stoic, and
civic-minded philosopher, 'Him' is an indolent, parasitical creature
of pure appetite, who confounds 'Me' at every step, denouncing conventional morality as illusion and vanity, praising grand acts of evil
for their sublimity, and suggesting that humanity resembles 'Himself'
more than the *philosophe* would like to admit. The book foreshadows
some of the great criticisms of the Enlightenment made by modern
philosophers.

The dominant trends in culture from the 1760s to the 1780s can be
traced both to the accomplishments of the *philosophes*, and also to
these criticisms and doubts. First among them was what can only be
called a Rousseauian obsession with sentiment, nature, and pastoral
simplicity. Actions, speech, and dress, it was increasingly argued,
should be unadorned, and offer a clear window onto a person's inner
feelings. Luxuries, and anything else which drew men and women
from their natural selves, should be fiercely rejected. Thus in painting,
the airy, voluptuous, and often complex tableaux of the rococo painters now gave way to stern, clearly delineated portrayals of simple
domestic scenes, set among the peasantry more than the upper

classes: for instance, Greuze's depictions of a village betrothal, and his parable of the punishment of a wicked son. Diderot helped promote the development of a new theatrical genre, the melodrama, which featured simple plots designed to tear at the heartstrings of the audience. Rousseau did more than anyone to advance the trend, above all through his epistolary novel *La Nouvelle Héloïse*, in which the characters practically wept their words onto the paper. Readers reacted with equally copious tears, with one writing to Rousseau: 'One must suffocate, one must abandon the book, one must weep, one must write to you that one is choking with emotion and weeping'.[14] The craze for the pastoral even reached the Court, where queen Marie-Antoinette dressed herself and her courtiers up as shepherds and shepherdesses. On one occasion, her pastoral steed having thrown her to the ground, the queen supposedly scandalized courtiers by loudly enquiring as to the proper etiquette a queen should follow in falling off an ass.

If the advocates of sentiment wanted to remove men and women from the artificial, stylized influences of Paris and the Court and return them to 'nature', the proponents of the neoclassical style, which reached its zenith in the 1780s, desired something else: to make them citizens. Rousseau himself had stressed in *Émile* the difference between these two goals: 'Forced to fight nature or social institutions, we must choose between making a man or making a citizen; we cannot do both at once.' In the 1780s, as the economy faltered, France's debts loomed ever larger, and existing political institutions seemed helpless in the face of imminent disaster, cultural critics began to link luxury, artificiality, Court manners, and political paralysis together as different sides of the same fundamental problem. And they concluded that the solution lay less in a utopian return to shepherding, than in a recovery of the manners and customs of antiquity, particularly the Roman republic. They wished, in other words, not merely to honour the ancients, and to profit from their wisdom, but actively to model their own lives and their own society on the ancient example. In this sense (if not, yet, in a directly political one), they can be called republicans.

The movement found its greatest artistic expression in the paintings of David. His 1789 *Lictors Bringing Brutus the Bodies of his Sons* concerned the Roman leader who had famously put his civic duty ahead of personal feeling to the extent that he ordered his own sons executed for their failings. David's masterpiece *The Oath of the Horatii*, the sensation of the artistic salon of 1785, presented a father and three sons taking a solemn oath to defend Rome, if necessary at the cost of their lives. David's works echoed some of Rousseau's writings (the *Social Contract* discussed Roman institutions at length), and also those of the *philosophe* Mably, who in his later years forthrightly advocated a republic as the best form of government. These paintings directly inspired a generation of revolutionaries.

Both of David's great Roman works juxtaposed strong, civic-minded men to weeping women in a state of collapse, and the pairing points to another key aspect of neoclassicism and emergent republicanism: their use of gender. In the neoclassical optic, the corruption of a society's proper customs and manners began at the moment when men and women abandoned the roles supposedly prescribed to them by nature: for men, to engage in public debate and to rush, like the Horatii, to the defence of the homeland; for women, to tend the hearth and raise the children. The recovery of Roman mores therefore theoretically entailed the exclusion of women from a cultural sphere in which they were exerting significant influence as *salonnières*, as patronesses (the king's mistress Mme de Pompadour in particular) and as artists and writers in their own right (for instance, the painter Vigée-Lebrun, and the novelist Mme de Lafayette). In practice, this exclusion was never accomplished. Nonetheless, the exclusionary impulse helped fuel the lampoonists' misogynistic portrayals of the queen as the embodiment of all France's ills, and foreshadowed the formal denial of the suffrage to women during the French Revolution, over the protests of early feminists. In addition, the change greatly damaged the salons, which had earlier served the Enlightenment so well. By the 1780s they had been partially supplanted by a newer cultural institution called the *musée* —a forum for public lectures and scientific demonstrations—which was far less open to female participation.

In the world of neoclassicism and republican thought, the supreme value was not just masculinity, however, but patriotism, defined as an ardent, all-consuming masculine dedication to the common good. And it was precisely in the *patrie*, the land of their birth, that the enlightened public opinion of the eighteenth century found its last and greatest cause. Already in the 1750s the crown itself had actively promoted a cult of the *patrie*, sponsoring unprecedented quantities of war propaganda to stoke the fires of French national fervour in the wars with Great Britain. It also promoted self-consciously 'patriotic' stage plays such as de Belloy's *The Siege of Calais*, a wildly popular 1765 melodrama about the Hundred Years War, and it gave large commissions to artists to portray the 'great men of the nation' on canvas and in stone. Poets followed suit, for instance an anonymous 1767 author who wrote (with more fire than talent):

Il faut pour la Patrie une chaleur sublime,	Our Country's love needs warmth sublime
Un amour qui soit passion;	A love that transcends reason.
Que l'indifférence est un crime,	Indifference is but a crime,
La tiédeur une trahison.	Tepidity plain treason.[15]

In the 1770s, of course, opponents of chancellor Maupeou labelled themselves the party of the 'patriots', and the label resurfaced in the final crisis of the regime, to the point that one young lawyer, in the heady autumn of 1788, even spoke of eating 'properly patriotic suppers'.[16] Voltaire quipped mordantly that in the long run, people would prefer being entertained to being praised for their choice of nationality, but in fact the public appetite for patriotism only grew.

If Voltaire was wrong on this question, it was for reasons that go back to the underlying changes in French culture and religion that have been discussed in this chapter. It was above all because love of the *patrie* had peculiarly powerful spiritual and emotional resonance in a nation where organized, revealed religion was losing its traditional place—where God himself now appeared as an unprecedentedly remote and disembodied idea. The teachings of the gospel might still provide comfort for many, even most of the French in the inner sanctum of their consciences, but religion no longer seemed to offer a reliable guide on the questions of how to order the terrestrial city, and of how to prevent each individual's pursuit of their selfish interests

[15] *Le patriotisme, poëme qui a été présenté a l'académie française pour le prix de 1766, Et dont on n'a fait aucune mention* (Paris, 1767), 11. Translation by William Doyle.

[16] Jacques Godard to Cortot, 7 Nov. 1788, in Archives Départementales de la Côte d'Or, E 642.

from tearing the country apart (significantly, images of horrific sixteenth-century civil wars remained a staple of French literature in the eighteenth century, notably in Voltaire's epic poem *La Henriade*). Nor did the creed of the *Encyclopédie*, the promise that science and reason could in time resolve these problems, provide an adequate alternative, particularly under the conditions of political and economic collapse that prevailed in the late 1780s. In those desperate days, when it seemed to many that France itself lay in mortal danger, the most resonant battle-cry, heard in hundreds of pamphlets and newspapers, was for the French collectively to surrender their individual interests, privileges, and prejudices, and to join together as one great family, becoming (in the words of the *Marseillaise*) their country's children, 'les enfants de la patrie'. In this way, the cultural shifts described in this chapter helped lay the groundwork for the French Revolution.

4

France overseas

Pierre H. Boulle and D. Gillian Thompson

At the beginning of Louis XIV's personal reign, France overseas consisted of a somewhat haphazard collection of territories under the half-hearted control of the metropolis. The principal possessions were New France and some islands in the Caribbean. By the end of the reign, France's empire was made up of colonies and commercial factories controlled from the centre and connected to the mother country by complex economic ties. It would continue to grow in the eighteenth century, when competition with the British for colonial empire reached its climax. By the mid-eighteenth century, France challenged British ambitions to control world trade. While Britain was victorious in North America and India, elsewhere, and notably in the West Indies, France more than held its own.

Throughout the period, the colonial empire was composed of three parts. The first was New France, the vast north-western Atlantic region of North America whose coasts and waterways were used by French fishermen, fur traders and missionaries, and the settlements within it. It included Newfoundland, Acadia on the Atlantic coast (the present-day Maritime provinces of Canada and eastern Maine), Canada on the St Lawrence river between Quebec and Montreal, and the Lower Great Lakes region. In 1663, a small French fishing settlement at Plaisance on the south coast of Newfoundland, 350 settlers at Port-Royal on the Bay of Fundy, and 2,500 settlers in Canada, most clustered near Quebec, Three Rivers, and Montreal, provided the basis for French territorial claims and involvement in the great North Atlantic fisheries and fur trade.

A second part consisted of the islands of the West Indies. Saint-Christophe (St Kitts, shared with the English), Martinique, Guadeloupe, and several nearby islands, including the minor outpost of

Cayenne off Guiana, were, in 1660, under the control of individual French proprietors, some of whom were already abandoning tobacco production for that of sugar. The French population of these islands approximated 10,000, of whom about 7,000 were indentured labourers. In the Greater Antilles, Tortuga and Saint-Domingue on the western part of Hispaniola were occupied by international communities of privateers and buccaneers, living off wild cattle left behind by the Spanish. Under nominal French control, these communities were gradually developing as permanent settlements.

Outposts in Africa, the Indian Ocean, and India constituted the third sector. In 1660, this was the least developed area, consisting only of a small settlement at Saint-Louis in Senegal and an even more uncertain one at Fort-Dauphin on Madagascar. Under the authority of trading companies to which the state had granted quasi-sovereign rights, the region developed in the eighteenth century into an important economic sector, focused on the African slave trade, new plantation colonies in the Mascareigne Islands, and trade with the Indian subcontinent.

Colonial policies and administration

By 1670, Colbert had gained control over the French economy by combining the office of controller-general of finances and the new office of secretary of state for the navy, responsible for both naval and colonial affairs. He considered external commerce to be 'the source of [public] finance' and labelled commercial competition among nations 'a money war'.[1] As early as 1664, Colbert had sought to establish long-range and colonial trade on a secure basis by creating two companies on the Dutch model: the West Indies Company for trade with Africa and the Americas and the East Indies Company for trade in the Indian Ocean and with the Far East. By expanding colonial settlements and establishing new trading posts, these companies were expected to wrest control of overseas trade from the Dutch and to

---

[1] *Lettres, instructions et mémoires de Colbert*, ed. P. Clément (8 vols., Paris, 1861–82), iii (I), 37, vii. 250; see also E. F. Heckscher, *Mercantilism*, 2nd edn. (2 vols. London, 1955), ii. 17–20.

create regular exchanges between the mother country and its overseas territories. To support these aims and shore up French commercial interests, the crown provided over 50 per cent of the companies' initial capital and expanded the navy.

Colbert's colonial goals were largely realized by 1683. The navy now had 276 vessels, including some 120 ships of the line, the colonies had been significantly transformed, and merchants in French ports, notably La Rochelle and Nantes, had begun to take up colonial trade. Although, in the process, the companies failed, it is unlikely Colbert saw this as a reverse, for he was not a rigid theoretician of mercantilism. Indeed, he had contributed to these failures by permitting private enterprise within the companies' monopolies. Thus, by 1669, he had granted special permission to private merchants to trade in the West Indies. Five years later, the West Indies Company itself was abolished and its Caribbean market fully opened to private enterprise in exchange for the profits of a new import duty. Similarly, the Company's African trade, at first transferred to the new Senegal Company, was soon opened to the private sector in exchange for the payment of a fee. In the process, the initial risk capital was lost, but colonial trade was assured. Only the East Indies Company survived into the next century, although it too was shorn periodically of its most profitable markets.

Colbert's less flexible successors pursued his policies more rigidly, but colonial trade continued to grow. Indeed, the colonial economy would have grown more rapidly had the king not prized his armies above his navy and had he not regarded colonies as valuable pawns to be sacrificed during the various wars and negotiations of his reign. Meanwhile, the division between overseas sectors would be reinforced when, following Colbert's death, his two economic offices were once again separated. Until the end of company rule, the controller-general of finances would oversee eastern trade, while, for the most part, colonies in the Americas would fall under the authority of the secretary of state for the navy.

The crown assumed direct government of New France in 1663, and of the Caribbean islands in 1674. The form of government then established in the colonies persisted relatively unchanged until the end of the Old Regime. At the head of each major colonial sector (New France and the West Indies, later subdivided into Greater and Lesser Antilles) stood a governor-general who served as military commander-in-chief responsible for the colony to the naval minister. Civil administration and finances were the responsibility of an intendant, also named by the crown. A sovereign council was created in each colony, composed of the main royal officials and leading inhabitants. While, in New France, this council was soon restricted to judicial functions, in the West Indies it assumed more prominence as a voice for planters. Subordinate officials were entrusted with colonial sectors not easily controlled from the centre (Plaisance, Acadia, Guiana, Guadeloupe, and later Louisiana and Île Royale). Such officials corresponded directly with the ministry.

The colonies to 1713

Colonial endeavours in the Indian Ocean and Asia were limited during the reign of Louis XIV. Although many dreams of conquest had contributed to the creation of the East Indies Company, its major expedition, undertaken in 1670–4 and involving 2,500 men on nine ships, resulted in failure. The expedition's arrival at Fort-Dauphin caused a Native uprising which forced the abandonment of Madagascar. The fleet then proceeded to India where its campaign against the Dutch ended in surrender. Yet the company made significant profits through trade. Furthermore, the period saw the beginning of the French occupation of the Mascareignes, when Bourbon Island (present-day Réunion) was settled by exiles and escapers from Fort-Dauphin. The company also gained concessions on the Coromandel Coast at Pondicherry, later the principal French factory in India, and in Bengal at Chandernagore.

By the early eighteenth century, fur traders and explorers, sometimes in defiance of royal policy, had pushed the boundaries of New France outward to include the upper Great Lakes region, headwaters of rivers running into Hudson Bay, and the valleys of the Mississippi and its tributaries to the Gulf of Mexico. Before the middle of the eighteenth century, such men had extended the boundaries still farther west to Lake Winnipeg and the foothills of the Rocky Mountains. Even in the seventeenth century, trade and settlement were essential elements of a French policy intended to prevent the advance of Anglo-American interests in the larger region.

The whole of New France was Native territory. Since the sixteenth century, Native populations had experienced cultural dislocation and been reduced to a fraction of their earlier numbers by European diseases, war between rival Native alliances, European wars, and migration. Because the Acadian and St Lawrence settlements normally did not occupy land in use by Native peoples, any animosities between French settlers and the latter tended to have a commercial rather than a territorial foundation. Intermarriage between colonists and Natives was rare. Native peoples would continue to experience losses, but nations, including the Mi'kmaqs, Abenakis, Ottawas, Iroquois and many others with whom French colonists had dealings, still numbered in the thousands and retained distinctive, superior physical qualities. As the Jesuit anthropologist Lafitau reported in the early years of the eighteenth century, 'they are tall—taller than we are—well-made, well-proportioned, of good constitution, nimble, strong and deft; in a word, in bodily qualities ... they may have advantages over us'.[2] Native peoples would not be outnumbered by Europeans in the territory of New France, however it was measured, until late in the eighteenth century.

In the late seventeenth and the eighteenth centuries, Native peoples remained powerful and independent, and could determine the outcome of events. They could threaten French and English settlements and trading posts, influence trading patterns, act as a buffer between rival European or Native groups, and serve as military allies of the French or English. Those who settled in the mission villages in the St Lawrence Valley, Acadia, Detroit, and the Illinois and upper Great Lakes regions adhered to syncretist forms of religion which included Catholicism. Jesuits and other resident missionaries were likely to have a sympathetic understanding of the culture and plight of Native peoples, to encourage them to create avowedly Christian communities separate from the world of commerce and war, and to expect them to take the side of the French in any dispute. But they were likely to choose their own course. From the beginning, the French depended on Native allies for furs and protection against Native enemies and for support against English attempts to take over the trade—and the continent. The creation of alliances for these

---

[2] *Moeurs des Sauvages américains* (Paris, 1724), quoted by P. Pluchon, *Histoire de la colonisation française*, vol. i, *Des origines à la Restauration* (Paris, 1991), 339.

purposes, gained and maintained through the judicious use of presents ranging from muskets, tools, and military medals to food, blankets, clothing, and other trade goods, and involving elaborate ceremonies based on Native traditions, was the cornerstone of French policy in North America. Such alliances were part of a network of mutual dependency, which could cause unforeseen obligations.

For the small settled French population of New France the century starting in 1663 was a period of steady growth. In Canada, partly subsidized immigration resulted in the arrival, in the 1660s and 1670s, of 2,500 people, most of them young, single adults, 40 per cent of them women. Hundreds of indentured labourers chose to stay in the colony, as did 400 regular soldiers disbanded in the 1660s and others in later decades, but overseas immigration remained insignificant until the 1750s. Three-quarters of the colonists came from the north-western and western provinces of Normandy, Île-de-France, Poitou, Aunis, Saintonge and Brittany. The Canadian population had grown, by the early 1680s, to roughly 10,000, and doubled every thirty years thereafter. Pre-1680 settlers were the ancestors of 70 per cent of the Canadian population of 1760. Canadian women tended to marry young and, if widowed, to remarry quickly, unlike their counterparts in France. The excess of births (55 per thousand per year) over deaths (30 per thousand per year) reflects the generally healthy environment and explains the large families that characterized New France.

Despite being under English rule in 1654–70, Acadia shared Canada's experience. Its French immigrants also came from western France. Startlingly, given that rural life awaited most colonists in New France, almost half the French immigrants to Canada and Acadia, and two-thirds of the women, came from urban areas: from Paris as well as from the ports of Rouen, Dieppe, La Rochelle, and Bordeaux. A large proportion were artisans, but social elites, including merchants, were also well represented. Acadians increased at about the same rates as Canadians. By 1680 Acadians numbered about 1,000 people, by 1713 between 2,000 and 3,000. While, by 1713, New France settlements were much larger than a generation earlier, the population remained small by any objective standard, and was still struggling to establish itself.

A fifth to a quarter of those who stayed in Canada could be found in its towns, which grew slowly to 1713, when Quebec had scarcely more than 2,000 people and Montreal about 1,300. A permanent military force of regular troops recruited for service in the colonies (*troupes de la marine*) was garrisoned in the towns, starting in the 1680s. Quebec, the administrative and ecclesiastical centre of New France, was often compared to a French provincial town. It was the residence of the governor-general, the intendant, and the bishop, and the location of the sovereign council, a seminary and the Jesuit college, where the local male elite was educated. A commercial deep sea port, Quebec was the home of many shipping merchants. Representing French commercial interests, with one foot in France, the other in Canada, they were not averse to marrying in the colony. Montreal was the great inland entrepôt of the fur trade and an important military base. Despite its mission origins, it was turbulent and avidly commercial. Its merchants provisioned *voyageurs*, the men licensed to convey trade goods through the interior. Its annual fur trade fair continued to attract hundreds of Native traders each summer to the end of the century.

A variety of people did the daily work of Canadian towns. Priests, like their counterparts in French towns, said public masses, administered the sacraments, preached, catechized and educated young men in town. Ursulines, the Congregation of Notre-Dame, Hospitallers, and other women religious, including, later, the Grey Nuns, educated young women and administered hospitals and other social services comparable to those of French towns. Royal administrators, military officers, merchants, artisans, tradesmen, shopkeepers, carters, labourers, domestic servants, and a handful of slaves did the towns' secular work and manual labour. The population was sharply stratified by occupation, income, and social rank. Military officers, increasing numbers of them born in Canada, were at the top. This nobility held the largest proportion of seigneuries. The church was also an important landowner. Government officials, the military establishment, prominent merchants, and leading clergy remained French, in attitude if not by birth, until the end of the regime.

The three-quarters to four-fifths of all immigrants who inhabited the countryside were the basis of the Canadian and Acadian populations. In Canada, seigneuries were divided into long-lot farms larger than peasant holdings in France, much of them, in the first generations, uncleared forest. Established, self-sufficient farms required the work of all members of a family, sometimes supported by wage labourers. As farms grew, wheat became the universal crop and was often used as a means of payment; other crops included legumes, barley, and oats. The average farm had poultry, pigs, and livestock, used oxen as draught animals, and would, in the eighteenth century, acquire horses. Seigneurial dues and tithes owed to the church were rarely onerous for an established family. In Acadia, whose largely absentee landlords exacted few seigneurial obligations, settlement had first developed in tidal areas near Port-Royal and, later in the seventeenth century, at the head of the Bay of Fundy. Acadian farms, dependent on dikes and the development of marshland, were self-contained and achieved high levels of production of cereals and apples, and then of livestock. Canadian and Acadian farmers, for whom the local parish church was the centre of community life, could feel isolated if, as was likely in the early years, they lived some distance from that church and their religious needs were met only sporadically by mission priests. Such experience bred self-reliance and general hardiness among the settlers.

The fur trade was the economic foundation of New France and the sole source of its exports in the seventeenth century. The export of beaver pelts, which then accounted for most of the trade, was a monopoly, leased to French financiers. Ever expanding, the beaver trade increased fourfold between 1660 and 1675–85, until, by 1696, a glut having developed in the European market, it had to be suspended for a short time. Free, but loosely regulated within the colony, the fur trade followed certain patterns. Trade goods were shipped from French Atlantic ports to Quebec, then to Montreal, to be sold to small companies of traders licensed to deal with Native suppliers in the interior. Furs were brought to Montreal and Quebec at the end of the summer and profits were shared among many participants along the lengthy trade routes.

New France was rarely at peace before 1713. The truce negotiated with the Five Nations Iroquois confederacy in 1667 was broken in the early 1680s, with attacks against French Native allies and colonial traders. The governor of New York, hoping to drive the French out of the Great Lakes region, encouraged these hostilities. The French fur trade was threatened by the English in Hudson Bay. In the east, the French supported the Abenakis, who fought against New England to preserve their land. In 1689–97, these conflicts merged with the war of the League of Augsburg. While Mohawk raiders terrorized settlers near Montreal, regular officers, commanding small parties of

Canadians and Native warriors, engaged in effective guerilla warfare against the English colonies. The English harassed Acadia and tried unsuccessfully to destroy Canada. In 1701, the Iroquois, having suffered major losses, accepted a negotiated peace involving many Native groups as well as the French, and agreed to remain neutral in any future French–English conflict, a strategic and commercially significant victory for the French.

With the French decisions to create a base on the Gulf of Mexico in 1699–1702, to control the Mississippi valley and to prevent the much larger English colonies from advancing beyond the Alleghenies, colonial war became part of a larger imperial conflict. The French plan involved the establishment or reinforcement of trading posts, settlements, and missions in the heart of the continent, the development of the fur trade south of the Great Lakes, and the founding of a colony in Louisiana. It disregarded economic and military arguments against the development of the fur trade to the south and economic ones in favour of a northern or north-western orientation. The founding of Louisiana was problematic. By 1710, with fewer than 200 people, it had none of the advantages that had assisted Canada or Acadia in the early phases, and its geography was hostile. Its survival long remained in doubt.

In the north, the War of the Spanish Succession involved fighting and privateering in Hudson Bay, Newfoundland, and Acadia. Forced to spare Albany to preserve Iroquois neutrality, Canadian and Native war parties spread terror in New England. The English retaliated with attacks on Port-Royal, which surrendered in 1710, but successive attempts to invade Canada by land and sea failed. When peace finally came in 1713, New France had been at war for close to thirty years, a situation which had slowed its development and strengthened the influence of the military establishment over the colonial government.

The West Indies and the sugar revolution

The years 1661–1713 were, for the West Indies, a period of both consolidation and transition, in which the French settlers suffered a number of painful adjustments. France's title to its West Indian possessions had been recognized by Spain in 1659. By then, the English had agreed to the division of the islands of the Lesser Antilles. Also, the Caribs, who had resisted French expansion on Guadeloupe and Martinique, had been persuaded to relocate on St Vincent, St Lucia, and Dominica, three islands the French and the English agreed to keep neutral. While such arrangements promoted stability in the French Caribbean settlements, their resources remained insecure and support from home, even during the first years of Colbert's regime, remained uncertain.

The first major adjustment was economic. The islands' principal crop had originally been tobacco, but the market for West Indian tobacco had largely collapsed by the 1660s and sugar was gradually replacing it. The assumption of direct power by the crown was not wholly welcomed by settlers. The Dutch were the principal traders in the seventeenth century. Not only did they provide the French islands with essential supplies, but Amsterdam remained the major outlet for any tobacco still produced there. French royal policy, the so-called 'exclusive', was to reserve colonial trade to metropolitan interests, but French commerce was not yet capable of supplying the colonies on its own. Consequently, the planters resisted Colbert's efforts to exclude foreign traders, sometimes by outright rebellion.

Even more disruptive were the various wars which pitted the French against the Dutch, the Spanish, and the English during the reign of Louis XIV. Previous wars had generally spared the West Indies, but the development of the French navy and the growing wealth of the islands meant that these colonies now became involved. St Kitts was periodically captured by one group of settlers or the other, until it was permanently ceded to the British in 1713. Martinique, by the 1660s the new centre of French West Indian administration, was also attacked and the even more fragile settlements on Guadeloupe, Cayenne, and Saint-Domingue were raided time and again, at great cost to their residents.

Yet war was not always to the disadvantage of the French, who preyed on enemy territory as much as they were preyed upon. The tradition of privateering among Saint-Domingue settlers assisted the navy in its campaigns against enemy colonies and fleets and yielded significant booty. When the slave trade was disrupted by maritime wars, raids could also replenish the supply of slaves. And, the cost of the ensuing War of the Spanish Succession notwithstanding, Louis XIV's acceptance of the Spanish throne for his grandson strengthened the French position in the West Indies by ensuring Spanish American support. This support enabled the islands to gain strength during the war, completing their transformation to sugar production, so that, by 1713, they were well on their way to becoming the most economically important segment of the French colonial empire.

Sugar cane and the techniques of its production were introduced into the West Indies by the Dutch around 1650, but the development of sugar production as the major industry of the French islands was delayed until the 1670s and 1680s by a lack of capital and labour. Sugar cane took longer to mature than any other colonial product, and its care and harvesting required much more labour. Once harvested, the cane was subjected to quasi-industrial processes to make it transportable to a metropolitan site for final refining. The equipment and the skilled labour needed for these processes could only be supported by large plantations with a substantial and cheap agricultural labour force. The introduction of sugar production, therefore, led to significant changes in the economy and society of the islands.

On Martinique and Guadeloupe, where arable land was already fully occupied, the concentration of land required by sugar production meant that many of the tobacco plantations were taken over and their owners obliged to leave. Many relocated on Saint-Domingue in the 1660s and 1670s. Moreover, indentured whites proved inadequate labourers on sugar plantations. Their numbers remained small and their temporary status—most had three-year contracts—rendered the labour force unstable. Permanently enslaved Africans provided a solution to sugar plantation owners, especially since the increase in the Dutch slave trade and the beginning of involvement of French merchants in the latter part of the seventeenth century led to a sharp, if temporary, decline in the price of new slaves in the West Indies. From the 1660s onward, the population of African descent grew dramatically. On Martinique, black slaves were a majority of the population by 1660; twenty-five years later, their number was more than twice that of whites.

Saint-Domingue turned to sugar later, as a result of changes in the administration of the tobacco monopoly in France. The 1674 decision of the new French tobacco farm to favour tobacco from Brazil and Chesapeake Bay had little effect on the economy of the Lesser Antilles, already shifting to sugar, but it temporarily ruined that of

Saint-Domingue, where tobacco remained the principal product. To survive, settlers, old and new, had to choose between emigrating to Dutch islands and resuming their old buccaneering and piratical practices. The significant booty obtained by the island's privateers from the 1697 expedition against the mainland port of Cartagena was reinvested on Saint-Domingue, where it provided capital to create sugar plantations and purchase slaves.

By the end of the century, a new kind of society existed on the islands, sharply divided between whites and blacks. The white elite consisted of royal officers and of leading inhabitants, possessing large plantations and commanding local militia units. Most plantations were run by resident owners, though some were controlled by agents. Other plantations were the property of the Jesuits and other religious orders which, like most of the rest of the islands' clergy, supported and benefited from the system which placed agricultural work in the hands of slave labour. Below this elite were merchants who, like those of New France, were often agents of French merchant houses, notably those of Bordeaux and Nantes, the two Atlantic ports which came to dominate the West Indian trade. Lesser planters, involved in the production of cotton, cocoa, indigo, and, later, coffee, formed another intermediate group.

At the bottom stood an increasing number of slaves, working the large and small plantations or serving as domestics and petty artisans in the towns. Distinctions were made between field hands, dominated by recent arrivals from Africa, and house slaves and craftsmen, often selected from the creole, or island-born, slave population. Despite the significant differences in the living conditions of these two groups, they were legally equal and wholly dependent on the master who had purchased them, or, worse, on a plantation manager. Life on the plantation was harsh, particularly on large estates where slave management was impersonal. Even house slaves were not immune to the whip or assignment to teams of agricultural labourers who cleared the land, planted and tended the cane, and harvested it, from dawn to dusk, under the direction of a trusted slave or indentured white. Food was insufficient, accidents were frequent, and disease was rampant. To these adverse physical conditions was added severe mental trauma, first caused by the forced withdrawal from a familiar African environment and by the abysmal conditions of the passage to America. Those who survived were then isolated linguistically and culturally by a conscious policy of mixing ethnic groups on a plantation, so as to discourage resistance. The end result was a slave society with an impoverished African culture surviving beneath half-understood white norms and languages. Even among more assimilated creoles, the dominant culture, including the Christian religion, remained fundamentally alien.

Regulating social relations between white masters and black slaves was the *code noir*, a set of laws first issued in 1685 and periodically reformed thereafter. The code supposedly created more humane conditions for slaves by requiring masters to provide them with religious instruction and a minimum of food and by prohibiting masters from mutilating or executing slaves, punishments which only the crown could inflict. Yet the code reinforced the hold of whites over blacks. Status was transmitted by the mother, so sons and daughters of white males and female slaves remained slaves. Manumission required the permission of local officials increasingly reluctant to grant it. A freed slave could be returned to servitude for helping a slave escape or for striking a white. As the protection of slaves from masters was rarely enforced, the overall effect was to harden the lines between blacks and whites, slaves and free. So powerful were the forces regulating slavery that even a relatively enlightened colonial governor found that his perspective changed once he reached the islands: 'I arrived in Martinique with all the European prejudices against the severity with which the blacks are treated . . . Such harshness had seemed revolting to me and to go against the rights . . . of creatures as human as we are, save for the colour . . . [Now, however] I have become firmly convinced that blacks must be led like cattle, and that they must be kept in the most absolute ignorance'.[3]

Two other groups were present in West Indian society. The first were mixed-race children of slaves and whites (called people of colour), many of whom obtained their freedom. Not yet numerous at the beginning of the eighteenth century (perhaps 3 per cent of the islands' population in 1700), this intermediate and unstable class of freedmen grew and increasingly rivalled the petty white planters,

[3] La Motte-Fénelon to ministry of the navy, 11 Apr. 1764, Archives Nationales (Paris), Fonds des colonies, F/3/90, fo. 106.

becoming slave owners themselves. The second group were the maroons, runaway slaves who formed free communities outside settled areas, from which they raided isolated plantations for supplies and new recruits, notably women. They were the target of periodic expeditions by the militia, undertaken in a vain attempt to eradicate them. Maroons were particularly numerous in Guiana, where they mingled with the original inhabitants, and on Saint-Domingue, where they lived in the no man's land between the French and Spanish parts of the island.

Peace and development to mid-century

The thirty years of peace which followed the War of the Spanish Succession form a hiatus in the intense colonial rivalry between France and Great Britain which characterized the period after 1688. France's involvement in colonial trade reached maturity as its ports, thirteen of which gained the joint monopoly of trade with the American colonies in May 1717, became increasingly involved in the overseas exchange of goods. The main beneficiaries were Nantes and Bordeaux, the first as the principal slave-trading centre, the second as the major eighteenth-century supplier of foodstuffs and manufactured products to the West Indies. Other ports, such as La Rochelle and Marseille, became important centres of colonial traffic as well. Until 1769, trade beyond the Cape of Good Hope remained the monopoly of Lorient, created by Colbert as the port of the East Indies Company.

Complex systems of exchange were created between France and its overseas holdings. West Indian commerce involved the exchange of sugar for slaves and food, generating both direct trade with France and the more risky, capital-intensive triangular trade between France, Africa, and the West Indies. Other triangular trades existed, one including the metropolis, the West Indies, and New France. Another, based on cod, linked the French Atlantic fishing ports, the Newfoundland Grand Banks, and various Mediterranean markets. The most complex system involved the exchange of French goods, including colonial products, in Spanish ports for silver piastres, and the shipment of this specie to India to purchase cotton goods and other finished products for sale in France or for re-export, notably to the African coast where they formed part of the cargo exchanged for slaves.

A major tenet of John Law's scheme to revive the French economy after Louis XIV's death was his plan to charge a single commercial company with responsibility for all colonial activities. The assets of Law's own Company of the West, created in 1715 for the settlement of Louisiana, were pooled in May 1719 with those of the East Indies Company and of several companies involved in African trade. The shares of the new Company of the Indies thus formed were sold on the open market, where intense speculation generated a huge amount of capital to buttress the paper currency issued by Law's bank. The boom was sustained temporarily by exaggerated claims regarding Louisiana, but when the Mississippi bubble burst in 1720, it dragged down Law's bank and threatened the existence of the company. The Company of the Indies survived because the crown sacrificed Law's bank to it, but it remained saddled with a substantial hidden debt, its fixed dividends of 8 per cent serving to cover a forced loan made to the king at 3 per cent. The shortfall was to be made up from the company's commercial profits. The years of peace permitted such dividends to be paid and, by 1740, the volume of trade done by the company equalled that of its British counterpart and nearly matched that of the Dutch company.

This success may be attributed in part to the disintegration of the Mughal empire in India, which led to a transfer of power to local rulers and to rivalries between them. By allying with local rulers, the companies obtained various benefits. From their concessions at Pondicherry, Chandernagore, and Mahé, the French extended their influence in the region by employing Indian craftsmen, merchants, and middlemen, as the British did from their factories. Such trade depended on specie, for Indians had no interest in most European goods. While some specie was Spanish silver, a substantial amount came from the sale of Indian goods to Red Sea and Persian Gulf ports. Like the British, the French companies allowed their agents to engage in this 'country trade'. Huge private fortunes were made, ultimately to be transferred to Europe as shares of cargo on company ships. Meanwhile, the specie gained in Arabian markets served to support the companies' activities in India. The French were particularly successful in exploiting local rivalries. With few European soldiers, in the

1730s and 1740s they created an unofficial empire in the interior of southern India and excluded the British from this region. Most important, as local ruler, governor-general Dupleix (1741–54) used tax revenues collected from the population to support company activities, thereby resolving the age-old requirement of the Indian trade for hard currency.

The French company also settled the Mascareignes in the first half of the eighteenth century. By 1713, Bourbon had nearly 1,200 inhabitants, half of them described as white. In 1721, the company introduced moka coffee plants and thereby provided Bourbon with a secure basis for its economy. The island produced 250,000 *livres* of coffee in 1727; by 1744, production had increased tenfold. The population, including slaves imported from Madagascar and Mozambique, grew to 6,000 in 1731, 11,500 in 1740, and 19,000 in 1761. From 1740 onward, slaves formed some 80 per cent of the population.

Lacking natural harbours, Bourbon was an unsatisfactory watering station on the way to India. The nearby island of Mauritius, abandoned by the Dutch in 1710, was claimed by the French company in 1715 and renamed Île de France. Its governor transformed the island in the 1730s, providing Port-Louis with facilities for ship repairs and promoting sugar and coffee production, as well as the growing of food and the raising of cattle to supply the company's fleets. Indeed, Port-Louis became the focal point of Indian Ocean commerce, the place where smaller ships trading with India, the Arabian peninsula, and even China congregated and transshipped their cargoes to larger, European-bound company vessels. A growing number of French slavers seeking captives on the east coast of Africa also used Île de France as a refreshment station, often bringing to it a load of slaves from Mozambique and picking up another on their way back to the West Indies. The population of Île de France was overwhelmingly unfree (82 per cent in 1736; 90 per cent in 1766).

The company failed to develop its monopoly of the African trade. It held the coast near the mouth of the Senegal river, but Senegal was more important as a way station than as a supply centre for the slave trade and the company's principal African revenues came from the collection of a fee for each slave landed in the French West Indies. Without company support, the French slave trade, in Nantes vessels and, to a lesser but growing extent, in those of such ports as

Bordeaux, La Rochelle, and Le Havre, was a 'flying trade', in which each ship dealt directly with African middlemen as it followed the coast from Senegal to Angola and beyond.

In the West Indies, the tightening of the colonial compact, which demanded that colonies provide surplus value to their mother country, perpetuated the sense of grievance colonials felt toward French merchants. In 1684, for instance, the French prohibited the final refining of sugar in the West Indies, a measure which led to disorders on Martinique in 1717 and on Saint-Domingue in 1722–3. Another grievance was the one felt by the islands placed under the dominance of Martinique. Martinique's geographical location and the convenience of making arrival declarations at the capital made it the usual first stop for transatlantic ships. Consequently, most goods, including the best slaves, were landed there. Guadeloupe and Guiana complained about this situation throughout the century, but Saint-Domingue evaded this problem when it gained its own governor-general in 1714. Thereafter, its larger area, which encouraged the development of sugar plantations, attracted direct shipments of slaves, so that by 1740 it had not only the largest white population in the West Indies but also the largest proportion of slaves (over 100,000 or 88.5 per cent of the population). It produced some 40,000 tonnes of sugar, more than all other French islands combined and as much as all the British West Indies.

The growing imbalance between white and black populations in the West Indies worried officials, who feared that the whites would be unable to maintain their dominance over the blacks. The problem of imbalance, however, proved insuperable, as the proportion of newly imported African slaves everywhere increased, and the government finally gave up attempting to resolve it. Equally troublesome to administrators was the growing number of free blacks and people of colour, a category which, on Saint-Domingue, nearly equalled the white population by the 1780s. In the absence of white women, sexual relations between white males and slave women were inevitable. The French governors strongly opposed the recognition of such relations. In the 1724 Louisiana version of the *code noir*, which became the standard throughout the West Indies, interracial marriages were forbidden. Although the church generally ignored the law, delinquents were ostracized by other whites and prevented from holding civil or military office. Nor could noble status be transmitted to mixed-race children, for 'such a grace', the secretary of state for the navy ruled, 'would tend to destroy the difference that nature has placed between whites and blacks and . . . to weaken the state of humiliation attached to this species'.[4]

New France after Utrecht

The Treaty of Utrecht of 1713, which ended the War of the Spanish Succession, kept French West Indian possessions relatively intact, at the expense of territory in North America. New France was greatly diminished under the terms of that treaty. France lost Newfoundland except for fishing rights on the French shore, and peninsular Acadia, now part of Nova Scotia. The part of Acadia between the Bay of Fundy and the St Lawrence became disputed territory, claimed by Mi'kmaqs, Maliseets, and Abenakis, supported by the French. The French also abandoned their claims to Hudson Bay. Now, as France and Britain rebuilt their own economies and competed for a greater share of world trade, New France was reduced to Canada, the new colony of Île Royale (Cape Breton Island) and its dependency, Île Saint-Jean (now Prince Edward Island). The thirty years of peace after Utrecht made possible the economic development of Canada and Île Royale, favoured the Acadian settlements under British rule in Nova Scotia and promoted the growth of the distant French colony of Louisiana. Yet the population of New France, despite rates of natural increase greater than those of metropolitan France, remained so small that advances were limited.

Louisbourg, capital of Île Royale, with 40 per cent of that colony's population, was, by the 1740s, the home of 2,000 people. A fifth of the residents were from New France, including the ceded settlements in Newfoundland and Nova Scotia, while most of the rest had come from those parts of France which had provided the first Canadians. Resident fishermen hailed from the coastline of the Gulf of St Malo and the Basque areas of southern France. Louisbourg women usually contracted their first marriages at less than 20, a couple of years

---

[4] Letter to the governor and intendant of Saint-Domingue, 27 May 1771, in M. L. E. Moreau de Saint-Méry, *Loix et constitutions des colonies françaises de l'Amérique sous le Vent* (6 vols., Paris, 1784–90), v. 356.

earlier than eighteenth-century Canadian women. As in Canada or Acadia, children formed a significant part of the population.

Louisbourg soon replaced Plaisance as the base for the north-western Atlantic fishery, that enormous industry which employed more than 400 French ships and 10,000 fishermen each year to supply French and southern European markets. It also trained future seamen for the navy. Previously, French ports had controlled the international trade, sending out fishermen accustomed to drying fish on Newfoundland's shores, expecting protection and perhaps trade from Plaisance, but otherwise scarcely dealing with New France. Now, it was Louisbourg that attracted fishermen who worked in nearby waters and processed their fish on shore. It was, however, local, shore-based fishermen and traders who took the greater share of the catch and exported growing quantities of dried cod to France and, increasingly, to the French West Indies. Île Royale cod accounted for up to a fifth of the entire North American fishery in the 1720s and 1730s. Its value was sometimes three times greater than that of the expanding Canadian fur trade of the period. Louisbourg had become a major entrepôt. Canadian merchants who supplied it received, in exchange, wine and manufactures or West Indian sugar, bought by Louisbourg merchants with Louisbourg cod. Local merchants were increasingly involved in New England trade as well.

The massive Vauban-style fortress of Louisbourg, the most impressive of the long line of French fortifications in North America, guarded the fishery and the maritime approaches to Canada and protected the port. It had a garrison of more than 500 soldiers. The governor of Louisbourg ensured the maintenance of good relations and of alliances with the Mi'kmaqs of Île Royale through the annual presentation of gifts. The citadel's chapel served as the parish church and male and female religious orders provided education and social services. Louisbourg was a dynamic small town in which a wide range of occupations was represented and where social gradations probably mattered less than in Quebec.

Louisiana on the Mississippi, like Canada, was a compact colony surrounded by a hinterland inhabited by Native peoples. Unlike Canada or Île Royale, it formed only rudimentary alliances with Native people and proved unable to cope with hostile neighbours. The royal government relied upon private finance to develop this colony, with dubious results. Under John Law and the Company of the Indies, large numbers of indentured labourers and convicts were sent to the Mississippi, giving the colony a bad name. Such colonists were followed by some 2,000 African slaves. Half the Europeans and over two-thirds of the slaves died of disease, and the economy was still faltering when the colony reverted to the royal government in 1731. Louisiana had a plantation economy, which produced tobacco and indigo, and a trade in deerskins, also for export. Its plantations were small compared with those in the West Indies, so that, as the colony developed and increasingly depended upon African and Indian slaves, social relations remained somewhat less rigid than those which characterized West Indian society. Louisiana, with its port and capital at New Orleans, and the Illinois settlements, numbered 9,000 people by 1763: 4,000 colonists of European origin and 5,000 slaves.

The years of peace beginning in 1713 brought population increase and economic growth to the Acadian settlements under British rule, as well as to the St Lawrence settlements. In both, agriculture increasingly produced a surplus for market. The key lay in the increase in population and in cultivated land. Acadians extended cultivated areas, including additional reclaimed tidewater land, and prospered. Largely neglected by their British governors, they traded surpluses of livestock, wheat, and flour with Louisbourg and Boston. By 1755, the Acadian population numbered some 13,000 people.

Canadian agriculture experienced the same phenomena on a grander scale. About 80 per cent of the population of nearly 35,000 by 1730 and 45,000 by 1740 lived in the countryside and worked the land. In 1749, the Swedish naturalist, Peter Kalm, travelling down the St Lawrence River, was delighted by the beauty of the farms and farm houses, which seemed to him to constitute 'a village'; indeed, he called the settlements between Montreal and Quebec, 'one continued village'.[5] On the eve of the Conquest, Canadians numbered about 70,000, of whom 60,000 lived in the countryside. Cultivated land, already significant in 1710, increased by 50 per cent by 1731–40. Peasants grew enough wheat and legumes to feed the colony, to provision the fur trade and the fishery, and, in good years, to export up to 16 per cent of their production. Earlier, smaller Canadian surpluses had gone to fishing ports in the Gulf of the St Lawrence, the

[5] *The America of 1750: Peter Kalm's Travels in North America, the English Version of 1770*, ed. and trans. A. B. Benson (2 vols., New York 1937), ii. 416–17; see also A. Greer, *The People of New France* (Toronto, 1997), 30–1.

West Indies, and, for a time, to Plaisance. Now, Canada frequently shipped significant volumes of flour, legumes, ship's biscuit, and some lumber to Louisbourg, and lesser amounts directly to Martinique and Saint-Domingue. Altogether, agricultural products, timber, and fish accounted for 40 per cent of Canadian exports in the 1730s.

Peace permitted the development of Canadian industries, as well as the expansion of trades. Complex, efficient flour mills were developed, as were iron mining and ironworks producing exportable iron bars and stoves for Canadian needs, sawmills supplying naval stores and some lumber for export, and a shipbuilding industry for the carrying trade. A growing fishery in the Gulf of the St Lawrence now extracted fish oil for export. Guilds were prohibited in the colony and artisanal life was more loosely regulated than in France. In the eighteenth century, urban trades increased in number, variety, and sophistication, so that most basic goods were now produced by local artisans. The building trades benefited from the expansion of towns and the construction of elaborate fortifications in Quebec and Montreal. Tanneries and shoemakers multiplied, and the presence of tailors, wigmakers, stocking makers, and silversmiths suggests greater refinement in the upper strata of society. As the Jesuit traveller, Pierre de Charlevoix, declared of Quebec: 'The governor's wife and the intendant's wife entertain circles as fashionable and witty as you will find anywhere'.[6]

After the crisis of the turn of the century, the fur trade was revived and again regulated, as part of the metropolitan government's new strategy for gaining control over the interior of the continent and limiting British influence there. Entrepôts, with Jesuit missions, were developed at Michilimackinac and Detroit for the Great Lakes region, and at Kaskaskia, in Illinois country, for the Mississippi valley. Furs and hides from the northern posts were shipped to merchants in Montreal and from there to France; those from the Mississippi region went out through New Orleans. Smaller, garrisoned trading posts were established or re-established over vast areas, to serve a new clientele as well as long-term Native trading partners and, if necessary, to prevent them from dealing with English colonists or the Hudson's Bay Company. In some posts, the trade was open to all and regulated through a system of permits (*congés*), but at a few strategic

[6] *Journal of a Voyage to North-America Undertaken by Order of the French King* (2 vols., London, 1761), quoted in Greer, *People of New France*, 44.

locations, the royal government retained a monopoly of the trade. In most posts, the trade was leased either to small companies of merchants or, increasingly, to the military commander in partnership with the merchants. Such monopoly holders had to bear the cost of supporting the garrison, other maintenance, and presents to Native peoples. As increasing numbers of men were needed to carry goods and furs between Montreal and this extended network of posts, traders came to rely on wage labour. The number of hired canoemen employed grew from fewer than 100 in 1700 to more than 400 annually after 1730. Beaver exports, a monopoly of the Company of the Indies since 1721, were greater than in the seventeenth century, but beaver pelts were no longer the only commodity in fur shipments. Hides and other furs exported by individual merchants may have accounted for as much as half the value of all furs exported from Quebec in the eighteenth century. In the 1750s, the Canadian fur trade produced more than 80 per cent of the furs and hides shipped out of North America. The trade was also a successful instrument of foreign policy. It sustained alliances with Native peoples and prevented Anglo-American traders from detaching such allies. When the supply of goods was interrupted by war in the 1740s, tensions arose but the French were able to regain the support of their Native allies and conclude new alliances with the Dakotas in the upper Mississippi and the Miamis south of the Great Lakes. The intelligent use of presents and the collaboration of traders were essential elements in the French occupation of the Ohio valley in the early 1750s. By then, they had excluded the British from the heart of the continent, still occupied by some 50,000 Native people and fewer than 3,000 French, and still, as the latter recognized, Native territory.

The colonial empire at war, 1740s–1763

Peace was shattered by the War of the Austrian Succession of 1744–8, the first European war since 1713 to involve the colonies. Hostilities in North America and in India continued with little interruption to 1760. Only in the West Indies and on the seas did the period between the Peace of Aix-la-Chapelle and the outbreak of the Seven Years War of 1756–63 represent a significant hiatus.

In New France, New Englanders, provoked by privateers from Louisbourg, in 1745 laid siege to the fortress with the aid of the British navy and captured it after a seven-week siege. In the following year, a French attempt to reconquer Île Royale and Acadia with a fleet of seventy-six ships met with disaster at sea. Threatened with invasion, Canada launched a series of raids against New England frontier settlements. In the end, the War of the Austrian Succession changed nothing in New France and left boundary issues unresolved, to serve as a cause of further conflicts. France got Louisbourg back at the peace conference; in response, Britain founded the naval and military base of Halifax in 1749. Thus far, wars in North America had been inconclusive affairs fought with limited means. The Seven Years War, however, involved unprecedented military resources. Largely as a result of the determination of Pitt, the British undertook to crush the international commercial power of France and, with the support of the English colonists, to bring about the destruction of New France. By 1754, two years before war resumed in Europe, shots had been exchanged on the Ohio and both the French and British colonies were on a war footing. The beginning of the end came in Acadia, now the scene of mass suffering inflicted on French colonists. The taking in 1755 of Fort Beauséjour, on the edge of peninsular Nova Scotia, by British regulars and the discovery there of supposedly neutral Acadians provided an excuse for a nervous British governor to proceed against a people perceived to be a security risk in strategically significant territory. The Acadian settlements were destroyed, and the Acadians, frequently separated from their families, were shipped to English colonies along the Atlantic coast, and often from there to England. In subsequent years, those who had escaped to Île Saint-Jean, Île Royale, and continental Acadia were rounded up and also deported. A minority found immediate permanent refuge in Canada, while others who survived the deportation gradually made their way to France, the West Indies, Louisiana, and Canada. Their terrible fate served as a warning to the Canadians of the consequences of defeat, and encouraged Canadians to accept the sacrifices demanded by the war.

The cost of the war to the people of New France was great. Beginning in 1753, thousands of Canadians were conscripted each year into the militia, draining labour away from agriculture. The presence of 4,000 regulars to reinforce the *troupes de la marine* and the militia added to the pressure on local resources. Then, in early 1756, even before war was again officially declared, the British navy conducted a sweep of the Atlantic, capturing some 500 merchant ships and thereby causing France to suffer from a dearth of sailors and vessels throughout the Seven Years War. Supplies from France were interrupted and severe food shortages followed.

In the early years of the war, the French, with the support of their Native allies, were victorious in the Ohio valley and captured Forts Oswego and William Henry. Yet the position was increasingly precarious. As the young Bougainville, *aide-de-camp* of the French commander and future explorer of the South Seas, stated in 1757: 'It is only thanks to the Indians that we maintain our position; they are the counter-weight that tips the balance in our favour'.[7] The tide turned in 1758, when Britain launched large armies against New France, while its navy prevented the exhausted colonies from receiving provisions and reinforcements from France. Louisbourg surrendered in July 1758 and, as in 1745, its inhabitants were sent to France. At the end of 1758, the French also lost control of Lake Ontario and had to evacuate their main base in the Ohio valley. In the following year, they abandoned their forts south of Lake Champlain and surrendered Fort Niagara. By then, the British had burned all the parishes below and surrounding Quebec—more than 1,400 farms—and their guns had destroyed four-fifths of the capital.

After the battle of Quebec in September 1759, at which Montcalm and Wolfe, the French and British commanders, were killed, many assumed that New France was lost, among them, the Native allies. Successively, those from the interior and from the mission villages of the St Lawrence valley made a separate peace with the British, as the nations from the Ohio valley had already done in 1758, and as those of Nova Scotia would do in 1760. After a desperate attempt by the French to recapture Quebec, in the early spring of 1760, three British armies converged on Montreal. The capitulation of the colony occurred in September 1760, but the fate of New France remained uncertain until 1763.

In India, the French retained the upper hand during the War of the Austrian Succession. A fleet from the Mascareignes scattered the

[7] 'Mémoire sur l'état de la Nouvelle-France 1757', in *Rapport de l'archiviste de la Province de Québec* (1923–4), 49.

British Indian squadron and forced the capitulation of Madras in 1747. This and victories in the Carnatic and Orissa placed the entire Deccan coast under French control. Although Madras was returned at the peace negotiations, in exchange for Louisbourg, rivalry between the French and the British companies continued unhampered. Dupleix pursued his policy of intervention in local affairs, while the British East India Company countered by allying itself to the opponents of Dupleix's allies. Until then, Dupleix's policies had been paid for with Indian revenues, but the continued competition forced him to ask for help from home. Its revenues and dividends seriously affected by the recent war, the company recoiled from such expenditures. In 1752, the king's commissioner, Silhouette, had already warned that '[military] successes notwithstanding, a less brilliant situation but one more peaceful and more favourable to commerce is what is desired' and summarized the company's policy thus: 'No victory, no conquest, a lot of trade goods and some increase in dividends'.[8] Dupleix was recalled in 1754 and the company signed an agreement of non-intervention in local affairs with its British counterpart. This neutrality agreement, however, fell victim to the resumption of war. The French did not, as promised, abandon their Deccan territories and the British again tried to eradicate them from India, a task facilitated by their naval superiority. By 1757, the British company had expelled the French from Chandernagore and assumed direct control over Bengal, thereby achieving for itself the fiscal power and security Dupleix had sought for the French company in the Deccan. Lacking sufficient support from home, the French faltered. The Deccan was captured in January 1760 and the last outposts fell early the next year.

In the West Indies, the French occupied St Lucia while the British captured several minor islands during the War of the Austrian Succession. This apparent equilibrium, however, concealed a serious disadvantage for the French, whose navy proved unable to protect commercial shipping against British capture. As a result, the French islands emerged from the war depleted and weakened, despite the permission reluctantly granted by colonial administrators to neutral and even enemy ships to trade with the islands during the war. The period 1748–55 was one of recovery and continued economic growth.

---

[8] Letter to Dupleix, 13 Sept. 1753, quoted in A. Martineau, *Dupleix et l'Inde française* (4 vols., Paris, 1923–8), iv. 318.

The importation of sugar and other tropical products reached new heights in these years, as did the slave trade. However, the experience of war had marked the islands' society, exacerbating planter grievances against the metropolis and determining the islanders' behaviour in the next conflict.

The stranglehold exercised by the British navy during the Seven Years War, especially after the defeat at Lagos in 1759, meant that French maritime commerce all but stopped for the duration of the war. The West Indies could no longer be supplied, save through neutrals and, increasingly, by opening their ports to enemy traders. Meanwhile, the British waged a war of conquest in Africa and the West Indies. Senegal surrendered in 1758; Guadeloupe fell in 1759; by 1762, only Saint-Domingue remained in French hands, and then largely because Spain's entry into the war on France's side diverted the expected British attack to Havana, captured in August of that year. The defence of the French islands had been half-hearted. On Guadeloupe, local leaders, faced with the threat of the destruction of their plantations by British troops, successfully urged a hasty capitulation. Their strategy proved economically sound, as the British governor, assuming Britain would retain the island after the war, wooed the planters, even providing them, by 1763, with new slaves in numbers estimated at between 18,000 and 30,000. The lesson was not lost on the other islands. Martinique offered only token resistance when attacked in 1762.

By 1760, France was nearing bankruptcy and its sole option was to sue for peace. The British having rejected overtures to this effect, the new principal minister, Choiseul, by August 1761, convinced Louis XV to sign the Family Compact which put the Spanish navy and Spanish possessions on the side of France. Even though Spain's entry into the war led to further British gains in the West Indies, it also forced Pitt's replacement by the peace party under Bute. Plenipotentiaries were then exchanged and negotiations, begun in early 1762, were completed in November. Peace was signed in Paris in February 1763.

The greatest loss suffered by France was New France. France retained only its fishing rights on the northern coast of Newfoundland and the islands of St-Pierre and Miquelon, where inhabitants from Louisbourg and Acadians resettled. Other territory east of the Mississippi was transferred to Britain, while Louisiana, reduced to the west bank of the river and New Orleans, passed to Spain. Canadians and those Acadians who were able to return to Nova Scotia tried to adjust to alien rule. Resistance came in the west, where Native groups from the Ohio valley and the Great Lakes region, led by the Ottawa chief Pontiac, attacked British garrisons in former French posts and killed 2,000 Anglo-Americans who had invaded their lands. The proclamation of October 1763, establishing the administrative framework of the new British territories, helped to bring about reconciliation by guaranteeing 'Indian country', forbidden to settlers, in territory extending through the Great Lakes region and west of the Allegheny mountains—even if it soon proved impossible to apply.

In India, the peace returned Pondicherry, Chandernagore, Mahé, and two other concessions to the French. These factories were to serve as unfortified commercial establishments, and the French renounced all acquisitions outside their confines. In Africa, Senegal, except for the tiny island of Gorée, was retained by the British. In the West Indies, France retained Guiana, which had been deemed by the British not worth attacking, and Saint-Domingue. Martinique and St Lucia were returned, as was Guadeloupe, the latter partly because British sugar interests feared the collapse of prices on the London sugar market if it were retained. Britain kept all its other West Indian conquests. Yet given Pitt's intentions, Choiseul could be satisfied by the settlement. At the cost of New France, France's most expensive and least economically profitable colonial possession, he had saved the major sugar islands of the West Indies, the essential element of the colonial economy. The Mascareignes, untouched by the war, buttressed this sector. With the preservation of the islands of St-Pierre and Miquelon and of Gorée, and the return of the five Indian factories, the minister had managed to retain a share in the cod fisheries, the slave trade, and Indian commerce. That only islands or demilitarized posts remained in French hands was to the good, for it meant less risk of incidents with Britain, at least until France had put its affairs in order and rebuilt its navy. The cession of Louisiana to Spain may be explained in this light, for Anglo-American ambitions beyond the Mississippi were already clear and it was hoped that Spain, with contiguous possessions, could better resist them than France.

The colonies after 1763

Even before peace was declared, French colonial recovery was being prepared. In response to colonial dissatisfaction, a commission had already been established to study the reform of colonial law. Choiseul pursued these efforts, issuing in 1763 an ordinance which reorganized West Indian civil administration and which was applied to the Mascareignes in 1767. He also prepared the way for the reconstruction of the navy: a shipbuilding programme was undertaken and, in 1764 and 1765, new naval ordinances modernized administration and reformed recruitment. Choiseul had family ties with the islands, and under him West Indians entered metropolitan public affairs in numbers. From the 1760s onwards, planters' representatives and ex-colonial officials wedded to colonial views were found in the upper echelons of naval administration and on commissions created to review colonial policies. No wonder colonial attitudes began to prevail. An early result was the modification of mercantilist policies. As the 1765 instructions to the newly appointed chief officials of Martinique stated: 'Circumstances may occur in which wealth and prohibition, which should go hand-in-hand in the colonies, will be in a state of incompatibility. The law of prohibition, however essential it is, must then nevertheless yield'.[9] This so-called 'modified exclusive' (*Exclusif mitigé*), promulgated between 1764 and 1767 at the instigation of Choiseul's adviser, the Martinique planter Dubuc, was based on the need to replace New France and Louisiana as sources of food supplies for the West Indies. Officially limited to the creation of two and then, by 1784, seven colonial entrepôts for foreign trade, this wedge into the metropolitan monopoly was extended unofficially by local arrangements permitting the supplying of food and slaves to the less advantaged areas of the West Indies. Monopolies, increasingly, were abolished. The one enjoyed by certain French ports over colonial trade was virtually abandoned when all ports capable of accommodating ships of 100

---

[9] Instructions to Governor Ennery and Intendant Peinier, 25 Jan. 1765, quoted in J. Tarrade, *Le Commerce colonial de la France à la fin de l'Ancien Régime: l'évolution du régime de 'l'Exclusif' de 1763 à 1789* (2 vols., Paris, 1972), i. 229.

tons' burden were included in the list. The monopoly of the Company of the Indies, weakened by a steep decline in the value of its shares, was increasingly challenged by private merchant interests seeking a place in the eastern trade. The company was ripe for restructuring. In 1764, the crown assumed direct control of the Mascareignes and opened their commerce to private vessels. Three years later, it took over rights to the slave trade in Africa. In 1769, the company itself went into liquidation, the Indian factories were placed under royal administration, and trade to the far east was opened to private shipping.

Not all Choiseul's projects were successful. His decision to entrust the defence of West Indian islands to regular troops paid by local taxes met with resistance, particularly when the inadequacy of the regulars forced Saint-Domingue's governor to recreate militias without removing the tax and, worse, to mix white and mixed-raced companies in the new regiments. The result was a rebellion in 1768–9, the repression of which added to planter grievances. The minister's plans to expand the empire were no more successful. Settlement projects, often involving the participation of reluctant Acadian refugees in France, were proposed; none succeeded. An early project, the creation of a white colony at Kourou in Guiana, led to disaster. Planned to replace New France as a source of supplies for the West Indies, the project attracted many volunteers, but fewer Acadians than had been expected. The number of colonists sent swamped the project, for few planners understood the deplorable conditions in Guiana and preparations proved woefully inadequate. The project was abandoned after two years of appalling mortality among the settlers.

For all this, Choiseul's reforms prepared France for the American War. If the Indian factories and the islands of St-Pierre and Miquelon were reoccupied by the British, the British navy for once met its match in the French fleet, notably in the West Indies where all British islands but Jamaica were seized. The French islands continued to be supplied throughout the war by French commerce, assisted by the American allies. The peace signed at Versailles in September 1783 did not reflect these successes, however. All the British islands, except for Tobago, were returned in exchange for St-Pierre and Miquelon and the Indian factories. Besides Tobago, the French recovered Senegal and more secure fishing rights on Newfoundland's French shore. These small gains could not offset the huge debt incurred during the war. Nor did the expected increase in trade with the new United States materialize.

A fragile economic boom

In the last decades of the century, the old colonial economy reached its greatest height. The Mascareignes achieved maturity as plantation colonies under royal government; in private hands, Indian and other far eastern trade increased. It was, however, the Atlantic trade surrounding the West Indies that experienced the fastest growth. The number of ships involved in the slave trade, coming from all the major ports and some very small ones, more than doubled between 1764 and 1789. The number of slaves they brought increased from an annual average of 15,000 in the 1760s to 28,000 in the 1780s. Over 90 per cent were taken to Saint-Domingue. Meanwhile Guadeloupe's economy reached its full potential after 1763, its economy overtaking Martinique's. The limited size of the two islands, however, impeded continued growth. By 1788, their combined population approached 200,000, 83 per cent of it unfree. Saint-Domingue, with nearly ten times the land, had nearly 500,000 inhabitants, 89 per cent of them slaves. Whereas free blacks and people of colour amounted to fewer than half the number of whites on Martinique and a mere one-quarter on Guadeloupe, their number on Saint-Domingue was approximately the same as that of whites. The other two islands, St Lucia and Tobago, had fewer than 35,000 people.

The domination of Saint-Domingue resulted in part from the availability of land and its under-exploitation in earlier periods. Substantial numbers of new immigrants arrived on the island after the Seven Years War—its white population nearly doubled between 1764 and 1775—seeking their fortune, first as managers of plantations for absentee owners, later as planters themselves. They opened new land, both in the plains where sugar was produced and in the hills, better suited to coffee. Yields were so large and the need for slaves so great that Saint-Domingue attracted slave ships at the expense of the other islands. Consequently, the production of that island grew rapidly, that of sugar doubling and that of coffee increasing fivefold between 1765 and 1788. By then, 81 per cent of the total production of the French

Antilles was grown on Saint-Domingue (indigo, 100 per cent; coffee, 87 per cent; sugar, 79 per cent; cotton, 76 per cent). Only cocoa was more important in the Lesser Antilles, but it made up less than 1 per cent of West Indian exports, in contrast to 70 per cent for sugar and 27 per cent for coffee. The re-export of West Indian products accounted for up to two-thirds of French external trade in the period and for the whole of its growth.

As a colony of recent arrivals, in contrast to the other islands, Saint-Domingue had a significant gender imbalance in both the white and the black populations. According to the 1775 census, only 29 per cent of white adults were female, which may explain the large percentage of children of mixed race on Saint-Domingue. The proportion of women was greater among slaves (44 per cent) but still less than equal, reflecting the weight of the African-born in that population.

Even within plantation economies, towns were not unimportant. St-Pierre on Martinique; Basse-Terre, the administrative centre, and Pointe-à-Pitre, the economic centre developed by the British during their occupation, on Guadeloupe; Cap-François and the new capital, Port-au-Prince, not to mention lesser towns such as St-Marc or Les Cayes on Saint-Domingue; Port-Louis on Île de France; St-Denis on Bourbon: all these towns provided their islands with a solid urban framework. Some were administrative centres, with civil, military, and religious institutions, including hospitals, barracks, and law courts. Most were centres of business, with offices for notaries and scriveners, taverns and inns, and above all port facilities, warehouses, and markets, including a slave market, though most new slaves continued to be sold on board ships. Towns were also cultural centres, the largest of which, by the second half of the eighteenth century, possessed theatres, masonic lodges, reading clubs, and newspapers. They compared in infrastructure and even in size—between 4,000 and 10,000 inhabitants in the late eighteenth century—with most medium-sized towns in France. The racial mix of their population, however, differentiated West Indian towns not only from their French counterparts, but also from their own countryside. The proportion of Creole non-whites was larger in town, and the ratio of whites to non-whites was much more even, as, with the exception of those who owned plantations, most freedmen lived in town, providing many of the petty services. Almost all working free women of colour laboured in towns, as tavern-keepers and innkeepers, petty retailers, seam-stresses, laundresses, and domestics. Some formal slaves had been left by their masters to ply a trade in town, in exchange for a share of their revenues. Towns were also visited by plantation slaves, on their masters' business or coming to sell the few vegetables and fruits they had managed to produce for market. Thus, towns were sources of information for the largely rural slave population, an important consideration in periods of disorder.

Yet, for all of the wealth it generated, the West Indian economy was fragile. Always in need of more slaves, planters became heavily indebted to slave traders, especially in the 1780s when the number of absentee planters drawing on plantation revenues increased. In the long run, slave traders took over plantations to recover their investment and began to sell their cargoes to themselves. West Indian indebtedness was thus transferred to France itself, with the added inconvenience that the ports' merchant elites lost the kind of liquidity which was fundamental to their success. While the West Indian economy boomed, the issue remained hidden, but it would emerge during the Revolution, when the economy of Saint-Domingue, wrecked by slave revolts and war with Britain, would collapse.

Despite their debts, the some 500 owners of large sugar plantations on Saint-Domingue and those of the other islands appeared to be enormously wealthy. As officers in the local military and, often, as advisers to or participants in the local government, but mostly as owners of estates with a large, dependent agricultural population and substantial numbers of domestic slaves, planters resembled the wealthiest nobles in France. Planters sent their children to be educated in France and, increasingly, visited France themselves, bringing slaves with them and purchasing estates there. Many assumed noble titles and claimed noble privilege. 'No-one can ignore that land-owners [*habitants*] born in the French islands of America enjoy in France the privileges of nobility,' argued one absentee planter in an effort to avoid a tax on domestics; 'they are all military officers and were born in the King's service'.[10] Yet significant cultural differences separated colonial and metropolitan societies. West Indian society enforced rigid social stratification based on race, particularly on

---

[10] Letter to intendant's subdelegate in Toulouse, n.d. [late 1770s], Archives Départe-mentales de Haute-Garonne (Toulouse), C2055.

Saint-Domingue, where 'colonial prejudice has adopted as a maxim that, however close [in colour] a non-white woman may be to a white, no white may issue from their procreation'.[11] While planters might educate their illegitimate children in France and assure them economic independence, they regarded people of colour as dangerous. A second cultural difference arose from the planters' resistance to dependence on the mother country, an 'American patriotism' stemming from an old resentment of the colonial compact. Attacks against the institution of slavery, in particular, tended to produce threats of West Indian secession, especially after the war of American Independence. Such attitudes created great difficulties in the late 1780s, when free men of colour, assisted by metropolitan humanitarians organized around the Friends of the Blacks (*Société des Amis des Noirs*), sought civil and political rights. Only in the short run did the views of the advocates of slavery—planters, spokesmen of slave-trading ports, and their aristocratic supporters—prevail and prevent reform of the colonial system.

Conclusion

Overseas possessions contributed significantly to the French economy from 1660 to the Revolution. The furs and fisheries of New France opened major European markets, as did the tropical crops of the West Indies and the Mascareignes. Colonial traffic and the re-exportation of colonial goods, principally sugar, to Mediterranean, Dutch, and German venues, were responsible for most of the growth of France's external trade. Moreover, the prestige gained from possessing an empire was, by the eighteenth century, an important component of great-power status.

And yet, the colonies had involved France in a century of warfare against Britain, a struggle which triggered the financial crisis of the 1780s and which, in the long run, was lost. More to the point, perhaps, the benefits of empire were obtained at some cost to the natural environment and at significant human cost, be it that of the Acadians,

---

[11] Moreau de Saint-Méry, *Description . . . de la partie française de l'isle de Saint-Domingue*, ed. B. Maurel and E. Taillemite (3 vols., Paris, 1958), i. 89.

caught between competing European powers, the West Indian indentured whites, many of whom died before the end of their three-year contracts, the participants in the unfortunate Kourou expedition, victims of incompetent metropolitan planners, the Native peoples of North America, who suffered loss of life, territory, traditional livelihoods and material security, or the plantation slaves, deprived of their humanity and victims of harsh, even mortal, exploitation.

5

The state and political culture

Julian Swann

'Louis by the grace of God, king of France and Navarre, to all those who will see these letters, present and to come, greetings.' With this phrase French kings began the preamble to all laws issued in their name, and once the terms of the legislation had been expounded they concluded with a majestic 'for such is our pleasure'. Taken together these few words conjure up an enduring image of the divine right monarchy of the old regime. In 1614, the deputies of the third estate had implored the estates general to declare it a fundamental law that the king 'is sovereign in his state, holding his crown from God alone, there is no power on earth, be it spiritual or temporal which has any authority . . . to depose the anointed person of the king'.[1] Their plea was, in part, a response to the assassination of Henri IV and to memories of the terrible civil wars of the previous century. Vaunting the power of the crown offered hope of preventing a repetition, and, once the Fronde had provided another glimpse into the abyss, few questioned the virtues of a powerful monarchy.

Enthusiasm for the divine right of kings dovetailed neatly with other theories stressing the sacred nature of monarchy. The king of France was no mere mortal. At his coronation he was anointed with oils from a phial that had, according to legend, been delivered to Saint Rémy by the Holy Spirit in the guise of a dove. Thereafter, like members of the priesthood, the king received communion in both

---

[1] Y. M. Bercé, *The Birth of Absolutism: A History of France, 1598–1661* (London, 1992), 58.

kinds. Finally, his sacred character was underlined by an ability to cure by touching those afflicted with the 'king's evil', scrofula. With such an imposing pedigree, bishop Bossuet could, without embarrassment, declare that kings 'are Gods and share in some way in divine independence'.[2]

Sovereignty was firmly in the hands of the crown and there was no parliament to check royal authority. The estates general of 1614 was the last to meet before 1789, and the ability of French kings to govern without a national representative body was a defining feature of absolute monarchy. Not that their rule was considered tyrannical or arbitrary. Royal theorists were unanimous in arguing that authority should be exercised in accordance with divine and natural law, respecting the teaching of the Catholic church and the lives and property of the subject. The king was expected to seek counsel before making decisions and was restrained by the fundamental laws of the kingdom. Despite their imposing title, they were not embodied in any constitutional document and were never formally written down. Instead they consisted of general principles such as the inalienability of the royal domain, the Salic law of succession (through the direct male line), and, after the conversion of Henri IV in 1593, that the king should be a Catholic. Taken together these safeguards were enough to persuade the French that they lived under an absolute monarchy, not a tyranny or, as eighteenth-century writers usually described it, a despotism.

King in council

From 1661, when Louis XIV took the momentous decision to rule as his own first minister, until the revolution of 1789, French kings governed through a remarkably stable ministerial and conciliar system. At its apex was the *conseil d'en haut*, where the king weighed the great affairs of military and diplomatic policy with a handful of counsellors known as ministers of state. Attendance was by royal invitation only, and many with vast departmental responsibilities were never called to

[2] J.-B. Bossuet, *Politics drawn from the very Words of Holy Scripture*, ed. P. Riley (Cambridge, 1990), 82.

council, or were summoned only intermittently to lend particular expertise. The other great council held in the presence of the king was that of dispatches, which was primarily concerned with the internal affairs of the kingdom. In addition to the members of the *conseil d'en haut*, it included the chancellor, who was head of the judiciary, and the controller-general of finances. Below them were the royal council of finances (which the king attended), the privy council, where he was rarely present, and, periodically, councils of conscience and of commerce. As their names suggest, these bodies dealt with more technical legal, fiscal, religious, and economic matters.

Amongst the ministers of state who served Louis XIV and Louis XV were the respected generals d'Huxelles, Villeroy, Villars, and Noailles, and leading ecclesiastics including cardinals Fleury and Tencin. The sun king was, however, reluctant to call upon the services of the princes of the blood. Placing these powerful men on the council was fraught with danger, as they viewed the king as the first among equals, and they were accustomed to pursuing their own policies irrespective of those of the crown. Louis XIV compensated the princes by showing exaggerated respect for their rank within the social and courtly hierarchy, and by rewarding their loyalty with titles, pensions, gifts, and sinecures. His successors followed in his wake, and before 1789 there was no serious repetition of the treachery and rebellion of the religious wars and the Fronde.

Alongside the ministers of state were the four secretaries of state (war, navy, foreign affairs, and the royal household) who, together with the chancellor and the controller-general of finances, dominated government after 1661. The title of controller-general was given to Colbert after the fall of the superintendent of finances, Nicolas Fouquet, the principal victim of Louis XIV's decision to rule as his own first minister. The immense energy and prestige of Colbert ensured that the tentacles of the controller-general reached into the most remote areas of the kingdom's fiscal and administrative system. Yet it was an office that lacked status within the ministerial hierarchy, something which had serious ramifications during the eighteenth century when the occupants of the post changed continuously. As a result, the finance minister could not restrain the spending of the secretaries of state, nor establish the personal authority needed to make the administration and its personnel bend to his will.

When it came to choosing his ministers Louis XIV was a model of consistency. Those favoured came overwhelmingly from the robe nobility, and especially the Colbert, Le Tellier and Phélypeaux families. Colbert and Le Tellier had come to prominence by serving Mazarin, but Louis XIV allowed them to found great ministerial dynasties and their sons, Seignelay and Louvois, followed them into government. When the king died in 1715, Colbert's nephews, Desmaretz and Torcy, were respectively controller-general and secretary of state for foreign affairs. The secretary of state for the navy was a Phélypeaux, the count de Pontchartrain, son of the chancellor and controller-general of that name and the father of Maurepas. The latter became secretary of state in 1723 at the age of 22, and, despite being disgraced in 1749, allegedly for writing rude verses about Madame de Pompadour, he returned as Louis XVI's mentor in 1774!

The ministerial clans engaged in fierce competition amongst themselves, but Louis XIV was able to count upon their undivided loyalty and in a personal reign of fifty-four years he only felt it necessary to disgrace three ministers. During the eighteenth century, instability became a feature of government with ministers dismissed by the score. The old ministerial dynasties began to lose their grip. New sources of recruitment were opened up, some of which would have horrified Louis XIV. He had never appointed members of the Court aristocracy to the offices of secretary of state, hence Saint-Simon's famous quip that they were held by the 'vile bourgeoisie'. The poisoned quill of the acerbic duke was inspired by his belief that government ought to be the preserve of aristocrats like himself, and after 1715 his dreams were partially fulfilled. During the regency of Philippe d'Orléans, Saint-Simon and other grandees participated in the *polysynodie*, a short-lived experiment in conciliar government. Its collapse in 1718 has often been attributed to the incapacity of the grandees. In reality, it was only a temporary setback to their ambitions. Louis XV was less wary of the great aristocracy than his predecessor. After 1750 its members were regularly appointed to the office of secretary of state, adding a further dimension to the faction fighting at Versailles, and causing friction with the robe nobility that had traditionally dominated ministerial office.

The royal Court

The palace of Versailles was one of the most potent and enduring symbols of Bourbon monarchy. Louis XIV made it his principal residence and the seat of his government in 1682, and his decision was long thought to be part of a cunning plan to tame the rebellious French aristocracy. Those that the king distrusted, such as the duke de La Rochefoucauld, found themselves appointed to offices that demanded daily attendance on his person, while the Great Condé was espied rowing ladies around the artificial lake. Domesticated at Court, they were separated from their provincial governorships and were unable to maintain the ties of personal loyalty and clientage that had been the basis of their military power. Court was also horribly expensive and the sums required to fuel the ostentatious lifestyle of a grandee potentially ruinous. When Louis XIV stepped in with financial gifts to soften the blow, these formerly independent warlords found themselves reduced to dependence. It is only necessary to recount the tales of fearsome battles amongst courtiers about precedence and etiquette to complete a sorry tale of an aristocracy trapped in a gilded cage.

Like all good caricatures there is a grain of truth in such a portrait, but Versailles offered as many advantages as it did inconveniences to the grandees. In a rigidly hierarchical society, proximity to the king was worth its weight in gold, reflecting the rank and status of the courtier. Here lies the explanation for the many seemingly petty quarrels about precedence or etiquette. Even minor details were potentially significant, marking out the distinctions between competing groups or families. Moreover any office or privilege that brought access to the monarch was coveted as a route to patronage and advancement with titles, offices, and sinecures providing ample compensation for the rather boring and menial task of waiting on the king. Competition was fierce and factionalism was a permanent feature of Court life, with cabals forming in the hope of capturing the king's ear and of monopolizing the patronage at his disposal. The ministries of Richelieu and Mazarin offered perfect illustrations of what could happen when a favourite ruled in the king's stead, and both had used their position to amass colossal fortunes, while ruling through an administration staffed by their 'creatures'. So absolute was their authority that other courtiers, including Louis XIII's mother, Marie de Medici, his brother, Gaston d'Orléans, and the prince de Condé were driven to revolt.

There would be no repeat of such behaviour during the personal reign of Louis XIV and the sun king was at his most masterful when it came to managing the Court. He cultivated an image of Olympian detachment by scrupulously protecting the respective ranks and dignities of the grandees. He was no less attentive to their incessant claims and counter-claims for patronage, realizing that the balanced distribution of his favour was the key to harmony. Finally, he rewarded the loyalty of his aristocracy by appointing its members to the highest positions in church and state as bishops, generals, diplomats, and court officials.

Versailles was, therefore, part of a royal strategy that reinforced the prestige of the most powerful families in the kingdom, more than making up for any loss of influence in the provinces. Louis XIV used every nuance of Court life to his advantage, but neither of his successors had his masterful touch. Whereas the sun king had been careful to keep the grandees satisfied with honours and commands appropriate to their station, Louis XV chose aristocrats such as the dukes de Choiseul, Praslin, and d'Aiguillon as his secretaries of state. Winning control of the ministry became one of the principal goals of the Court cabals and the bitterness of their rivalries undoubtedly contributed to the political instability that preceded the revolution. Louis XVI, on the other hand, was unable to preserve an image of impartiality. The queen, Marie-Antoinette, gradually gained control over both ministerial appointments and patronage, attracting vicious criticism from those excluded from her charmed circle in the process.

Despite the effectiveness of Versailles in projecting the image and authority of the monarchy, it was not without cost. By withdrawing to the great palace and to others dotted around Paris, successive kings cut themselves off from their subjects, and from an older tradition of monarchy built upon regular public display. This was particularly damaging during the eighteenth century when neither Louis XV nor Louis XVI made more than a handful of sorties beyond the Île-de-France. They thus failed to cultivate public affection, or to imitate monarchs such as Frederick II of Prussia or George III of

Great Britain who were so adept at associating themselves with the lives and patriotism of their subjects.

State and administration

Although absolute in theory, the power of French kings was much more limited in practice. France had no common legal code or administrative system, many of its people spoke languages other than French, and individuals, towns, corporations, and provinces all possessed a bewildering array of privileges. Before 1789, the kingdom was divided into the historic provinces that had been added piecemeal to the crown over the centuries. Dynastic accidents had led to the acquisition of Burgundy and Brittany, in 1476 and 1532 respectively; Louis XIV conquered Franche-Comté in 1678; and Lorraine did not become part of France until 1766. When they inherited or captured a province, or even a town, monarchs recognized their existing privileges. These rights were guarded jealously, and one of the most predictable sights of a new reign was the procession of local worthies petitioning the king for their confirmation.

Provinces were divided between the *pays d'états*, such as Artois, Brittany, Burgundy and Languedoc, which had preserved the right to assemble the local estates, and the *pays d'élection* where that privilege had lapsed. Royal authority in the provinces was represented by the governor, who was usually a prince of the blood or a great aristocrat. Before 1660, an able governor could rule as a minor potentate, using his prestige and patronage to win the personal allegiance of local nobles and office-holders. Condé and the other *frondeur* princes had used their governorships as recruiting grounds for their campaigns against Mazarin. The political finesse of Louis XIV, who kept the princes at Court rather than in the provinces, and the growing strength of the royal army gradually rendered noble revolts obsolete, but the governors remained important. Many civil and military appointments were in their personal gift, and their rank and proximity to the king made them highly attractive as power-brokers for provincials seeking the favour of the government.

A governorship was a lucrative and prestigious position, but it was not a sinecure. In moments of crisis, the incumbent was expected to come to the aid of the province. When the terrible winter of 1709 threatened Lyon with famine, the governor, Villeroy, sent troops to secure grain from neighbouring Burgundy. His actions produced a clash with the governor of that province, the prince de Condé, who on several occasions made plain his refusal 'to see Burgundians starve to feed Lyon'.[3] Burgundy was a Condé family fief, and in 1775 his successor came to the aid of Dijon, arguing furiously with the controller-general, Turgot, whose doctrinaire pursuit of free trade in grain had caused hardship and unrest in the city. In more prosperous times, the governors contributed to the embellishment of the artistic, cultural, and economic life of the provinces, sponsoring public buildings, learned academies, and new industrial ventures.

In theory, the crown had thousands of office-holders to carry out its business, including, among others, the members of the parlements, courts of aids, chambers of accounts, bureaux of finances, and the grand council. In addition to acting as the highest courts of appeal within their jurisdictions, the parlements traditionally policed public order, watched over the supply of essentials such as bread and firewood and supervised the administration of prisons and hospitals. The courts of aids heard appeals against tax assessments and investigated abuse in the fiscal system, especially relative to the *taille*, while the chambers of accounts verified the accounts of tax-collecting bodies such as the provincial estates or bureaux of finances. The grand council, on the other hand, was a tribunal for the adjudication of disputes within the legal system, especially those involving the parlements or between a parlement and the lower presidial courts. It also heard certain privileged cases such as those affecting the religious orders.

On paper, the king possessed an impressive officialdom, but it should not be confused with a modern bureaucracy. Since the sixteenth century, French monarchs had sold judicial and administrative offices to the highest bidder, and in return for an annual payment allowed office-holders to pass on their charge to their descendants or sell them on. To make them attractive, offices came complete with privileges, including hereditary nobility for the most exalted, and membership of a corporate body. This system, known as venality, was

[3] Archives Départementales de la Côte d'Or, C 3144, fos. 298–9.

a lucrative source of income for the crown, and it was a boon to the upwardly mobile. The great ministerial dynasties, and many of the most dynamic servants of the Bourbon monarchy, acquired nobility through the purchase of office.

There was, however, a price to pay. The only means of removing the office-holders was through reimbursement and the chronic state of the royal finances prevented even Colbert from achieving that aim. As a result, the government was obliged to work with these powerful corps, whose recruitment was beyond its control and which were frequently more concerned with their own, or provincial, interests, than those of the king. Even when such clashes were avoided, often large assemblies of office-holders were difficult to manage, and they were ill-suited to providing the rapid decision-making and unbiased local information that the government needed. It was, in part, to circumvent these problems that the crown became increasingly attracted to the solution offered by the intendants.

The period from 1660 to the revolution was the golden age of the intendants, who were commissioners appointed by the king. They were sent to one of the fiscal and administrative regions known as generalities to act in matters pertaining to 'justice, police and finance'. As the boundaries of generalities roughly coincided with those of the provinces, intendants had often been the clients of governors and even after 1661 it was advisable for them to tread carefully. In 1694, D'Argouges, intendant of Burgundy, made the fatal mistake of crossing the Condé family and was recalled. Long afterwards his successors trembled at the mention of the governor. Elsewhere their more fortunate colleagues were able to take advantage of the wide-ranging nature of their commissions to become the driving force of provincial administration.

The majority of intendants were recruited from the ranks of the robe nobility. A typical candidate had been educated in the law before passing a brief spell in one of the parlements. From there he bought the office of master of requests, acting as the king's judge and reporting to the royal council, where he could hope to impress a patron ready to open the doors of an intendance. Once in place, the intendants faced a truly daunting task. First they were expected to act as the eyes and ears of the government, and Colbert and his successors expected an almost daily flow of information. Even the most cursory glance through the voluminous correspondence they generated reveals that the duty was performed conscientiously. Official files overflow with reports on, for example, the state of the harvest, the condition of the highways, and the behaviour of provincial institutions and their members. Fiscal matters were, however, uppermost in the minds of the intendants. They were expected to draw up the rolls of the *taille*, and later those of the new direct taxes—the capitation, tenth, and the twentieth—and oversee their collection. Keeping abreast of this crucial task obliged them to make regular tours of their generality, and the ideal intendant was a peripatetic beast. Knowledge of local terrain helped reduce fraud and evasion, kept local officials on their toes, and provided the basis of the reports despatched to Versailles.

The intendants were also burdened with a variety of other duties. They supervised the raising of the militia regiments, implemented commercial schemes, inspected fairs and markets, and settled local judicial disputes. Many other tasks could be added to this list, and it is not surprising that they acquired a reputation for omnipotence. During the seventeenth century, men such as Pellot, intendant of Poitou, Bouchu, intendant of Burgundy, or Basville, in Languedoc, laboured away for decades as trusted servants of the crown, while in the next century their successors such as Turgot or Bertier de Sauvigny, respectively intendants of Limoges and the generality of Paris, were amongst the most enlightened administrators of their age. That these later examples are drawn from the *pays d'élections* was not a coincidence. It was there that the intendants had the greatest freedom to act upon their own initiative. In the *pays d'états*, on the other hand, a strong tradition of local self-government reduced their authority considerably.

To deal with such an imposing workload, the intendants were forced to recruit local deputies, called subdelegates, to assist them. Colbert frowned on the practice, but by 1700 they had become part of the administrative furniture, and at the end of the old regime the thirty-three intendants were served by over 700 subdelegates. Yet these were hardly imposing numbers when we consider both the physical size of the kingdom and its burgeoning population of some 28 million. Without denigrating their immense efforts, it is clear that the intendants were also restrained by social and political realities. Mostly recruited from the narrow circle of the Parisian robe nobility, they were frequently the clients of ministers. Moreover despite official regulations stipulating that intendants should not spend more than three years in one generality, or be sent to their own regions, these rules were regularly flouted. Even when the intendant had no personal connections in the province where he served, maintaining the guise of an inflexible agent of the central government was likely to prove counter-productive. If he antagonized local elites, he risked provoking not only opposition to his policies, but also a flood of angry correspondence to his masters in Versailles. To thrive, an intendant needed to cultivate support by showing a willingness to listen to the local population and, where appropriate, to intervene with the government on its behalf. Problems with raising the militia or arrears in taxation were commonly explained away by the poverty of the region, or the paucity of the harvest, and ministers were always on the lookout for evidence that an intendant was 'going native' and neglecting his primary duty of serving the king.

Within the *pays d'états*, the power of the intendant was more restricted. Together with the governor, he represented the king at the assemblies of the provincial estates, presenting the royal demands to the deputies of the three orders. The estates had preserved the right of consent to taxation, and the most pressing problem was to secure the necessary approval for a 'free gift' (*don gratuit*), and, after 1695, the capitation and other direct taxation.

Traditionally the voting of monies was a protracted business, often strung out over weeks, with the governor and intendant obliged to use all of the charm, patronage, and threats at their disposal in order to produce an offer acceptable to the king. Louis XIV found the practice of haggling with his subjects demeaning, and by the late 1670s he had effectively ended it. When the provincial estates met, they no longer engaged in a lengthy ritual of offering the smallest free gift compatible with decency and then gradually increasing it until compromise was reached. Instead, they accorded the full amount requested by the king by acclamation. This was not the result of Louis XIV's threats, or the despotic nature of 'absolutism'. When the estates showed respect and obedience, the king rewarded them by reducing his demands. The monarch thus received the outward signs of submission that he craved, while the estates had a real incentive to comply. With the periodic exception of Brittany, this model of mutually beneficial cooperation endured without significant modification until 1787.

Provincial estates which continued to meet were, therefore, power-ful and independent institutions. When they were not assembled, they delegated their authority to permanent commissions, and these bodies, not the intendants, carried out the vast majority of fiscal and administrative tasks. The intendants were forced to work with the commissions, and their role involved more supervision and negoti-ation than in the *pays d'élection*. Despite these qualifications, the intendants were impressive royal servants, and they did achieve a remarkable amount given the obstacles they faced. They offered a first taste of uniform government in the sense that every generality had an intendant from 1689, when Brittany finally fell into line with the rest of the kingdom.

Although the intendants have captured the historiographical head-lines, there were others toiling away in important, if less glamorous, administrative posts. Secretaries of state and controllers-general came and went, but their teams of clerks (*commis*) remained in place. First clerks such as Malet, Mesnard de Conichard, or Marie de Villiers were amongst the most prestigious of several hundred who laboured for the ministry, and they were probably the inspiration for the econo-mist Gournay when he coined the term *bureaucracy* in the middle of the eighteenth century. These were not venal appointments, and tal-ent and technical expertise as well as the patronage of a minister were essential ingredients in a successful career. Not surprisingly, many clerks stayed in their posts throughout the revolutionary and Napo-leonic periods, providing the backbone of the state. Similar patterns are detectable amongst both the engineers of bridges and roads, who were responsible for the impressive expansion of the road network during the eighteenth century, and the inspectors of manufactures. Entrance to these posts was increasingly by competitive examination, and proven competence and professionalism were required for advancement. The old regime state was therefore an uneasy amalgam of traditional and more modern forms of administration which were frequently in competition with one another.

The fiscal military state

From 1660 until the Revolution only one decade, that of the 1720s, was entirely peaceful, and the French state had been forged by the demands of war. The great conflicts of Louis XIV's reign saw the kingdom fighting desperately against ever more powerful coalitions. To do so required mobilization of men and materials on a hitherto unseen scale. During the Thirty Years War, the rival armies often resembled little more than mercenary bands, and to put 50,000 troops in the field was a major achievement. Thanks to the painstaking work of the secretaries of state, Le Tellier and his son Louvois, the situation was transformed. Rigorous attention to the perennial problems of arming, housing, and feeding troops allowed ever larger forces to be raised, and, more importantly, to be kept on a war footing even in peacetime. In what might justifiably be called a military revolution, the army rose to a staggering 360,000 by the early eighteenth century. No less remarkable was the growth of the navy, which, at its peak in the 1680s, briefly challenged the maritime hegemony of England and the Dutch republic. The cost of these forces and the campaigns they waged was astronomical, and by the end of the War of the Spanish Succession in 1713 France was in debt to the tune of 2,000 million *livres*. Although the size of the army declined to a peacetime level of 160,000 by the reign of Louis XVI, war was no less expensive and the bill for the War of American Independence alone amounted to over 1,000 million *livres*.

The means by which the monarchy raised the revenue for these campaigns says much about the nature of the old regime and the reasons for its eventual demise. The *taille*, which was paid by the third estate, and especially the peasantry, was the principal direct tax. In the course of the century after 1690, direct taxation was extended to include all lay members of French society. In 1695, the introduction of the capitation marked the end of noble fiscal exemption, and it was followed by the tenth (1710–17, 1733–6, 1740–8) and its successor the twentieth (1749–89). Only the Catholic church was able to preserve its independence, and continued to vote its own 'free gift' to the king.

In the *pays d'élection*, it was the intendants who drew up the tax rolls and oversaw the fiscal administration, but in the *pays d'états* that task fell to the permanent commissions of the provincial estates. Within individual parishes, it was the peasants who organized the collection of the tax and they were held jointly responsible for producing their allocation. If anyone absconded, or refused to pay, it was left to their fellow parishioners to make up the difference. These sums passed to local receivers, who had bought their office from either the crown or the provincial estates. They had done so in pursuit of profit, and in addition to their fees substantial sums stuck to their fingers and to those of the receivers-general who oversaw their activities for the generality as a whole. Nor was the royal treasury filled with public servants. Those funds that were not consumed at a local level flowed into central funds (*caisses*) that were themselves controlled by office-holders acting in their own interest as well as that of the king. This intermingling of public and private motives was even more blatant in the field of indirect taxation. The crown leased the collection of customs and excise duties to syndicates of tax farmers, who paid a cash advance and often an interest free loan as security to the king. Naturally enough, they had a vested interest in extracting the maximum from taxation because every penny they received over and above that paid for the lease was profit.

Tax revenues were rarely sufficient in themselves to cover royal expenditure, and the government was obliged to borrow heavily to meet its engagements. After 1688, it became increasingly clear to French statesmen that they were at a financial disadvantage relative to the Dutch and the English, who could float loans far more cheaply. The absence of a national parliament, and its own justly deserved reputation for sharp practice, account for the monarchy's discomfort. It did, however, compensate partially through a ruthless exploitation of both venality and the wider system of privilege. Between 1689 and 1713, new offices were created in profusion, encompassing every profession from judge to that of taster of spirituous liquors. Nor was the sale of office the only way funds could be extracted from venality. Once a profession had been venalized, it was relatively easy to extort fresh funds from its members by threatening to create new offices, or to reduce its privileges. Both policies threatened to undercut the market price of existing offices, and to protect their patrimonies the endangered owners proposed cash gifts for the withdrawal, or moderation of the crown's demands. If their appeal was granted, they would then borrow privately using their collective prestige, salaries, and privileges as collateral. As the king usually thanked them for their public-spiritedness by graciously confirming those rights, they had the security required to borrow at comparatively low rates of interest. It is easy to imagine how unpopular these measures were, and they were not helped by their method of implementation. Private *traitants* paid for the right to sell offices much as farmers-general leased the right to collect taxation. Not surprisingly, they were adept at finding new areas to venalize, or in suggesting existing corps that might be squeezed further, and they were consequently detested.

Through its fiscal expediency, the monarchy reinforced the system of venality and privilege that it had created. Historians have often wondered why, for example, the *pays d'états* survived after 1661, and the answer is to be found, in part, in their ability to raise credit. They were continually obliged to advance money to the crown in order to 'buy out' unwanted offices, or deflect royal interference in their affairs. This was a provincial variation on the general theme of the royal extortion of corporate bodies. During the eighteenth century, however, the system was extended with the king ordering the provincial estates to borrow on his behalf. Using their far superior credit, they were able to raise funds at only 4 or 5 per cent, receiving in return a portion of the receipts from the capitation or twentieth with which to pay the interest and amortize the capital. For the estates and their creditors it was almost too good to be true. They were being offered a regular and secure investment opportunity which they seized with alacrity. Provincial estates also profited from royal penury by negotiating what were termed *abonnements* for the capitation and twentieths. In return for a cash advance to the crown, that was usually much inferior to the actual value of a particular tax, they received the right to levy it themselves. As the estates were controlled by urban office-holding and noble elites, the fiscal burden was then deflected onto the peasantry.

By milking the system of venality and privilege the monarchy raised billions, but by reinforcing the power of the office-holders and alienating its taxes to the pampered elites of the towns and the *pays d'états*, it made necessary reform even harder to achieve. Moreover the use of extortion and fiscal blackmail to raise funds had its costs, confirming the government's reputation for bad faith—the very reason why the public was reluctant to lend to it in the first place! That such a ramshackle fiscal system did not collapse before 1788 is a tribute both to the monarchy's resourcefulness and to the patience and resilience of its subjects. But the relative decline of France as a military power after 1750, and the initial outbreak of revolution in 1789, had fiscal origins.

The critics of state power

If historians are today more conscious of the limits of royal power, contemporaries nevertheless feared the strength of Louis XIV's state. As memories of the Fronde receded and wars took their toll, critical voices were once again heard. Some came from predictable sources, notably the Huguenot victims of religious persecution. In a fiery pamphlet, *The Sighs of France Enslaved*, the exiled Calvinist pastor, Pierre Jurieu, accused Louis XIV of acting tyrannically not only by persecuting his Protestant subjects, but also by stripping the nobility, towns, and provinces of their liberties. Similar conclusions were reached by Fénelon, tutor to Louis XIV's grandson, the duke de Burgundy, and his fellow dukes, Chevreuse and Beauvillier. They formed a Court-in-waiting, and as Louis XIV's reign dragged on they busied themselves with plans for reform. They lamented the loss of representative institutions, and planned to reintroduce provincial estates into the *pays d'élection*, to abolish the intendants and even to call an estates general. Another target of their ire was the centralization of the royal administration, and its alleged secrecy and lack of accountability. Criticizing the king directly was clearly not advisable, and it was the secretaries of state who bore the brunt of the attack, being charged with the crime of 'ministerial despotism'.

What united critics of Louis XIV was the belief that French government had become arbitrary, authoritarian, and unrepresentative. These dissident voices were largely confined to the ranks of the exiled Huguenots or to aristocratic salons before 1715, but in the course of the eighteenth century criticism began to seep into the public domain. The parlements were particularly important to this process, repeating the attacks on ministerial despotism and the arbitrary and inefficient nature of the royal administration in their many remonstrances. These texts were published and widely disseminated amongst the literate public, and, after 1750, they were accompanied by

a wider debate about the desirability of reviving provincial representative institutions. In private, some radical spirits dreamed of a
restored estates general, and the first public calls for such an assembly
were heard by the end of the reign of Louis XV.

Given the traditional image of absolute monarchy, it seems
incongruous that such ideas should have been circulating throughout
the seventeenth and eighteenth centuries. Yet both contemporaries
and many subsequent historians were dazzled by the first twenty
years of Louis XIV's personal reign, assuming that the monarchy
was indeed as powerful as the theorists and propagandists claimed.
In fact, the years between 1660 and 1685 were something of an
aberration, a brief period of calm in an otherwise choppy sea.

The parlements

While the existence of dissident voices should never be ignored, the
French monarchy was nevertheless viewed by the majority of its
subjects not as a despotism, but as a government tempered by the
laws. In addition to the moderating influence of the Catholic church,
they took comfort in the existence of corporate bodies that restrained
the crown. The most significant of these were the parlements. The
parlement of Paris was the highest court of appeal in a vast jurisdiction covering approximately one-third of the kingdom. By 1789,
there were also twelve provincial parlements, sitting in cities such
as Aix-en-Provence, Bordeaux, Grenoble, and Rouen. Judges in the
parlements were venal office-holders who had, in many cases,
invested fabulous sums for the privilege of belonging to one of these
august institutions. In terms of prestige, the parlement of Paris was at
the apex of the judicial system, and the dignity of its members was
reinforced by their association with the princes of the blood and the
peers who participated in their assemblies on great public occasions.

Parlements were not representative institutions, but nor were they
mere law courts. Whenever the monarch issued new, or revised,
legislation, including that affecting fiscal matters, it was sent to the
parlements for registration. The judges then examined the law to
ensure that there were no conflicts with existing jurisprudence.
Where they found none, the law was added to the court's registers

and was published and enforced by its officers. If, on the other hand, they found grounds for an objection, they could delay its implementation while they petitioned the sovereign with remonstrances. On certain contentious subjects, notably their own privileges, taxation, or religious affairs, the judges often repeated this process several times before registration. Should the king wish to accelerate matters, or to end an unseemly squabble, he could command obedience at a 'bed of justice'. In Paris, this quaintly named ceremony was attended by the king in person, together with the princes, peers, and great officers of the crown, while in the provinces it was the governor who presided. The disputed legislation was presented by the chancellor who, after listening to a justification of the parlement's resistance from its first president, made a tour of the assembly, before approaching the king and declaring the law registered. It was an elaborate charade which, through the performance of ritual, disguised the imposition of the royal will.

If the crown was patient, however, and allowed the judges to deliberate and even remonstrate where necessary, it could usually count upon achieving prompt registration. By submitting laws to the scrutiny of the parlements, it also gained significantly in the process. While there was theoretically nothing to stop the king from issuing laws as *arrêts du conseil*, he rarely did so because contemporaries were almost unanimous in believing that registration conferred a solemnity and authority that laws would otherwise lack. Despite the frustration of both Louis XV and Louis XVI with the obstructionism of the parlements, the monarchy enjoyed a symbiotic relationship with these great law courts, and without them would, in all probability, have faced a rendezvous with the estates general before 1789.

It is true that in 1673, Louis XIV curtailed the power of the parlements by obliging them to register laws before presenting remonstrances. His decision horrified former frondeurs like Jean Le Boindre, who wrote that as 'the French had changed their laws and their monarchy, they might as well change their name'.[4] He was obliged to brood in silence, and despite his anger we should note that the king never challenged the legitimacy of either registration in the parlement or remonstrances. Over the period as a whole, the

---

[4] J. Le Boindre, *Débats du parlement de Paris pendant la minorité de Louis XIV*, ed. R. Descimon and O. Ranum (Paris, 1997), 355.

relationship between the crown and its judges produced more debate and conflict than might be expected within a theoretically absolute monarchy. Without ever being revolutionary, the parlements expounded a set of legal principles which, while not incompatible with royal sovereignty, acted as a brake on its exercise. Central to their claims was the right to 'free verification' of the law. If, for example, the king refused to hear remonstrances, arrested or exiled judges, tried to cut short parlementary assemblies or held a bed of justice, he was almost certain to provoke an angry response. Bound together by their esprit de corps the judges were tenacious opponents. They were most easily roused in defence of their own honour and jurisdiction, quarrelling with rival law courts, the clergy, and any other institution brave enough to risk their wrath. Self-interest played a significant part in their thinking, especially on fiscal matters, but it was not their sole motivation. They did have a wider conception of their role which included the presentation of public grievances. As the parlement of Paris noted in 1718, in the absence of the estates general, 'your Parlement, sire ... is the only channel by which the voice of your people can reach you'.[5]

Those who were anxious to see an institutional check on the powers of the crown were happy to concur, overlooking the venal nature of the parlements to accord them a representative role. This was most apparent in the case of the parlement of Paris which was not only presented as a substitute for the estates general, but even as the true parliament of France. This argument first surfaced during the Fronde in a controversial pamphlet entitled the *Judicium Francorum*, which gave a novel twist to radical theories first advanced during the sixteenth-century religious wars. Whereas Huguenot resistance theorists had argued that the estates general was the descendant of ancient French parliaments that had met in the age of the Franks and the Gauls, the author of the *Judicium Francorum* claimed that the parlement of Paris was that true parliament of the kingdom. During the personal reign of Louis XIV any supporters of this theory kept their thoughts to themselves. In 1732, however, the *Judicium Francorum* was dusted off and reprinted by Jansenist lawyers anxious for support in their campaign against the religious policies of cardinal de Fleury. The parlement reacted angrily, ordering the

[5] J. Flammermont, *Les Remontrances du parlement de Paris au xviii* siècle* (3 vols., Paris, 1888–98), i. 101.

pamphlet to be lacerated and burnt by the public executioner. Yet when the religious troubles flared again during the 1750s, the ideas contained within the *Judicium Francorum* were popularized in a more substantial work, the *Lettres historiques* of 1753–4, written by the Jansenist lawyer, Louis-Adrien Le Paige. Within months, his theories had been integrated into the remonstrances of the parlement which, in August 1756, boldly declared that it had an unbroken 1,600-year history dating back to the 'birth of the French monarchy'.[6]

To bolster these fanciful claims, the Parisian judges reached out to their colleagues in the provinces by declaring their affiliation to the mother parlement in Paris. Rather than forming separate institutions, the provincial courts were 'classes' of the one and indivisible national body. Having conjured up a national parlement, it was but one small step to transform it into a parliament by challenging the ritual of a bed of justice. In 1756, Le Paige published a pamphlet which took his theories to their logical conclusion by claiming that those present had the right to give their opinions openly, and not, as was currently practised, sit silently while the chancellor counted their imaginary votes. If one believed that the parlement of Paris really was the successor to the Frankish assemblies, it was difficult to find fault with his argument. Unfortunately, as many were well aware, the origins of the parlement were to be found in the thirteenth and fourteenth centuries, not at the side of Clovis or Charlemagne.

Yet whether they shared Le Paige's historical vision or not, many judges were prepared to endorse aspects of it because he confirmed their belief that the parlement held a special place amongst the kingdom's institutions. Montesquieu had already popularized the notion of the parlements as intermediary powers, ensuring that France was a monarchy and not a despotism, and the judges themselves were forever reminding the king that they were the guardians of the 'fundamental laws'. Indeed so insistent were their references to the latter, that Louis XV once asked chancellor de Lamoignon what they meant. With understandable embarrassment, he was forced to admit that he was unsure. Lamoignon had no need to reproach himself. For the parlement, the beauty of such concepts lay in their very vagueness. Quarrels with rival corps, or even the crown, could acquire a whole new dimension by being invested with the gravitas of

---

[6] Flammermont, *Remontrances*, ii. 26, 73.

a defence of the fundamental laws. Many of the constitutional arguments advanced by the judges during times of conflict were therefore rhetorical strategies, intended to achieve more limited objectives than their evocative language suggests. As part of a privileged professional and social elite, they were instinctively conservative and with very few exceptions devoutly monarchist. It was, however, frequently a more legalistic and restricted conception of monarchy than that held by the Bourbon kings and their ministers.

Because of its symbolic and political importance and proximity to Versailles, the parlement of Paris was regularly drawn into the high political world of the Court. Its deliberations during the Fronde, for example, were nearly always graced by the presence of princes of the blood, or members of the peerage. They realized that the parlement gave legitimacy to their opposition to the regency government. Louis XIV was determined to avoid a repetition of such behaviour. He worked assiduously to confine the judges to their legal duties, and tried to limit their contacts with Versailles by forbidding them from sitting on the councils of the princes.

When the parlement was once again permitted to remonstrate before registration in 1715, its political power was restored and the barriers separating it from Versailles fell into disrepair. By cementing links of faction and clientage with the judges, ministers and courtiers could hope to influence their deliberations. If the parlement obstructed legislation, the credit of a minister could be challenged and he might even be disgraced, thus creating an opening for those who had plotted his fall. Predictably it was the controller-general who was most vulnerable, and attempts to introduce new taxation or reform the fiscal system were, from his perspective, fraught with danger.

Within the parlement similar calculations were also being made. The great robe dynasties of, for example, Joly de Fleury, Lamoignon, Maupeou, Molé, and d'Ormesson competed for the highest judicial offices of chancellor, first president, and procurator-general. Their rivalries and jealousies continually affected the behaviour of the parlement. When Lamoignon de Blancmesnil became chancellor in 1750, his defeated rival, first president de Maupeou, was accused, not without some justification, of encouraging opposition in the court to embarrass his new superior. After 1768, when Maupeou's son was named chancellor, he quickly discovered that he had bitter critics amongst the other robe clans that resented his good fortune. The willingness of Louis XV to choose his controller-general directly from the benches of the parlement, as occurred in 1763 and 1769, stoked the flames of internal rivalries yet further, because there was no shortage of would-be candidates for such a powerful post.

Finally, after 1750, the parlement of Paris sought to draw the princes and the peers into its disputes with both the clergy and the crown. The judges issued invitations to participate in their deliberations in, for example, 1752, 1756, 1760, and 1766, which were quickly countermanded by an angry Louis XV. His action infuriated the grandees, many of whom were encouraging the parlement and hoping to exercise a more direct role in its affairs. The king's discomfiture provided a perfect illustration of how the tight political control exercised by the sun king had been allowed to lapse. As Louis XVI stumbled through the pre-revolutionary crisis of 1787–8, it was a dangerous combination of princes, parlements, and people that would prove his undoing.

Corporate politics

In the hierarchical and corporate society of the old regime, the monarch reigned supreme. It was he who created and confirmed the rights, distinctions, and privileges of his subjects, and acted as the arbiter of their claims and disputes. Arguing about who should take the lead in a procession, dress in a particular fashion, or be allowed to sit, on what, and in the company of whom, are just a selection of the myriad disputes that were a daily feature of life in France before 1789. One of the most notorious quarrels involved the dukes and peers and the presidents of the parlement of Paris. The affair hinged on whether or not the presidents should remove their bonnets in the presence of the peers. Despite its seemingly superficial nature, this was a crucial issue as it would seal the respective positions of the disputants in the social hierarchy. As for the parlement of Dijon, it spent several months in exile for refusing to allow the local military commandant to sit in the governor's armchair. It prompted one Burgundian wit to note that, just as much passes between 'the glass and the nose', so too does it 'between the arse and the armchair' (*entre les fesses et le fauteuil*).[7] In the world of the law, jurisdiction was a perennial cause of contestation. The parlements and the church were continually at loggerheads about appeals, when secular courts overturned the verdicts of their spiritual counterparts (*appels comme d'abus*). They were not alone. Protecting honour and status was an obsession at every level of society, and corps of wigmakers or winemakers were no less anxious to uphold their dignity and precedence than the most exalted judge or cleric.

For the king, however, the sight of his subjects locked in struggle was reassuring. They looked to him to resolve their bickering, providing living proof of the old proverb that he was the father of his people. The crown allowed some of these quarrels to continue for generations, but its procrastination was the result of more than just an exercise in divide and rule. Any firm decision was liable to produce at least one disappointed party, whose loyalty might then be in question. Delay, on the other hand, kept all sides on their best behaviour, for fear that a false move would prove fatal.

In these corporate struggles, access to the king and members of his council was vital, either to assist a favourable verdict, or to block an unfavourable one. The church was in a particularly happy position, and could exert influence through the king's confessor, Court sermons, and the intervention of courtly prelates as well as via the official route of episcopal deputation. The parlements and provincial estates also enjoyed privileged access to the monarch, and by the later eighteenth century the presentation of remonstrances was an almost daily event. While even the most lowly corps or group of office-holders could petition the king, they could be less confident of receiving a hearing. If they were not careful, their remonstrances would accumulate unread on the desks of the first clerk or masters of requests. To avoid that fate, they required the good offices of an intermediary, who could convey their message to a higher authority.

Foremost amongst the power-brokers of the old regime were the provincial governors and intendants. With their ability to open the doors of ministers and even the king, they were an indispensable ally for an embattled corps. Others who might play a similar role were local bishops, or aristocrats, willing to plead their cause at Versailles. When two institutions from the same province were in conflict,

---

[7] Bibliothèque Nationale MS Fr 10435, fo. 34.

potential power-brokers could expect to be contacted by both sides, if only out of a desire to neutralize their 'good offices'. The first clerk and the masters of requests, who controlled the flow of information to ministers and the royal council, were another coveted source of influence. Wherever possible, corps sent deputies to court in order to wait on these officials and to be on hand to forestall any ambushes prepared by their rivals. The more affluent amongst them sought to insure their position by keeping influential power brokers on a form of retainer. In addition to the sums traditionally dispensed on the governor, controller-general, and intendant, the estates of Burgundy petitioned successfully for the right to pay a pension of 3,000 *livres* to the first clerk, Mesnard de Conichard, in 1769. Less powerful institutions had to limit themselves to the occasional gift and regular displays of deference in the hope of protecting their interests. As for the power-brokers, they had the satisfaction of seeing their place in the social and institutional hierarchy, the basis of their influence, reinforced.

Approaching the powerful was not the only strategy pursued in the Darwinian world of old regime politics. During the Fronde the Parisian law courts had joined together in opposition to cardinal Mazarin, and the parlement of Paris threatened the government of Louis XV with the theory of a 'unity of classes' on several occasions after 1756. Yet when chancellor Maupeou implemented his dramatic remodelling of the judicial system in 1771, the parlements never dared to put their theory into practice. When their offices were threatened with additional taxation, the kingdom's bureaux of finances also explored the prospect of an association in 1774. This, and other similar projects, came to naught because once such bodies went beyond a rhetorical expression of equality, they found themselves confronted by the imposing obstacles of particularism, privilege, and precedent.

In the *pays d'états*, friction between the provincial estates and the local parlement was a perennial feature of administrative life. Fiscal matters were especially controversial, and the parlements denounced what they perceived as abuse in the collection of taxation. Their protests were not always altruistic, and they would have liked nothing better than to act as the censors of local government. Brittany was the one exception to this conflictual picture, and after 1750 the provincial estates and the parlement of Rennes mounted joint opposition to taxation. This resistance was almost solely the work of the numerous

Breton nobility who dominated both institutions. Any noble who could prove that his family had belonged to the second order for at least 100 years was eligible to sit in the estates. Hundreds took advantage of the privilege. By day, they gathered to denounce royal policy, while at night they expected to eat, drink, and make merry at the king's expense. As these sessions could continue for weeks, it is easy to understand the crown's subsequent frustration. The sheer number of nobles made it difficult to employ the traditional tactics of patronage and bribery that were so successful in Burgundy or Languedoc. Moreover, as many of the Breton nobility were comparatively poor, they were especially sensitive to increases in direct taxation and they had the ideal platform from which to voice their discontent.

If horizontal cooperation across corps was rare, it was far easier to achieve within a hierarchically ordered profession. During the reigns of both Louis XV and Louis XVI attempts to curb the powers of individual parlements through disciplinary edicts or exiles resulted in a complete cessation of the legal system within their jurisdiction. The parlements were capable of commanding obedience from the lawyers, advocates, and junior legal officers, whose actions were conditioned by a mixture of respect and self-interest. The judges were powerful men and their social rank and position inspired loyalty. Anyone tempted to break ranks, and that included those judges inclined to put duty to the king above *esprit de corps*, risked social ostracism and a premature end to their career.

Old regime politics can appear an elite affair, and it is true that nobles and office-holders held centre stage. They were nevertheless eager to mobilize popular support. The most dramatic instance of this was provided during the Fronde, and, on one occasion, the first president of the parlement of Paris could inform the disbelieving regent, Anne of Austria, that '50,000 armed Parisians were ready to march at his side'.[8] The genie of popular political activity, which came so close to being unleashed during the Fronde, was safely bottled for most of the next 150 years. Indeed one of the more remarkable features of the period is the relative absence of political violence. Driven to extremes by the policies of Richelieu and Mazarin, French elites, in both the towns and the countryside, had connived in popular revolts, either by secretly encouraging them, or by refusing to use

---

[8] Le Boindre, *Débats du parlement*, 251.

the forces of coercion at their disposal. Where revolts occurred after 1661, notably in Brittany in 1675, they were repressed with severity. Louis XIV punished the parlement of Rennes for failing to uphold his authority with sufficient vigour, by transferring it to distant Vannes where it spent the next fifteen years. It was a clear lesson to others, but French elites had little reason to complain about their treatment. The king offered order on generous terms and most were grateful to accept.

Displays of support for those engaged in conflict with the crown were therefore carefully choreographed. During the reign of Louis XV, the provincial parlements drew comfort from elaborate celebrations marking the end of their periodic quarrels with the crown. In a carnivalesque atmosphere, the various corps and guilds would parade in their finery to salute the judges. The streets were bedecked with flowers and banners, and lit in the evening to allow fireworks, music, dancing, banquets, and other distractions for the ordinary people. In 1761, the townspeople of Besançon were treated to the spectacle of a mechanically operated angel crowning the judges with laurels as they returned from exile. Two years later, their neighbours in Dijon witnessed a triumphal chariot, pulled by six black horses, and containing twenty-four local beauties, dressed as nymphs, who threw sweets to the crowds as they toured the city to bestow laurels on local judges after a battle with the provincial estates.

These were very traditional expressions of communal solidarity designed to highlight and reinforce the social hierarchy. If they strengthened the hand of the parlements in their dealings with the crown, they never challenged the authority of the king directly. Victories were not won over the monarch himself, and the crowds that cried 'long live the king, long live the parlement' were rejoicing at the re-establishment of a harmony disrupted by those shadowy figures who had temporarily 'deceived the king'.

The public and its opinions

Old regime politics was dominated by clientage and patronage, with corporate bodies struggling to maintain their status within a structure still defined by the personal authority of the king. Yet the impact of cultural and economic change during the eighteenth century did produce a more politically conscious public, with the education, wealth, and leisure time needed to follow the military and diplomatic affairs of Europe and the religious and parlementary crises of France. It is true that the Fronde had produced an outpouring of political literature, most of it incredibly crude and hostile to the queen mother and Mazarin, but it was a brush fire whose blaze was as brief as it was intense. By the eighteenth century, the climate had altered profoundly. Not only was the total volume of political literature produced much greater, but it was also sustained over a far longer period and was accessible to a greater number of people. In addition to government newspapers and court circulars, the curious could peruse foreign periodicals, clandestine pamphlets and publications, notably the Jansenist *Ecclesiastical News* (*Nouvelles ecclésiastiques*), parlementary remonstrances (which were published despite an official ban), royal replies to those protests, handwritten broadsheets, and many other forms of literary ephemera. All told, it was a healthy diet to put before the public that gathered in the salons, academies, masonic lodges, reading rooms, coffee houses, and other places of sociability to read about or discuss current affairs.

The monarchy had always been anxious to influence public opinion, as its elaborate ritual and visual propaganda made plain. For all his imperiousness, Louis XIV was even prepared to have an appeal for public support read from the pulpits in 1709, when the harsh peace terms offered by his enemies forced him to continue waging war. Defending the royal authority against the parlements and other critics in print, as his successors were obliged to do, was, however, more difficult because it allowed the reader to make a choice that was not necessarily favourable to the crown. Both contemporaries and subsequent historians have thus described public opinion as a new tribunal that threatened to replace the king as the arbiter of conflicting political claims.

There is no doubt that all sides were conscious that popular support was a valuable weapon. On at least one occasion, the parlement of Paris was so determined to put its case to the public that it published its remonstrances, which was in itself illegal, before they were presented to the king! Ministers were no less adept, leaking information to the press and timing official announcements to maximum advantage. Policies required explanation, not only to those charged with implementing them, but also to ordinary subjects. With the kingdom awash with print, an increasing quantity of which was far from deferential, the government's task was more onerous than ever before. In the aftermath of defeat in the Seven Years War, Louis XV went as far as to commission projects for the abolition of the *corvée* and the re-establishment of provincial estates in a bid to restore public support. It says much about his disappointing reign that these imaginative plans never left the drawing board.

Public opinion was not, however, the decisive factor in late eighteenth-century politics. Even today, despite the attention of armies of psephologists and well-heeled market researchers, it remains a fickle and elusive creature, and interpreting the effects of political literature on the eighteenth-century public is problematic. Before the reign of Louis XVI, appealing to the tribunal of public opinion, while common, did not necessarily achieve a great deal. It is difficult to cite a significant example of public sentiment radically altering royal policy, and although in 1709 Louis XIV sought to explain his actions, he would never have made peace because it was popular. A great deal of ink was spilt by the government of Louis XV justifying its declaration of war against Great Britain in 1756. Yet an outraged public reaction was not enough to persuade the king or his grandson to abandon the hugely unpopular Austrian alliance contracted in the same year. Finally, although opinion was overwhelmingly against chancellor Maupeou—whose allegedly despotic remodelling of the parlements in 1771 earned him the title of grand vizier—it was the death of Louis XV and not public hostility that brought about his fall. Like Mazarin before him, Maupeou seemed living proof that the confidence of his master, not public popularity, was the key to power in the old regime. Yet his dismissal by Louis XVI signalled a change: the new king was worried that to retain the chancellor would begin his reign on a note of unpopularity. When, eleven years later, he went so far as to consult his subjects in an assembly of Notables, the move was wittily remembered by the count de Ségur as the royal 'resignation'.

Finally, it has been suggested that the highly contentious nature of political and religious debate in the eighteenth century began to filter down the social scale, touching those excluded from the still rarefied world of print. In 1757, the long-running religious and parlementary crises caused by Jansenism inspired a mentally confused domestic servant, Robert-François Damiens, to make an attempt on the life of Louis XV. As police spies trawled the kingdom for possible accomplices, they discovered others praising Damiens and the more successful regicide, Cromwell, and, in the case of the military deserter Bellier de La Chauvellais, claiming that in the same circumstances he 'would have stuck his knife into the heart of the sacred bugger'.[9] Before Damiens struck, the marquis d'Argenson had recorded in his diary the appearance of regicidal placards in Paris, proclaiming, among other things, 'stir in yourselves the spirits of Ravaillac', a reference to Henri IV's notorious assassin. Disturbing as it was for Louis XV to attract such opprobrium, he could reassure himself that he was not the first to be so maligned. In 1709, the royal family had been serenaded with the insulting verse:[10]

Le grand père est un fanfaron,	Grandfather a braggart,
Le fils un imbécile	The son a mere fool,
Le petit-fils un grand poltron	The grandson a coward,
Ah! la Belle famille!	Fine family rule!
Que je vous plains, peuples français	Unhappy French people,
Soumis à cet empire	Subject to this sway,
Faites ce qu'ont fait les anglais	Just do like the English,
C'est assez vous le dire!	No more need I say!

Verbal abuse and insulting ditties, ballads, limericks, and other doggerel had long been directed at the monarch, his ministers, close family, and mistresses as well as at the elites of the kingdom by their social inferiors. The government was sensitive to this opinion, as its employment of an army of spies testified, but its direct political influence was minimal. Instead, the popularity of the monarchy ebbed and flowed, and the despair and anger with Louis XIV in 1709 was replaced by a tide of public affection for his great-grandson. Louis XV squandered that resource, and by 1774 he had sunk low in public esteem. Yet the accession of Louis XVI transformed matters, and the young king was genuinely popular. His own tragic fall from grace came after 1789.

---

[9] D. Van Kley, *The Damiens Affair and the Unraveling of the Ancien Régime, 1750–1770* (Princeton, 1984), 247.

[10] Quoted in M. Bouchard, *De l'humanisme à l'encyclopédie: l'esprit public en Bourgogne sous l'ancien régime* (Paris, 1930), 283. Translation by William Doyle.

Conclusion

If the ghost of Louis XIV had returned to haunt the corridors of Versailles during the 1780s, he would have found life much as he left it. Louis XVI reigned as an absolute monarch, holding council meetings as his forefather had done and ruling through the same apparatus of intendants and office-holders and the still ramshackle fiscal system that was about to bring the whole edifice crashing down. With hindsight, it is the relative weakness of the monarchy in the eighteenth century that is striking. Yet attempts at reform met with opposition because the subjects of Louis XV and Louis XVI feared that the famous intermediary powers would not be enough to prevent a strong government from degenerating into despotism. In his justly celebrated remonstrances delivered to the young Louis XVI on behalf of the Parisian court of aids, Lamoignon de Malesherbes declared: 'no one should dare to leave you in ignorance of the fact that the unanimous wish of the nation is to obtain either the Estates General or at least the provincial estates'.[11] His bold and eloquent plea was a sign that well before 1789 the French were moving towards the conclusion that there could be neither taxation nor legitimate government without representation.

[11] K. M. Baker (ed.), *The Old Regime and the French Revolution* (Chicago, 1987), 65.

6

Politics: Louis XIV

William Doyle

Although Louis XIV had been on the throne since 1643, come of age in 1651, and been crowned in 1654, in 1660 he was still a figurehead. No king had both reigned and ruled in France for half a century. Government under Louis XIII, and then his widow Anne of Austria, had been in the hands of energetic and insinuating cardinal-ministers. Mazarin, inseparable from the regent-queen, was even the young king's godfather, and proved a genuine substitute for the royal parent he could scarcely remember. But the cardinal, though assiduous in initiating him into affairs of state, still took all the important decisions. And so it was this wily, acquisitive Italian adventurer who bequeathed to Louis XIV the issue that would dominate his entire reign: the Spanish Succession. Mazarin regarded the peace of the Pyrenees of 1659, which brought an end to twenty-four years of war against Spain, as the crowning achievement of his career. The peace was sealed the next year by the marriage of the king to the infanta Maria Theresa, thereby giving him and his heirs potential claims on the throne of Spain.

It was true that before the marriage the future queen renounced her succession rights, as her husband's own mother had when she came from Spain in 1615; but such routine renunciations by Habsburg princesses marrying outside the family had never yet been tested. And meanwhile on 26 August the exultant king of France brought his bride to his capital city. There he made a formal and glittering entry, as his predecessors had done on great occasions since the Middle Ages. A magnificent procession took two hours to rumble westwards into Paris, and the accompanying festivities took eight more. And on this occasion the young king shared the glory with none but his queen. The queen mother watched from a balcony; Mazarin was too ill to take part. It was to be seven more months before Louis XIV began to rule his kingdom in person, but in retrospect the royal entry into Paris of 1660 was almost as momentous in its significance. After it, triumphal entries went out of fashion. Public ceremonial would be supplanted by royal ceremoniousness. The fickle acclaim of the Parisians would be shunned for the predictable deference of court-iers. A peripatetic monarch—the entry of 1660 ended a year-long progress through the southern provinces—would henceforth confine his journeyings largely to the Île-de-France. Even the magistrates of the parlement of Paris, who almost marred the occasion by refusing to take part, would not so openly defy authority for another two generations. The entry was the last act of a style of monarchy soon to disappear.

Personal rule

The transition, when it came, was abrupt—though not, if we are to believe the royal memoirs, unpremeditated. When Mazarin died on 9 March 1661, the king instructed the secretaries of state to report directly to him. Nobody thought this could last, but it did. From this moment until the day he died fifty-four years later, Louis XIV governed according to precepts most clearly expounded to the grandson who became king of Spain in 1700: 'Do not let yourself be governed, be the master; never have either favourites or a prime minister; listen to, consult your Council, but decide yourself: God, who has made you a king, will give you the necessary wisdom so long as your intentions are good'.[1] These attitudes had been largely moulded by the experiences of the king's youth, when over-mighty subjects had made him from time to time a fugitive in his own king-dom. In 1648 the parlement of Paris, the leading law court of the realm, had led a revolt of venal office-holders against an extortionate state. Supported by the people of Paris and an insubordinate clergy, they had driven the royal government from the capital. And this first Fronde, which had exposed the limits of the queen's and Mazarin's

[1] 'Instructions au duc d'Anjou (1700)', in J. Lognon (ed.), *Mémoires de Louis XIV* (Paris, 1927), 268.

power, engendered another, this time led by princes of the blood royal, who sought to capture the authority of a monarch now nominally out of tutelage to a regent. They were even prepared to cooperate with the Spanish enemy to achieve their ends, and they briefly secured the expulsion of Mazarin from the kingdom. Divisions among the rebels, and their flirtation with treason, soon opened the way for his return, however, and between 1652 and his death the cardinal steadily rebuilt his power in the king's name. He also made persistently clear to his godson where the blame lay for five years of rebellion and civil war, which had lost him the chance of an early victory over the king of Spain. And so, when Louis XIV took personal control of his realm, he had no illusions about the rivals on whom he must stamp his authority. Never again must office-holders, the city of Paris, or the higher nobility be allowed to dictate to their sovereign.

In time, firm adherence to these principles would bring its own reward; but in 1661, apart from general goodwill towards a confident young king unafraid to deploy his own authority, Louis XIV had only one effective body of support to rely on in confronting such massive vested interests. This was Mazarin's network of clients and dependents, suddenly deprived of their patron. But even this powerful nexus, whose members had their hands on all the key financial and jurisdictional levers of the state, was debilitated by long-standing rivalry between Nicolas Fouquet, superintendent of the finances and procurator-general of the parlement, and Jean-Baptiste Colbert, intendant of finances and the manager of the cardinal's vast personal fortune. Choosing between them was the king's first major policy decision. Fouquet's mistake was to assume that the young monarch's attempt to rule by himself would soon flag, and that Mazarin's power would then pass to him. Believing his personal credit to be indispensable to the royal finances, he lived on the same luxurious scale as the two cardinal ministers, and his house and garden at Vaux-le-Vicomte, where he entertained the king with unparalleled lavishness in August 1661, outshone anything a subject had ever built before. But by the time of the famous visit, Colbert had convinced the king that Fouquet's wealth had been acquired at royal expense, and that his whole management of the finances was suspect. A few days later an astonished Fouquet was arrested. After a show trial lasting three years he was condemned to life imprisonment and his goods confiscated. At the same time almost 500 other financiers were hauled before a 'chamber of justice' and fined for alleged malversations as far back as 1635. In practice, the war begun then could not have been waged without them, but they must have known the risks. Chambers of justice were an occupational hazard for financiers when wars ended or reigns began. Extremely popular with resentful taxpayers, these tribunals were at the same time a roundabout way of cancelling debts to the crown's leading creditors. This one also made a spectacular break with the hated regime of the dead cardinal.

Behind it, however, men raised up by Mazarin continued to be the king's principal advisers: Hugues de Lionne, the kingdom's most experienced diplomat; Michel le Tellier, the organizer of military victory; and now Colbert, entrusted with the royal finances. They met regularly as ministers of state in the king's innermost council; but not by right, merely by his verbal invitation. Even the chancellor, traditional head of the administration, was now excluded from innermost policy-making. Louis XIV never changed this system. Nor did he frequently change his ministers. When they died, he preferred like a good patron to replace them with their sons or near relatives. The one occasion when he chose a minister he did not know personally (Arnauld de Pomponne in 1671) he later recognized as a mistake. Government through such a small circle did not preclude rivalries, and sons succeeding fathers prolonged them down the generations. Antagonism between Le Telliers and Colberts marked much of the reign. But the king positively fostered a competition which prevented the dominance of anybody but himself.

Authority asserted

In recognition of their services, he heaped his ministers with titles and honours, and their wider families with patronage. Socially, however, they remained relative newcomers, and this was quite deliberate. 'It was not in my interest,' the king wrote to his son, 'to take subjects of more eminent quality. Above all things, I had to establish my own reputation, and let the public know, by the very rank from which I took them, that my intention was not to share my authority with them. I was concerned that they should not harbour for themselves higher hopes than it pleased me to give them: which is difficult for people of high birth'.[2] Undoubtedly princes, peers and other great nobles of old stock resented the power thus vested in men whom they regarded as social inferiors. Yet they had few other grounds for discontent with the way the king treated them. Louis XIV regarded himself as the first gentleman of his kingdom. In his taste for war, hunting, and luxurious pastimes he set an example that nobles were eager to follow. And he gave the greatest of them a focus for their ambitions and pleasures in a lavish Court where, by assiduous attendance and catching the royal eye they could accumulate commands, sinecures, pensions, and ecclesiastical patronage for themselves and their relatives to maintain and enhance the prestige of their birth. Indeed, the expenses of living at Court made pursuit of such handouts essential.

Over the reign the pattern of Court life solidified. The king spent increasing amounts of time at his hunting lodge at Versailles, and by the late 1660s it was being regularly extended to accommodate his growing entourage. A decade later it was proclaimed the principal permanent royal residence, massive new building works were begun, and the Court moved there in 1682, even though the works were still far from finished. Whole ministerial wings were added, for ministers and their offices had to be where the king was. This made them equally accessible to those who lived at Court, further increasing its attractions. Accordingly the greater nobility progressively abandoned their old provincial power bases to reside almost permanently at or near the Court. They remained important conduits of provincial patronage, and the greatest of them would reappear from time to time representing the king's person as governors. But with the old elites no longer resident, their networks of clientage, in which so much of the disorder of earlier generations had been rooted, withered away. Provincial life was left to the dominance of the ennobled office-holders of the sovereign courts. But they, too, were soon abandoning their old defiant ways. They liked a king who ruled with confidence, and knew his own mind. What they had really wanted since the century began was secure and transferable tenure of their offices without the threat of financial ruin, together with uncontested exercise of their companies' jurisdiction. The years after 1661 seemed to promise more of both. The advent of international peace meant that many of the more

[2] *Mémoires*, 30.

insensitive ways of blackmailing money out of office-holders were abandoned; and they had the satisfaction of seeing the financiers who had thought them up humiliated by the chamber of justice. The king's determination to restore order to lawless regions like the Auvergne also gave magistrates plenty to do, and he was soon taking care to interfere less in the everyday processes of justice than those who had governed during his minority. All this made the courts less inclined to resist attempts in the 1660s to fix office prices and curb the magistracy's rights to obstruct new legislation. When in 1673 they were forbidden to remonstrate until after registering new edicts, they scarcely raised a protest. Nor did they offer serious resistance to the steady spread, throughout the 1660s and 1670s, of the omnicompetent intendants who had overridden the ordinary courts so heedlessly under the two cardinals, and for whose removal all venal officers had so insistently called during the Fronde.

Although Colbert had been dead for six years before the last intendant was finally established in Brittany in 1689, the generalization of these permanent, resident agents of central government in the provinces was inseparable from his work. The use of commissioners with wide powers over justice, police, and finances had a long history, and had become more frequent over the early seventeenth century. Previous intendants, however, had usually been appointed to deal with limited and extraordinary situations. They had mostly been charged with securing funds for war, and containing the unrest provoked by such demands. These would remain essential duties, but Colbert saw their role as much wider. Initially they sometimes needed the support of provincial governors, especially in provinces like Brittany or Languedoc, where representative estates retained tax-raising powers and therefore the capacity to bargain. But Colbert's intendants, largely his own clients and enjoying his unequivocal support, were soon able to make clear that they were not there to negotiate. They were there to state the king's requirements, and to recommend rewards for those who complied promptly. And, as magnates abandoned their old power bases for the even greater rewards of the Court, the intendants enabled the king to build up an unprecedented monopoly of patronage reaching into the remotest parts of his kingdom.

Government under Colbert

The key to this system was local knowledge. Colbert's appetite for it was insatiable. He expected all intendants to write to him at least once a week with their appraisals and recommendations; and periodically he launched general enquiries into specific problems, such as a census of venal offices of 1664, or a search for usurpers of nobility begun in 1666. Colbert wanted to know, so far as was possible, the complete state of the king's resources. His 'grand design', in which he was inspired by the work of Richelieu, was to seek every opportunity of maximizing these resources. Basically this meant both enriching the king's subjects and taxing them more effectively; but no general theory underlay this tireless quest. Whereas he tried to diminish privileges which shrank the number of taxpayers (hence his attempts to reduce the number of venal office-holders and false nobles) he would just as readily extend privileges elsewhere if they seemed likely to create wealth. Thus he granted a number of manufacturing monopolies, and created trading companies with exclusive rights to French commerce with the East and West Indies, the northern seas, and the Levant. Colbert believed that the king should and could act positively to promote the prosperity of his realms. For almost a quarter of a century he sought actively to stimulate French economic activity. Yet he did not believe that what could be achieved was limitless. Wealth was ultimately measurable in precious metals, whose quantity in the world was finite. As the largest and most populous kingdom in Europe, France had a 'natural' right to the lion's share she did not yet have. Trade, therefore, was 'a perpetual combat in peace and war among the nations of Europe as to who should win the most of it'.[3] The products and services of foreign rivals must be kept out of French markets by tariffs and exclusion, while French products must force themselves upon these same rivals. War was in the logic of such policies. So whereas, as superintendent of the king's buildings, Colbert was reluctant to spend money on Versailles, he did not stint on fortifications or harbours to boost and protect the king's power.

---

[3] Quoted in C. W. Cole, *Colbert and a Century of French Mercantilism* (2 vols., New York, 1939), i. 343.

And as (from 1669) secretary of state for the navy, he built up a fleet, underpinned by policies for manpower, munitions, and forests, which by 1680 was possibly the strongest in Europe. Nor was there any doubt who it was primarily directed against. For Colbert, France's natural enemies were her commercial rivals—which meant the English, but above all the economic superpower of the day, the Dutch.

A warrior king

Although his personal rule began in the glow of peace, Louis XIV dreamed from the start of military glory. 'I saw . . . wars', he later reminisced,[4] 'as a vast field where at any moment there might arise great occasions to distinguish myself'. During the first few years of his personal rule he lost no opportunity to pick diplomatic quarrels and demand deference from other rulers. Then, in 1665, there arose a genuine pretext for a full-scale conflict. The death of Philip IV of Spain, leaving the unhealthy son of a second marriage as his heir, allowed French diplomats to manufacture a claim on behalf of their queen to inherit the Spanish Netherlands by right of 'devolution' to the child of a first marriage—especially since the huge cash dowry agreed in 1659 had never been paid. The claim was outrageously specious, but when the Spanish treated it as such, French armies invaded Flanders with the king at their head (1667). Only a secret proposal by the new Emperor Leopold of Austria that they should divide the whole Spanish empire between them when (as seemed likely at any moment) Charles II of Spain should die, persuaded Louis XIV to break off the war with modest territorial gains. But by then his aggressive behaviour had alarmed the English and the Dutch, hitherto sworn enemies, into an alliance to preserve Spanish rule in the southern Netherlands.

The king was outraged. Despite their Protestantism, their republicanism, and their commercial rivalry, he had been prepared to support the Dutch against England and their former Spanish masters. Now they had betrayed him. From the moment peace was concluded

[4] *Mémoires*, 142.

in 1668, accordingly, Louis XIV began to work towards the diplomatic isolation of the Republic in preparation for an all-out attack. When Charles II of England offered a secret alliance in return for subsidies and a promise to convert to Catholicism, the occasion seemed heaven-sent. It was too soon for Colbert, who thought another 7–8 years were needed to restore the finances ravaged by previous wars to full health; but the king was now under the growing influence of Le Tellier's bellicose son and designated successor as secretary for war, Louvois. Aware, as Colbert sometimes forgot, that 'His Majesty must not be served any better than he wants to be,'[5] Louvois encouraged the king's warlike dreams. When Colbert tried to moderate them he almost found himself dismissed. By the beginning of 1672 he had accepted that war was inevitable, and that he would need to find the resources to pay for it. At the end of March the king joined his armies to lead an onslaught which he was convinced the impertinent republican 'cheese mongers' would be unable to resist.

He was right: unwilling until the last minute to believe the French would attack them, the Dutch were militarily unprepared. They lost a string of fortresses, and the province of Holland was only saved by a man-made flood when the dykes were deliberately opened. Even then the republic offered to surrender all that the French had conquered; but Louis XIV disdainfully returned to France to await an unconditional surrender. The unexpected effect was to galvanize them into defiance. The 22-year-old Prince of Orange, untested heir to the command of the republic's armies, was swept to power by a wave of popular patriotic defiance. William III, a general more dogged than talented, was to prove Louis XIV's nemesis repeatedly down to his death in 1702. He at once went onto the attack, and this began to persuade other rulers that French power was not perhaps irresistible. As the fighting degenerated into a stalemate of sieges, Dutch diplomacy and subsidies were patiently deployed to build up an anti-French coalition. Within a year, the emperor, Spain, and a number of smaller powers were coming together to join the Republic in resisting further French expansion; and in 1674 Charles II of England was compelled by domestic pressure to withdraw from his French alliance.

[5] Quoted in P. Sonnino, *Louis XIV and the Origins of the Dutch War* (Cambridge, 1986), 96.

As a result, Louis XIV gained nothing from his war against the Dutch. When the two original antagonists concluded peace at Nijmegen in 1678 it was France which made all the concessions. By then the focus of operations had long been further up the Rhine, and Europe had learnt that French ambition might be contained by a coalition. But French war aims had shifted with the widening of the conflict, and in this perspective the peace of 1678 proved perhaps the greatest triumph of Louis XIV's entire reign. For when Spain was lured into the conflict, he was given the perfect pretext for renewed incursions into the southern Netherlands, and for overrunning the indefensible landlocked province of Franche Comté. At the peace, the latter was finally ceded to France, along with remaining Spanish enclaves in Artois, and a number of strategic towns in Flanders. The insolent republicans of Holland might remain unbowed; and a marriage alliance of 1678 between William III and a Stuart princess in line for the English throne was ominous for the future. But the war had produced a vast extension of Louis XIV's realms at the expense of the Habsburgs, he had been present at a number of successful sieges, and felt entirely justified in accepting the city of Paris' suggestion that he should be known henceforth as Louis the Great.

Domestic dissidence

Although he was relentlessly hard-working, Louis XIV loved to be depicted as effortlessly successful. The first twenty-five years of his personal rule witnessed a determined effort to glorify the achievements of the 'sun king' (outshining the mere 'planet king' of Spain) with a lavish programme of building and patronage of the arts and sciences. The king was also anxious to appear as the serene restorer of order after the domestic chaos of mid-century. That was, indeed, his genuine ambition, but the reality fell short of it. The 1660s were a difficult decade economically, and there were outbursts of popular unrest over taxation in every year except 1667 and 1668. The Dutch war, lasting longer than anyone expected, renewed financial pressures not seen since Mazarin's time. Colbert was forced to reactivate many of the expedients he had tried to abandon, such as the creation of new venal offices and blackmail of their holders. Above all he imposed new taxes, including an extension of the salt monopoly and a stamp duty on all official paper. The result, in 1675, was a massive series of revolts along the entire western seaboard, already suffering from the cessation of trade with the Dutch. The magistrates of the parlements of Rennes and Bordeaux lost control so totally that they were suspected of complicity with the rebels. These upheavals echoed the anti-fiscal disturbances during earlier wars, but this time there were seasoned regular troops to use against them. A brutal military terror in which thousands died was followed up by billeting the soldiers on the better-off citizens of the provincial capitals, while their sovereign courts were exiled to remote small towns. More systematic than previous repressions, the example did much to ensure that revolts did not recur, even during the infinitely harsher and more extortionate later years of the reign.

The persistence of popular disobedience reinforced the king's instinctive suspicion of any potential rebels and 'republicans'. Mazarin had taught him particularly to mistrust the well-connected religious clique known as Jansenists, whose persistent refusal to acknowledge papal and episcopal condemnations of the writings of a Flemish bishop who had died in 1638 had raised knotty doctrinal and jurisdictional problems throughout the 1640s and 1650s. The young monarch understood few details of these quarrels, but in his eyes the refusal of Jansenist writers and the nuns of their spiritual headquarters, the abbey of Port-Royal, to make an unequivocal declaration of orthodoxy looked like inexcusable defiance of legitimate authority. Royal pressure, with papal support, brought about a truce in these conflicts under the 'peace of the church' of 1669. But the crypto-Calvinism which continued to be imputed to the Jansenists kept suspicions alive in a decade when the king's principal enemy was a Protestant republic.

For overtly Protestant subjects the situation was far worse. Although toleration was guaranteed to them under the edict of Nantes (1598), the million-strong Huguenots had a long record of armed rebellion, and were presumed to sympathize with their regicide and republican co-religionists in England and Holland. Catholic opinion was united in its disapproval of the privileges vouchsafed to them by the edict, even though since 1629 these had amounted to little more than the right to freedom of worship in the privacy of their 'temples'. Initially the young king took pride in respecting this situation. His grandfather Henri IV, he declared, had loved the Huguenots, his father had feared them, but he did neither. He was determined, however, to do them no further favours, and the letter of the law was almost invariably interpreted against them throughout the 1660s, to bring about professional exclusions, impediments to baptisms, marriages, and burials, and destruction of churches. When the Dutch war brought some unexpected respite, the Huguenots proclaimed ostentatious loyalty, but resisted cash incentives now offered for conversion to Catholicism. And so the king's triumphal mood of 1679 brought a return to judicial harrassment. Two decades of pressure had only produced a marginal fall in Huguenot numbers, and for a king seemingly able to impose his will on Europe it was an embarrassment not to be able to enforce religious conformity on his own subjects. And, increasingly at odds with the pope over their respective authority in the French church, and shown up by his own (diplomatically well-motivated) reluctance to join the emperor in a crusade against Turkish advances in the Balkans, he was anxious to demonstrate his Catholic zeal. Accordingly in 1681 Protestants began to be selectively subjected to the rigours of billeting—the notorious *dragonnades*. Despite severe prohibitions, many fled the kingdom to escape them, horrifying the Protestant countries to which they went with their stories. But wherever *dragonnades* occurred they produced thousands of apparent conversions, and by 1685 it was just possible for the king and his ministers to believe that the problem had been solved and there were no more Protestants left in France. This, at any rate, was the pretext for the edict of Fontainebleau, which revoked the edict of Nantes in October 1685.

The chorus of Catholic approval and celebration was deafening. Only the pope, at variance with Louis XIV over other matters, was lukewarm in his commendation. Nevertheless it was the most disastrous single decision of the reign. As a result of it, 140,000–160,000 religious refugees left the kingdom between 1685 and 1690, carrying with them an image of the king of France as a cruel and bigoted tyrant. Those who went to Holland used Dutch distribution networks to disseminate a penetrating critique of absolute monarchy and its claims which reached far beyond sympathetic Protestant countries, and eventually penetrated back into the intellectual life of France itself. The exodus signalled a decade of economic disruption in the areas left by the refugees, and Huguenot skills and energies permanently benefited the economies of the lands where they settled, among them some of France's most formidable competitors. The diplomatic consequences were equally damaging: the Calvinist elector of Brandenburg forsook his French alliance, decisively shifting the balance against France in Germany; while the shock to Protestant opinion in England did much to tip the scales against the catholiciz-ing James II, and so prepare for his replacement by Louis XIV's arch-enemy, William III. It was not even as if French Protestantism was eliminated. Most Huguenots were unable to leave the country, and persecution only made some of them more fanatical, especially in rural areas. In the Cevennes of Languedoc, where there were few Catholics, the economic hardships and renewed fiscal pressures of the 1690s made the zeal of Catholic persecutors eventually intolerable. In 1702, the murder of one of them marked the outbreak of a full-scale guerrilla war of resistance: the war of the *Camisards*. It lasted for two years and tied down an army of 30,000 at a time of renewed inter-national warfare. The conflict was eventually contained, but more by negotiation than force; and the survival of French Protestantism, despite all Louis XIV's efforts, was symbolized a few weeks before his death by the first general synod since the revocation, held 'in the desert'. Huguenot ministers would continue to be hanged, and their faithful followers sent to the galleys, for two more generations; but French Protestantism had survived the hostility of the most powerful monarch who had ever ruled the kingdom.

The arrogance of power

The revocation was only the most spectacular assertion of Louis XIV's seemingly limitless pretensions in the decade after the peace of Nijmegen. Triumph though it was, the peace disappointed him, and he dismissed Pomponne, the minister who had negotiated it. It is true that the more ostentatious routines of royal life began to be muted in the 1680s. In 1682 the Court was finally established at Versailles, and by the time the queen died the next year her husband had ceased to frequent the mistresses who had outshone and humiliated her almost since her arrival in France. His regular companion was now the pious Mme de Maintenon, who had been governess to the children of earlier mistresses; and soon after the queen's death he married her morganatically. Under her influence he became genuinely more devout himself—as his Protestant subjects had good cause to regret. But none of this made him a more obedient son of the institutional church. The relentless search for new revenues during the Dutch war had led him in 1673 to seek an extension of the regalian rights whereby the crown enjoyed the revenues of vacant episcopal sees. His aim was to levy them uniformly throughout the kingdom rather than, as up till then, mainly in the north. But two southern bishops objected, appealed to Rome, and Innocent XI took up the case. Intransigence on both sides soon raised momentous general principles, and in 1682 the king convoked an extraordinary general assembly of the French clergy which proclaimed four 'Gallican articles' strictly circumscribing the pope's temporal authority within France, and hinted at more general limits. In response, Rome refused canonical confirmation of new bishops; and throughout the 1680s the Most Christian King found his relations with the visible head of the church deadlocked. Louis XIV did not give way, occupied the papal enclave of Avignon, and three popes later a more accommodating pontiff at last accepted the French position (1693) . Throughout the quarrel Rome's only supporters among a supine French clergy had been Jansenists, reviving all the old suspicions in the royal mind. The peace of the church intended to lay them to rest therefore lasted barely more than a decade, and by the early 1680s leading Jansenists, like the Huguenots they loved to denounce, were leaving for exile beyond the king's reach.

Yet the king was increasingly unwilling to recognize clear limits to that reach. Dissatisfied with the territorial gains of 1679, he spent the next five years fabricating jurisdictional claims to vulnerable territories along the fragmented eastern frontier. Special courts were established, called 'chambers of reunion' to review the status of isolated enclaves of Spanish or imperial territory and seek precedents for French suzerainty. They never failed to find them, whereupon these 'dependencies' would be occupied and rapidly fortified. The climax of this policy of piecemeal strategic annexations came in 1681 when the free imperial city of Strasbourg accepted French 'protection'. A French army of 180,000 men, which had remained on a war footing after 1679, made any thought of resistance fruitless. Besides, the emperor, whose rights were most challenged by these acts of

undeclared war, was preoccupied by rebellion in Hungary, and Turkish advances in the Balkans which only stopped when they reached
the gates of Vienna in 1683. Spain for its part tried to resist French
aggression by declaring war, only to lose Luxembourg in 1684 as a
result. Nevertheless the siege of Vienna proved a turning point. It was
raised by an imperial army commanded by the king of Poland, and
the Turkish host melted away. The emperor now had some freedom
to turn west, buoyed by a groundswell of German resentment at
continued French advances. Louis XIV, who in 1683 had perhaps had
dreams of succeeding to an imperial crown snatched from the
Habsburgs by infidels, was forced to recognize that his moment of
maximum advantage had passed. He chose to consolidate his gains
before the Austrians imposed final defeat on the Turks; and by the
truce of Regensburg (1684) he secured provisional recognition for
twenty years of his gains since 1679 at both imperial and Spanish
expense. In return he promised no more attempted reunions during
the same period.

The truce of Regensburg marked the high point of French territorial expansion under Louis XIV. But all parties were anxious about
its provisional character, and the princes of Germany sought further
security in forming a defensive alliance, the League of Augsburg. The
Revocation of the edict of Nantes ensured that France's last major ally
in Germany, Brandenburg, joined it in 1686. The emperor, now victorious in the east and with the empire unprecedentedly united
behind him, was able to block a French candidate for the archbishopric of Cologne and stiffen the resistance of a new elector palatine to
French dynastic claims on a share of his inheritance. Colbert had died
in 1683, and with him no longer there to urge caution on the king and
Louvois, it was decided that growing imperial confidence must be
thwarted by forcibly turning the truce of 1684 into a permanent
peace. The means was to be a lightning occupation of the Rhineland;
and the second half of 1688 presented a seemingly ideal moment. The
headlong attempts of James II to catholicize England had produced
appeals from beleaguered Protestants for the intervention of William
III. The French could have prevented this by striking into Germany
through the Netherlands, but they saw more advantage in letting the
Dutch commander sail into a probable civil war beyond the Channel.
It proved another disastrous miscalculation. While the French
armies united Germany against them over the winter of 1688–9 by

ferociously ravaging the Rhineland, James II abandoned his throne, and William III was able to bring the combined wealth and power of the British kingdoms and the Dutch Republic into a grand coalition against France. Louis XIV would win no more easy victories. The rest of his reign would be an uneven struggle to hold on to the gains of his earlier years.

The Nine Years War

It was 1672 over again. A war intended to end in glory within months ran on for years; but this time there were no compensations. And the conflict coincided with some of the worst natural disasters of the century. In 1692 and 1693 there were massive harvest failures followed by acute famine and epidemics in many parts of the kingdom. Over the years 1693 and 1694 the population fell by almost two million. Yet this depleted economic base was forced to bear the burden of financing a war funded on the other side by the massive resources raised by the credit of the commercial maritime powers. All the mid-century expedients eschewed by Colbert, and only partially revived against his better judgement during the Dutch war, were now fully reactivated: indirect taxes on every conceivable commodity and transaction, the sale and regular manipulation of ever-increasing numbers of offices, unprecedented sales of annuities (*rentes*) and in 1695 a new, direct poll tax, the capitation, from which even nobles enjoyed no exemption. And one of the main casualties of the war was the one expensive weapon on which Colbert had always been willing to spend—the navy. Since his death his son and successor Seignelay had maintained the pace of naval construction and training, and the successful landing of an army in Ireland in 1689, and a victorious encounter with the Dutch off Beachy Head the next year, seemed to vindicate the effort of a generation. But by the end of 1690 Seignelay was dead, and within eighteen months an Anglo-Dutch force had scattered the main French fleet within sight of its home shores at La Hogue (1692). The king professed himself undeterred, but from that moment French maritime strategy began to shift from battle fleets to privateering, and what was left of Colbert's navy was sent to prey on Dutch and British trade, far from the narrow seas. Its impact in this role was not negligible, with 5,700 enemy vessels taken in the course of the war; but there were none of the glorious victories that the king relished so much.

Nor was the record on land much better. After the battle of the Boyne (1690) French troops and their *protégé* James II were driven out of Ireland. Easy early victories in the Rhineland were partly reversed after a French army surrendered occupied Mainz (1689). Most fighting now took place in the Netherlands, always Louis XIV's most cherished territorial objective, but the one conquest that William III (even more than its Spanish sovereign) was determined to deny him. William was defeated in several extremely bloody battles, but always came back. Uncertain of winning, his French antagonist stopped campaigning in person after 1693. Only on secondary fronts against weak opponents, in Savoy and Catalonia, did French troops make significant progress, but by then the effect was merely to bring long-drawn-out peace negotiations to a conclusion. At the peace of Ryswick (1697) Louis XIV was forced to recognize that many of the international objectives which he had pursued for almost three decades were unachievable. Most of the territories annexed in the reunions were surrendered. Of the gains of that period, only Strasbourg was now universally recognized as French. Lorraine, an independent duchy embedded in French territory and occupied and exploited by the French ever since 1670 in the hope of ultimate annexation, had to be given up. The proud war aims of 1688 were simply forgotten, nor did the French raise serious objections when in a supplementary agreement of 1698, the Spaniards allowed the Dutch to garrison a series of 'barrier fortresses' in the southern Netherlands.

The peace came about through exhaustion on all sides. The scale of the struggle, the size of the forces involved, and the cost, were all unprecedented. And whereas the allies emerged with positive gains to show, France had almost none. But even before this outcome became clear, a number of Louis XIV's own subjects had begun to question the attitudes and policies that had brought the kingdom such tribulations. They were not rebels: apart from desperate Protestants, everybody now realized that rebellion was the surest way to stop the king's ears. Most of them were in fact courtiers, and they hoped to change royal policies by persuasion rather than confrontation. This in itself was recognition of how far Louis XIV had changed the political reflexes of his subjects. Nevertheless these critics deplored much of the drift of his personal rule. They condemned government by will and force, rather than by custom and negotiation. They lamented the aggressive promotion of industrial and commercial advantage, and neglect of the land and those who worked it. Above all, they questioned the reckless pursuit of military glory without counting its cost. Among them were churchmen, like Fénelon, magnates like the dukes de Chevreuse or Beauvillier, and even warriors like the great military engineer Vauban. They expected little enough from a king set in his ways as he approached 60, but they placed all their hopes in the ultimate succession of his grandson the duke of Burgundy. Members of the circle had been entrusted with the young prince's education, and they hoped to mould him in a different image from that of the reigning king. It was a blow to them when Fénelon, whose achievements as Burgundy's tutor were recognized in 1695 by appointment to the archbishopric of Cambrai, became involved with Quietism, a mystical cult recently (1687) condemned by the pope. In 1697, as peace was made, he was exiled to Cambrai and remained there for the rest of his life. Peace, in any case, removed the strongest reasons for discontent; and the events of the next few years made clear that most of the major princes of Europe, including Louis XIV, were determined that it should be a lasting one.

The Spanish Succession

This is shown by the frenzied efforts made between 1697 and 1700 to avoid a further war over the Spanish Succession. Having defied expectations for over thirty years, Charles II of Spain was now visibly in terminal decline, with no heir apparent. The treaty of 1668 for partitioning the Spanish empire between the Bourbons and Austrian Habsburgs had not survived the intervening decades of conflict between the two houses, so both maintained credible claims on the entire inheritance. The Nine Years War had taught Louis XIV, however, that Europe would never accept so vast an extension of French power, and he now sought ways of persuading Leopold I that the Habsburg claim was equally unacceptable. Buoyed up by continuing victories over the Turks, the emperor was in no mood to compromise; but the French king believed that without the financial support of the maritime powers the Austrian Habsburgs would not be able to fight for their claims. This meant that France must negotiate first with William III; and he, too, was anxious to avoid conflict in ways which kept France out of the southern Netherlands. Accordingly, in 1698 the two rulers rapidly agreed that they would support the candidacy for the Spanish throne of the young grandson of the emperor who was elector of Bavaria. Unfortunately the next year the elector died. Under a second partition treaty which was immediately negotiated, France agreed to recognize the emperor's younger son the archduke Charles as heir to Spain, the Indies, and the Netherlands, leaving Spanish possessions in Italy to the dauphin. The French hope was to exchange these territories almost immediately for the duchies of Lorraine and Savoy; but this took no account of the fact that the Italian dependencies of Spain were the only territories of Charles II's patrimony which really interested the Austrians. There was no hope that Leopold I, who made a victorious peace with the Turks that year, would accept this treaty, on which he was not in any case consulted. Not consulted, either, were the Spaniards whose empire was thus being disposed of. Their reaction was to blight the whole project by inducing their moribund king to make a will. In it he left his entire dominions to Louis XIV's second grandson, Philip duke of Anjou. If this disposition was refused, the whole bequest was to go to the archduke Charles.

This will became public when Charles II finally died in November 1700. The last revenge of a king on whom he had preyed from the moment of his accession, it left Louis XIV with no real choice. He had to accept, even if that meant tearing up the second partition treaty. And war was far from inevitable even then. The emperor could not credibly contest the will without the support of the maritime powers, but they both accepted it. As so often before, however, Louis XIV miscalculated how foreigners would view his actions. He might plead that French law put it beyond his power to exclude Philip V from the French line of succession, but his insistence on proclaiming the fact raised fears abroad that French dreams of 'universal' monarchy had not been abandoned. He might feel honour-bound to recognize the right of James II's son to the British thrones when the Stuart exile died in 1701, but this was to deny the legitimacy of William III's title and the revolution from which he derived it, in contravention of promises given at Ryswick. And if flooding the Spanish Netherlands with French troops could be portrayed as securing the inheritance of a now-friendly monarch, the Dutch barrier fortresses were out-flanked, and the republic left as defenceless as in 1672. And so, although William III died in 1702, by then the former coalition was coming together once more, this time with the objective (which Charles II's will had been designed to prevent) of partitioning the Spanish empire so that France should never gain control, direct or indirect, of the European dependencies her rulers had always coveted. Later, after French armies suffered an unprecedented string of defeats, allied war-aims expanded to encompass the expulsion of Philip V from the throne of Spain and his replacement by the archduke Charles. The king of France, meanwhile, had war aims for the first time forced upon him. He fought to keep Philip V on the throne in Madrid and, later, to hold on to the territorial gains which it had taken him a lifetime to accumulate.

Louis XIV's last war proved longer and even more terrible than its predecessor. As before, it was war on a worldwide scale, with clashes throughout the Americas and as far away as India. More than any of the reign's previous wars, this was a conflict about trade. At stake was commercial access to Spain's worldwide empire, which the maritime powers feared might become a French monopoly. The war at sea was fought mainly by privateers on all sides, and the 2,800 enemy ships taken by French corsairs represent perhaps the greatest consistent success of the war. As always for Louis XIV, however, the sea was secondary, and he poured most of his resources into the army. Yet despite bringing almost 400,000 men under arms at the height of the conflict, he now faced unprecedentedly numerous opponents who were equally well organized and in some respects better equipped. The British and Dutch under Marlborough, and the Imperials under Prince Eugene were able to defeat the French in open battle for the first time at Blenheim (1704) in Germany; then at Turin (1706) in Italy, and Ramillies (1706) and Oudenarde (1708) in the Netherlands. The archduke Charles was also sent to Spain, where the ever-dissident Catalans offered him a bridgehead against Philip V. As early as 1705 the French had begun to negotiate, but the triumphant allies were in no hurry to settle too soon. Only towards the end of 1708, with Lille in their hands and France wide open to invasion, did they come seriously to the table; and then it was only to dictate terms.

In 1697 France had been fought to a standstill. In 1708 she had been defeated. Louis XIV now offered to surrender Lille and Strasbourg, and to recognize the archduke as Charles III of Spain. The latter's older brother, since 1705 the emperor Joseph, would take Spain's European territories. In other words Louis XIV offered to abandon the dreams and ambitions of his entire reign. But the allies now wanted even more. They demanded the surrender of a number of 'cautionary towns' to guarantee that the French king would keep his word. Above all they required him to provide troops to help drive his own grandson out of Spain. But this was a humiliation too far, and he saw no alternative but to fight on. The once-proud absolute monarch even issued an appeal to his hard-pressed subjects for their support: 'I wish my people to know . . .' he wrote, 'that they would enjoy peace if it depended on my will alone to procure them a benefit which they so rightly desire, but which must be won by renewed efforts, since the immense conditions which I would have agreed to are useless for the re-establishment of public tranquillity'.

The war effort

Some of the depredations of the Nine Years War were made up for with remarkable speed between 1697 and 1702. As harvests improved, trade recovered and credit became cheaper. Venality ceased to expand, and there were punitive prosecutions of financiers and government contractors—a sure sign that a sustained period of peace was now expected. The Spanish king's will blighted these signs of promise, and even before the coalition re-formed the search resumed for 'extraordinary affairs' to pay for renewed hostilities. Between 1702 and 1708 the credit of the king's subjects was squeezed to the limit, either through the sale of new *rentes* or by forcing office-holders to borrow in order to buy off various expedients of fiscal blackmail. By 1708 the only offices that anybody would buy were ones created at the expense of others, and even then the buyers would usually be holders of the ones threatened. Indirect taxes on commodities and transactions also rose to unprecedented levels. Coinage was routinely debased, and from 1701 the government began to pay bills in unsecured paper (*billets de monnaie*), which it made legal tender, to little effect when they began to lose value. The king even melted down his own plate to make coins. By all these efforts the cost of the war was borne with more or less difficulty down to 1708. But by then, as military disasters accumulated, the controller-general of finances Chamillart was in despair, and begged to be relieved. He was replaced by Desmaretz, a nephew of Colbert who hoped to return to the more rigid financial principles of his uncle. His first two years, however, were spent coping with the results of natural as well as military disaster.

If the harvest and winter of 1693–4 were the worst climatic catastrophe of the seventeenth century, those of 1708–9 were the worst of the eighteenth. Frosts were so severe that seeds were killed in the ground; all watercourses, and even the sea, froze; and at Versailles itself the royal family was unable to keep warm. 'It has never been so cold in the memory of man,' wrote the duchess d'Orléans in January 1709,[6] 'nobody recalls a Winter like it.' Two months later it was still going on, with transport and milling immobilized, and thousands dying in the streets. Even when warmer weather returned, it was too late to ripen much of the harvest, so that famine conditions persisted well into 1710. Public order broke down in many places, and in Paris the dauphin was attacked in his coach. The resulting slowdown in economic activity had a catastrophic effect on tax returns. 'To speak truly,' reminisced Desmaretz seven years later,[7] 'the armies of the state were kept on foot by a kind of miracle in the year 1709.'

All Europe was affected by the disaster, so the allies found themselves in no position to deliver a knockout blow. At Malplaquet in September, where 35,000 men fell, the French withdrew, but in good order, and the allied momentum was stopped. The allies now placed their hopes in French financial exhaustion, but in this too they were deluded. For some years thoughtful analysts, including the veteran military engineer Vauban, had been advocating a direct tax on all incomes, a 'royal tenth'. Chamillart had thought it impossible to impose, but in 1710 Desmaretz introduced it for the duration of the war. Together with 24 million raised from office-holders for the abandonment of the old *paulette* on heredity in 1709, he was able with the aid of the tenth to raise an extra 111 million between 1711 and 1714.

---

[6] *Princesse Palatine: une princesse allemande à la cour de Louis XIV* (Paris, 1962), 118.

[7] Quoted in A. de Boislisle (ed.), *Correspondance des contrôleurs-généraux avec les intendants des provinces* (3 vols., Paris, 1874–9), iii. 676.

And while France fought on, the allied coalition fell apart. The British Tories, who won the 1710 election, were committed to a quick 'peace without Spain'; and the next year the death of the emperor Joseph brought the archduke Charles to the imperial throne. The maritime powers no more wanted a Habsburg universal monarchy than a Bourbon one, and now sought a settlement that would divide the Spanish empire. When in July 1712 the French defeated Eugene at Denain, the coalition finally broke up. Peace negotiations, in progress since January at Utrecht, now became serious, and in April 1713 France made peace with all her enemies except the emperor Charles VI and his German satellites, who only settled at Rastadt eleven months later. Under this settlement, Philip V retained Spain and the Indies, but renounced his rights in the French succession. Most of Spain's European dependencies, in Italy and the Netherlands, went to the Austrians; and the Dutch kept their barrier fortresses. Yet the unprecedented efforts of Louis XIV's subjects since 1708 brought their master rewards that he had been prepared to surrender then. A Bourbon now sat securely on the throne of Spain. Although most of France's footholds in North America were lost to the British, who also demanded the destruction of the defences of Dunkirk (that nest of privateers), Lille was recovered, Strasbourg held, and, in posthumous revenge on his most inveterate enemy, Louis XIV was allowed to annex William III's old principality of Orange. It was still little enough to show for the generation of warfare so confidently launched in 1688. No wonder the dying king in 1715 confessed to his heir that he had loved war too much.

The final years

By then that heir was his last great grandson, a child of barely 5 years. The dauphin had predeceased his father at 50, in 1711. His son, that duke of Burgundy in whom reformers had placed so much hope, and now briefly did so again, died himself early in 1712. So in turn did his elder son. Devastated, the king sought to reinforce the succession in 1714 by admitting to it two legitimized sons of earlier mistresses, the duke du Maine and the count de Toulouse. There was general outrage at this contempt for the law by which the king himself sat on the throne; but it was a decision that could be (and was) reversed after his death. More difficult was his determination to impose the bull *Unigenitus* as a law of the state.

This was the king's solution to the problem of Jansenism. His renewed hostility to 'those Port-Royal people' after 1679 had driven most of their leaders into exile. But when French troops overran the southern Netherlands in 1701 they captured the papers of Pasquier Quesnel, the leader of a new generation of Jansenist polemicists. They revealed a Europe-wide network of Jansenist agents, and many still active in France. The king, now reconciled with Rome, urged the pope to issue new fulminations against them, and all the faithful were duly ordered to accept the bull *Vineam Domini* of 1705. With ominous rumblings about papal pretensions in France, the clergy and the parlements did so; but the ageing nuns of Port-Royal (forbidden to recruit newcomers since 1679) insisted on equivocating. As a result, in 1709 Port-Royal was closed down, and two years later the very buildings were levelled by explicit royal order. But this was still not enough for the devout king and his Jesuit confessor. They demanded that Clement XI issue a comprehensive condemnation of Jansenist doctrines in the form of a bull directed against the devotional writings of Quesnel. Louis XIV promised that there would be no jurisdictional resistance, and in 1713 a reluctant pope finally promulgated *Unigenitus*.

There followed the most sustained outburst of defiance (at least among Catholics) since 1675. The bishops objected, and the parlement prevaricated, all in the name of those very Gallican principles which the king had invoked against the pope in 1682. The apparatus of censorship was swamped by a flood of polemical pamphlets denouncing the 'constitution'. The fury into which the astounded king was thrown probably helped to bring on his final illness. Certainly when he died on 1 September 1715 it was after a series of angry and violent threats against the parlement, and in the midst of preparations to convoke a special clerical assembly to enforce full acceptance of *Unigenitus* as a law of church and state. Jansenists, whom he had identified as his most dangerously 'republican' subjects in 1661, were openly flouting his will again as he lay dying, and they would set the agenda for domestic politics for most of the equally long reign of his successor.

The great reign and its legacy

Louis XIV might not have thought so, but even the opposition which he encountered during his last year on the throne was a paradoxical tribute to his achievement. It was the product of a new generation which, thanks to him, could not remember the sort of disorders which had flickered their last in the 1670s, and had no fear of their return. And the jurists and clerics who resisted him did so not to diminish or seek a share of his authority, but to preserve it against the claims within the kingdom of a foreign prince, the pope. They accepted, in other words, that the king of France was an absolute monarch who shared his power with nobody, and was only answerable to God for its exercise.

This doctrine was scarcely new when Louis XIV assumed personal power in 1661, but no king for over a century had been in a position to live up to it. Louis XIV, strong-willed, self-controlled, and long-lived, made the attempt. Thereby he established a working paradigm of monarchy which dazzled the rest of Europe and continued relatively unchanged in France for three generations after his death. The kingdom would be governed not from Paris, but Versailles; and the main agents of royal will in the provinces would be the intendants. The focus of politics would be at Court, but the magnates who dominated it socially would remain largely excluded from executive power: magistrates and career administrators would form the backbone of ministries down to the 1780s. The monarchy and its servants would remain largely committed to the policy objectives laid down by Louis XIV: continental hegemony, obstruction of the Habsburgs, territorial consolidation, state control of economic activity, religious uniformity. Time and cultural evolution would eventually lead increasing numbers of French subjects to question these principles; but they would never lack articulate and influential defenders until absolute monarchy itself collapsed.

The main problem with Louisquatorzian monarchy was that it required a Louis XIV to run it. Neither of his succeeding namesakes inherited his indispensable qualities. Both proved unable, for instance, to rise above the forces of Court factionalism and ministerial rivalry as he had, to give a consistent steer to government. And both were hobbled by problems which he bequeathed to them. They never escaped, above all, from the financial aftermath of the great wars between 1688 and 1713. Many debts contracted then were still being serviced three generations later, and were only liquidated by the Revolution. The debt represented by venal offices was now so great that it was impossible even to dream, as Colbert once had, of buying their holders out. Pursuit of the grandiose foreign policy traditions established before 1715 exacerbated the burden of debt steadily, until in 1788 the state collapsed under the strain.

Financial need in turn would provoke increasing opposition from the parlements, whom Louis XIV had not so much emasculated as ignored. The magistrates of Paris were stirring into renewed political activity over *Unigenitus* even before he died, and Jansenism would be the main issue in domestic politics for another half-century. It would only die away when the Jesuits whom Louis XIV had so consistently favoured were expelled from his former kingdom; and by then the struggle against a bull first issued at his personal insistence would have engendered ideologies of opposition that struck at the very foundations of absolute monarchy itself.

7

Politics: Louis XV

Julian Swann

According to pope Benedict XIV there was no greater proof for the
existence of providence than to see France prosper under the rule of
Louis XV. Few were as gentle or ironic as the pontiff in their assessment of the king. For the duke de Choiseul, who was the linchpin of
his government for more than a decade (1758–70), Louis XV was
'soulless' with the mind of a 'spiteful child'. Worse still 'he would, like
Nero, have been enchanted to watch Paris burn . . . but lacked the
courage to give the order.'[1] In the popular memory, the king is famous
for uttering the phrase 'after me the deluge', which, while almost
certainly apocryphal, conjures up an image of a monarch intelligent
enough to foresee the tragedy of 1789, but too lazy to do anything
about it. Napoleon, on the other hand, once declared that he 'found
the crown of France in the mud' and many have assumed that it was
Louis XV who let it drop. Mme de Pompadour was only the most
important of a string of mistresses, many of whom were little more
than girls housed in the *Parc aux cerfs* ('deer park') in circumstances
reminiscent of a brothel. Finally in 1769, the ageing monarch scandalized his subjects by falling for the charms of Mme du Barry, a
courtesan of ill-repute, who was installed in Versailles as his official
companion. With such a record, Louis XV has, not surprisingly, been
represented as the embodiment of vice, the very incarnation of the
abuses allegedly rotting the core of the old regime. It may therefore
come as a surprise to learn of the existence of another very different
interpretation of his reign. There is a venerable school of historical
scholarship which maintains that in his later years the king threw off
his lethargy, sponsoring reforms capable of saving the monarchy had

---

[1] J. P. Guicciadini and P. Bonnet (eds.) *Mémoires du Duc de Choiseul* (Paris, 1983), 192.

not a premature death cut short the experiment. That the historical reputation of Louis XV remains so contentious says much about both the troubled personality of the king and the long-term significance of his reign.

The regency, 1715–1723

Popular rejoicing greeted the news of the sun king's passing, but for a perceptive observer any sense of relief was liable to be tinged with apprehension. His successor was a child of 5 and previous royal minorities had been blighted by civil war. With the government close to bankruptcy, it would require a regent endowed with ability and luck to avoid a repetition. As the king was an orphan, it was the senior prince of the blood, his uncle Philippe duke d'Orléans, who would act as regent. Affable, intelligent, and a talented general, the regent was also a libertine and a rake who had fallen foul of the starchy atmosphere of Versailles during Louis XIV's twilight years. His unorthodox lifestyle even gave birth to vicious rumours accusing him of poisoning his relatives when tragedy struck the royal family in 1711–12. The old king treated these slurs with the contempt they deserved, but he never accorded Orléans his total confidence. Just prior to his death, Louis XIV drew up a secret will limiting the power of Orléans as regent while promoting that of his bastard sons, the duke du Maine and the count de Toulouse. His actions have been interpreted as a sop to Mme de Maintenon, permissible on the grounds that the wishes of a dead monarch were not binding on his successors. It is true that a similar testament written by Louis XIII had been ignored, but there was no guarantee that history would repeat itself.

In defusing the crisis, Orléans displayed his political flair. Hours after the king's death, he announced that a bed of justice would be held the next day, 2 September 1715, for the formal declaration of the regency. Rather than take chances, Orléans struck a deal with leading parlementaires by promising to restore their right of remonstrance before the registration of laws in return for annulling the will. When combined with the conspicuous deployment of troops and liberal dispensation of patronage to the other princes and Court grandees it was enough to ensure victory. The parlement of Paris, with the princes and the peers assembled, overturned Louis XIV's testament, recognizing instead the right of Orléans to the full title and powers of regent. Many years later a frustrated Louis XV bitterly reproached the regent's grandson, blaming Orléans for his difficulties with the parlements. It was an unjust reprimand. In 1715, after more than twenty sombre years of war, France was seething with discontent. The decision to undo Louis XIV's legislation of 1673 restricting the right of remonstrance was sensible and perceptive. It opened an important safety valve and won Orléans vital allies at a crucial moment.

The regent was equally dextrous in his handling of the grandees. The aristocratic thinkers of the Burgundy circle had been critical of Louis XIV's 'ministerial despotism' and in addition to their hopes of restoring the old nobility to political power had been discussing the summoning of an estates general. Orléans defused the threat with aplomb. He informed the grandees of their appointment to key positions on a series of seven new councils that became collectively known as the *polysynodie*. The councils, which included foreign affairs, finance, and the navy were not executive organs. They merely acted as discussion chambers, preparing reports and recommendations for the regency council where real power lay. Not surprisingly, initial enthusiasm soon waned and in 1718 they were abolished without dissent. Yet *polysynodie* had more than served its purpose by bringing potentially disruptive groups into government while the regent consolidated his grip on power.

An ability to balance the competing interests of the court factions was one of the regent's most telling assets, and he succeeded in persuading the powerful that cooperation with his government was more lucrative than opposition. The truth of this maxim was demonstrated by the treatment of the defeated bastards. In July 1717, the regent overturned Louis XIV's edict placing them in succession to the throne. A year later they were stripped of their 'royal' status and demoted to the level of peers. Orléans was generous in victory and Toulouse remained a trusted adviser on naval matters. Maine, on the other hand, was drawn into plotting against the regent with the Spanish ambassador, Cellamare. When the conspiracy was discovered, Maine, together with his equally compromised wife, was imprisoned in the Bastille.

As the struggle with the bastards demonstrated, the French succession had been in the balance since 1712 and Orléans had to tread carefully. If Louis XV succumbed to one of the all too prevalent childhood illnesses Europe faced a grave international crisis. According to the Salic law—one of the fabled fundamental laws of the kingdom—the crown passed to Philip V of Spain. The fear of a king reigning in both Madrid and Versailles had made his renunciation of the French throne one of the principal clauses of the peace of Utrecht. If the treaty was upheld, the crown passed to Orléans, an outcome with obvious attractions to the British and Dutch governments. Some historians have therefore been critical of the regent's foreign policy because of its emphasis upon an entente with the maritime powers consummated by the signing of the Triple alliance in 1717. The target of the new allies was Philip V who had launched a crusade to recapture Spanish possessions in Italy lost at Utrecht. Nothing revealed the new diplomatic order better than the sight of French troops marching into Spain in order to check him.

Yet the regent's diplomacy was not part of a cunning plan to advance the interests of the House of Orléans. France needed peace, not a quixotic expression of Bourbon family solidarity that would have almost certainly resulted in war with Austria and the maritime powers. Had Louis XV died then even the closest admirers of the regent realized that Philip V would be king. The most Orléans could hope for was to replace him in Madrid. The support of the maritime powers would be a huge advantage in these circumstances as all sides realized. However, if the regent occasionally dreamed of life in the Escorial, there is no evidence that he allowed his personal interests to conflict with those of Louis XV.

With peace abroad, Orléans was free to concentrate upon internal problems. The most pressing was a truly astronomical state debt of some 2,000 million *livres*. Following the precedent set by Colbert and Louis XIV, he established a chamber of justice in 1716 to investigate the excess profits allegedly extorted by the financiers during the wars. The substantial sum of 220 million *livres* was raised, but it was still only a drop in the ocean of state debt. The chamber did, however, please the magistrates who served on it and the public who saw these despised 'fat cats' get their just deserts. Although welcome, something more substantial than a public relations triumph was required, especially after the tenth tax lapsed in 1717. It was in these circumstances that the regent displayed the unconventional side to his character by placing his confidence in the Scottish adventurer, John Law.

In a meteoric career, Law rose from obscurity to a brief and eventful dominance of the kingdom's financial affairs. With official encouragement, he established a private bank in 1716 and began to issue bank notes. These were subsequently accepted as legal tender, and the phenomenal success of the enterprise persuaded the regent to accept its conversion into a state bank in December 1718. With external peace and strong demographic and economic growth, the moment was propitious for such an experiment. As the paper currency began to circulate it gave an inflationary boost to the economy and, as Law intended, interest rates fell. He then turned his attention to the second major plank of his scheme, the creation of a monopoly trading company—the Mississippi company—financed by his bank. An already grandiose project was rendered even more imposing by the acquisition of the rights of the general farm and the tobacco monopoly. To crown the edifice, the bank also took over responsibility for state debt.

Law was clearly seeking to emulate the banking and commercial ventures of the English and the Dutch. Unfortunately for France, his scheme was overambitious and his economic analysis riddled with flaws. Convinced of the benefits to be gained from the increased circulation of money, he printed ever larger numbers of bank notes, quickly outstripping the productive capacity of the economy. Nor was he helped by the regent's proclivity for scattering the company's shares like confetti as part of his constant battle to keep the Court grandees on his side. A speculative frenzy, soon followed by rampant inflation was the predictable result with company shares reaching dizzy heights on unsubstantiated rumours that the Mississippi delta would be Louis XV's El Dorado.

Here alone were enough reasons for the project to falter and there were plenty of political obstacles to add to the equation. By promoting Law, the regent alienated the Court bankers and farmers-general as well as the head of the council of finance, the influential duke de Noailles. The parlement also raised its voice against Law's untested schemes and was exiled to Pontoise for its pains. Yet despite desperate efforts to shore up the bank's credit, the speculative bubble burst in May 1720. For those perceptive enough to convert their paper into more tangible assets before the crash, the scheme brought fabulous profits. Similarly those individuals or institutions that had been able to repay debt with inflated notes had reason to thank Law. The state itself had prospered in this fashion, reducing its debt substantially in the process. Of course, for every beneficiary of Law's system there were countless victims left holding a currency not worth the paper it was printed on. As a result, he has been blamed for the monarchy's subsequent inability to establish a state bank. In reality, the problem was more profound. Years of broken promises and fiscal expediency had created a perfectly legitimate suspicion of the crown's fiscal operations. Without public accountability, hopes of transplanting English or Dutch banking practice to French soil were doomed to failure. Once Law was exiled, French financial administration continued as before.

Religious divisions posed a no less perplexing problem for the regent. The bull *Unigenitus* condemning Jansenism was a poisonous gift from Louis XIV that had damaging repercussions throughout the reign of his successor. A religious sceptic, and by nature a conciliator, Orléans sought a compromise. Influential opponents of the bull, such as the archbishop of Paris, cardinal de Noailles, and the *parlementaire* priest Pucelle, were invited to sit on the council of conscience. Meanwhile pope Clement XI was approached in an ultimately vain attempt to persuade him to clarify disputed aspects of *Unigenitus*. What undermined the pursuit of peace in the church was the depth of religious feeling on both sides. In April 1717, over 3,000 clerics, including Noailles, and a majority of the theological faculty of the Sorbonne, appealed against *Unigenitus* to a general council of the church. Nothing was more certain to light the blue touch paper in Rome, and in September 1718 an outraged pope unleashed a rocket in the form of the encyclical, *Pastoralis Officii*, which excommunicated the appellants. He found staunch supporters in the French church, known as the *constitutionnaires*, who called for unequivocal acceptance of the 'constitution', as the bull was known. In sermons, pastoral letters, and polemical pamphlets the theological storm raged and with his policy of conciliation in tatters, the regent changed tack. In August 1720, he issued a declaration imposing silence on all disputes arising from *Unigenitus* and acted firmly against those who disobeyed. It was not a permanent solution, but the regent was spared further frustration by his premature death in December 1723. He had finally paid the price for a life of epic overindulgence. Yet Orléans deserves to be remembered as something more than a rake. Thanks to his equanimity and good sense, he had given France the most trouble-free regency in its history.

The 'golden age' of Fleury

Although Louis XV was crowned at Reims in October 1722, he was only just entering his teens and with the regent's death power passed to the duke de Bourbon. His brief ministry is primarily remembered for his decision to marry the king to Maria Leszczynska, daughter of the dethroned king of Poland, and it ended abruptly in December 1725 with the duke's exile to his chateau at Chantilly. His disgrace was the first independent act of the young king, who replaced him with his tutor, cardinal André-Hercule de Fleury. Orphaned at the age of 2, king of France and focus of the attendant regal and courtly paraphernalia at 5, Louis XV suffered a traumatic childhood that left him inclined to shyness, fatalism, and melancholy. The grandfatherly Fleury, already a venerable 73 in 1726, was an indispensable source of emotional support for his royal charge and Bourbon had made the mistake of trying to separate them. He was not alone in underestimating Fleury, who was commonly believed to be too old or unambitious to turn his hold over the king to advantage. It was a grave mistake because once in power he was almost impossible to dislodge. Acting as first minister, the cardinal directed the affairs of France for the next seventeen years. He had the complete confidence of Louis XV, and he kept a sharp eye on the activities of the secretaries of state by sitting in on their meetings with the king. Any minister unfortunate or foolhardy enough to cross Fleury risked dismissal, as the talented Chauvelin discovered to his cost in 1737.

In his approach to international politics, Fleury was generally pacific. Like the regent, he viewed the English alliance as the basis for European stability. Although the alliance between the two powers lapsed after 1731, they were able to maintain a mutually beneficial détente. France was thus free from the threat of hostile European coalitions that had brought her so close to defeat between 1689 and 1713. When war did break out over the disputed Polish succession in 1733, Fleury was able to draw maximum advantage.

The death of Augustus II provided the opportunity for the deposed Stanislas Leszczynski, now the father-in-law of Louis XV, to reclaim the throne. Poland formed part of France's traditional stable of secondary powers subsidized in order to threaten the flanks of Austria. If Stanislas could be re-established in Warsaw, it would be a major diplomatic coup, and would silence slanderous tongues who mocked the marriage of Louis XV and a minor Polish princess. What prevented this happy outcome was the intervention of Russia. Since Peter I's victory in the Great Northern War, Poland had been reduced to the level of a Russian protectorate. Empress Anna had no desire to see that position reversed, and she backed the rival candidacy of Augustus III of Saxony. With Russian aid, he soon worsted Stanislas, who took refuge in the port of Danzig. Fleury, who was astute enough to realize the futility of waging war in such circumstances, did no more than send a token force in an abortive attempt to relieve him. Instead, the war was fought against Russia's ally, Austria, in the traditional theatres of Germany and Italy. Helped by a renewed alliance with Spain, France won a series of rapid victories, forcing the emperor Charles VI to sue for peace. The defeated Stanislas was compensated with the duchy of Lorraine. It was a triumph for Fleury. An intendant arrived to administer the duchy, which became officially part of France on the death of Stanislas in 1766. There were other gains for the Bourbons in Italy, and the only cost to France was recognition of the pragmatic sanction, naming Maria Theresa, daughter of Charles VI, as sole heir to the Habsburg hereditary lands.

One short, successful war was the only interruption in an otherwise peaceful generation. Without needing to implement drastic reforms, the government was able to repair much of the damage inflicted by Louis XIV. The controllers-general, Dodun (1722–6) and, especially, Orry (1730–45), restored balance to government finances that were showing a modest annual surplus by the late 1730s. No less impressive was the stabilization of the French currency, the *livre tournois*, which after 1726 was no longer subject to manipulation by the crown. The development of a modern road network, which was one of the great ornaments of the age of Louis XV, also gathered pace under Fleury. Thanks to the painstaking efforts of chancellor d'Aguesseau, progress was made in judicial reform, primarily by ironing out inconsistencies in civil law. These were worthy achievements, but it has to be said that the cardinal's administration was profoundly conservative. With France still basking in her reputation as the continent's foremost military power a certain complacency was understandable, and while the ministry tinkered with the edges of the existing system, it never contemplated radical change.

Fleury's rule was therefore a period of relative calm. What stopped it from becoming soporific was the continuing furore surrounding *Unigenitus*. The regent's efforts to impose silence on clerical bickering had failed and the row continued with a powerful and influential group of bishops claiming that complete submission to the 'constitution' was essential for salvation. A small, but no less fervent number believed the very opposite and they were backed by a more substantial body of opinion in the parish clergy. An unshakeable faith in the righteousness of their cause was the inspiration for Jansenists throughout the eighteenth century. As a minority within the church, they might have been nothing more than a nuisance were it not for the fact that the opposition to *Unigenitus* was fed from other streams.

Most significantly, the bull offended those in the church and especially the parlements who were loyal to the Gallican tradition. The four articles promulgated by Louis XIV in 1682 had given legal expression to the widely held belief that the French church had rights and liberties independent of Rome. *Unigenitus*, with its clumsy phraseology, most strikingly in the notorious article 91 in which the pope reserved the theoretical right to excommunicate the king, challenged those principles and only Louis XIV's threats and coercion had persuaded the magistrates to register the bull. After his death, they were much less malleable and any alteration to its status risked provoking opposition.

Fleury had personally accepted *Unigenitus* without demur. He was not, however, a religious bigot. Like many others, he believed Jansenism to be a danger to church unity and acted accordingly. His strategy was to starve the movement of leadership, much as Louis XIII and Louis XIV had done with the Huguenots. Constant pressure was exerted upon leading appellants, notably cardinal de Noailles, with the aim of persuading them to accept the bull. Noailles spent more than a decade grappling with his conscience before finally capitulating in 1728. Other outspoken critics of *Unigenitus* were exiled to distant seminaries and, in the case of Soanen, bishop of Senez, deposed. Thereafter Fleury used his control of ecclesiastical preferments to ensure that only those of orthodox, preferably moderate opinions were promoted. Finally, he sought, not altogether success-fully, to suppress the publication of sermons and theological tracts that had done so much to fan the flames of controversy.

As these measures began to bite, the cardinal felt confident in his ability to end further quibbling by issuing a declaration, in March 1730, making *Unigenitus* a law of church and state. Opposition within the parlement of Paris was fierce. The Jansenists, led by Pucelle, played on the Gallican and legal sensibilities of their colleagues to such good effect that the government was obliged to hold a bed of justice. It was a pyrrhic victory for the crown. An angry parlement, frightened that Fleury intended to remove its traditional right to hear appeals against convictions in the ecclesiastical courts, waged a bitter war against the bull's partisans in the episcopate. After two years of strife, Fleury struck out in August 1732, issuing a law restricting the parlement's right of remonstrance. The regent had employed a similar tactic in 1718, threatening the magistrates with a return to the draconian era of Louis XIV. Such a danger concentrated minds wonderfully, and in 1732, as in 1718, a compromise was reached that involved the suspension of the law. It was, however, a stark warning of the havoc religious controversy could wreak on the delicate relationship between the crown and the parlement.

Thereafter calm was gradually restored. Fleury stuck fast to his policy of isolating the Jansenists and tried to avoid trouble in the parlement by evoking contentious cases to the royal council. He was helped by a radical offshoot of Jansenism, the convulsionary move-ment, which flowered in Paris after 1727. It emerged as the cult of a pious deacon, François de Pâris, whose tomb in the cemetery of Saint Médard became the setting for miracle cures and bizarre worship, featuring speaking in tongues and all manner of writhing and contor-tions. Hundreds of pilgrims flocked to the scene either to marvel or mock at these wondrous sights. Neither Fleury nor the ecclesiastical authorities had need of a Jansenist saint and they closed the cemetery. The parlement of Paris did contain a handful of disciples of Saint Médard, but the overwhelming majority was shocked and embar-rassed by the convulsionaries. This undoubtedly contributed to the less combative stance of the magistrates after 1732, and when Fleury died in 1743 there were good grounds for believing that the worst of the religious crisis had passed.

Louis *le bien-aimé*

To the dismay of the ambitious, Fleury's vigorous constitution enabled him to govern until he was well into his eighties. He carefully chaperoned the king, controlling access to his person and appointing a ministry loyal to himself. Aware that there was little chance of unseating the cardinal, the court cabals were rendered relatively powerless. Only towards the end of his life did he begin to lose his grip. When Charles VI died in 1740, Fleury was personally inclined to honour the pragmatic sanction. His hopes of peace were dashed by the opportunistic Frederick II of Prussia, who brazenly seized the Austrian province of Silesia. With the Habsburg empire seemingly on the brink of partition, Fleury was unable to restrain the war party at Court, headed by the charismatic count de Belle-Isle, grandson of Louis XIV's disgraced minister, Fouquet. As French armies marched into Germany, they brought a quickening of the diplomatic and political tempo that symbolized the transition from the more leisurely pace of life under the cardinal. He died on 29 January 1743; France would learn to mourn his passing.

With his mentor gone, Louis XV was finally, at the age of 32, obliged to quit the shadows and assume his *métier* of king. His first, and in some ways most important, decision was whether or not to replace Fleury. He chose not to do so, and instead, following the precedent of 1661, announced that he would rule as his own first minister. Unfortunately, unlike Louis XIV or Frederick II, Louis XV was not a young man impatient to exercise power. The king was intelligent and punctilious in his performance of his official duties and had a regal bearing that commanded immediate respect. He was not, however, a natural ruler. Instead he jealously guarded his own authority without bringing vision to government. Unwilling to trust his own ministers, he spent most of his personal reign directing a 'secret' foreign policy at odds with official diplomacy. By turns fatalistic or authoritarian, he could strike out boldly one day, only to retreat in the face of opposition the next. No policy or minister could ever be considered secure and both the Court and the royal council were beset by intrigue. Senior ministers such as Machault d'Arnouville, d'Argenson, and Choiseul, to name but a few, were disgraced and there were ten finance ministers between 1750 and 1774. Perhaps the only point of stability was provided by the presence of Mme de Pompadour. Between 1745 and her death in 1764, this cultured and resilient woman was inseparable from the king. She dominated the distribution of court patronage and her political influence increased as the years progressed. Yet even Pompadour was only one powerful figure among many seeking to monopolize the confidence of the king. In such circumstances, stable government proved elusive and it is not surprising that perceptive observers dreamed of a return to the golden age of Fleury.

In the early years of his personal reign, Louis XV was shielded from the pitfalls of Versailles by the impact of war. Despite the perfidy of Frederick II and the attacks of the French and their allies, Maria Theresa refused to play the role of sacrificial lamb. Displaying great courage, she rallied her subjects, driving an audacious French force led by Belle-Isle from Prague in 1742. He saved his army with a brilliant tactical retreat, but his hopes of delivering a mortal blow to Habsburg power were dashed. Yet despite Britain entering the conflict on the side of Maria Theresa, the War of the Austrian Succession would bring glory to French arms and to Louis XV. Under the command of marshal de Saxe, the French won a series of battles in the Low Countries. Brussels was taken in 1746 and Saxe was soon threatening the Dutch republic. Alarm bells rang in London as well as in Amsterdam, bringing their governments scurrying to the peace table at Aix-la-Chapelle.

Louis XV shared in the triumphs of his great general. The king's first campaign was uneventful; his second, in 1744, almost ended in catastrophe. As he advanced eastwards to join his armies, he was stricken by a sudden and terrifying illness. For several days he lay on what all feared would be his deathbed at Metz. The panic that gripped France was only outweighed by the joy and relief that swept the kingdom when news of the king's recovery was made public. On a tide of euphoria, his subjects thanked God for saving their king who was now popularly acclaimed 'Louis the well-beloved' (*bien-aimé*).

A year later, the king was crowned with the laurels of victory at Fontenoy. There Saxe achieved perhaps his greatest triumph defeating the British after a bloody and close run encounter. Despite coming under enemy fire, the king refused to leave the field and Voltaire and countless lesser bards sang the praises of the warrior king, who, as he surveyed the human carnage of Fontenoy, exclaimed: 'see what such a victory costs, the blood of our enemies is always the blood of men, the true glory is to spare it.'

These pacific sentiments were genuinely held and they counter the claims of critics like Choiseul that the king was heartless or cruel. When peace was signed at Aix-la-Chapelle in 1748, Louis XV was generous to the point of recklessness. To the amazement of Europe, he handed back his conquests in the Low Countries in return for French possessions lost to the British in North America. Gains in Nice and Savoy were also relinquished, and, to add insult to injury, he agreed to expel the immensely popular young pretender to the British throne, 'bonnie prince Charlie', from France. His moderation contrasts sharply with the arrogance of Louis XIV and guaranteed that there would be no repetition of the great coalitions against France of 1688 to 1713. Yet to patriotic French opinion, it seemed as if blood and money had been sacrificed in vain. Nothing better captures the public mood of anger and resentment than police reports of children taunting each other with the rhyme 'you're as stupid as the peace'.

The mid-century crisis

Historians are forever on the lookout for turning points and watersheds. If any year in the reign of Louis XV deserves such a label it is 1748. A successful war had deflected attention from his conduct of government and that was about to change. Within only a few years, the king was being compared to the ineffectual Henri III, and his government ridiculed for its incompetence and factionalism.

The first sign of trouble to come was provided by the attempted reforms of the finance minister, Machault. In 1749 he decided to replace the wartime tenth with a new tax, the twentieth. It was a bold innovation, proposing not only to levy a new direct tax in peacetime, but also to include the hitherto exempt French church and relatively undertaxed nobility and *pays d'états*. Fully implemented, the twentieth would mark a crucial step towards fiscal equality. Initially the omens were good. After making remonstrances the parlement of Paris registered the law without difficulty. The other parlements and the provincial estates also yielded, leaving the church alone in its opposition to Machault.

With the lines between church and state so firmly drawn, Louis XV and his minister were in a potentially powerful position. A successful raid on the coffers of the church would have undoubtedly sweetened the otherwise bitter pill of new taxation for the population at large. The campaign to tax the clergy also attracted a broad coalition stretching from Voltaire and the anti-clerical *philosophes*, to those Gallicans and Jansenists in the parlement of Paris who were keen to curtail the privileges of the clergy. If the king had stood firm, it is nearly certain that ecclesiastical resistance would have been overcome and that his name would have joined the others in the pantheon of enlightened absolutists. Instead, Louis XV grappled with his usually elastic conscience before caving in to the remonstrances of the bishops and the devout party at court. The church thus preserved its fiscal privileges and a golden opportunity was lost.

Had Louis XV's capitulation to the clergy over the twentieth been part of a broader strategy to preserve peace in the church it might have been comprehensible. Alas, the bishops who were so forceful in opposing Machault were simultaneously stirring the pot of religious controversy. The chief troublemaker was the new archbishop of Paris, Christophe de Beaumont, an implacable opponent of Jansenism devoid of any sense but that of his own righteousness. His appointment to such a critical see would have been unthinkable under Fleury, and it was an early signal that the cardinal's adroit handling of religious affairs would not be matched by his successors. Together with other zealots, Beaumont began systematically to deprive the Jansenists of the sacraments on the controversial basis that submission to *Unigenitus* was a 'rule of faith'. His favoured tool was the confession note, a certificate confirming that a penitent had been confessed by an authorized priest. Failure to produce a note was tantamount to admitting opposition to *Unigenitus* and resulted in a denial of the last rites.

Words scarcely suffice to describe the horror of such a punishment for a devout catholic as it carried the risk of eternal damnation. Even condemned criminals were not denied the consolation of the sacraments, and the public was stunned to see elderly religious, many of whom were distinguished by their piety and good works, treated so harshly. An estimated 10,000 mourners attended the funeral of one

victim, and public anger led the diarist Barbier to declare 'the majority of Paris . . . is Jansenist'.[2] Against all good sense, Beaumont had
succeeded in reviving religious controversy and there was no Fleury
to douse the flames. With his Court and council divided, Louis XV
failed to provide the necessary leadership and even today it is impossible to be sure about his own view of Beaumont's actions. Nor was
there anyone in the ministry to speak in his name. The result was drift
and procrastination interspersed with fruitless efforts to negotiate a
compromise.

As this new wave of persecution broke, the Jansenists turned once
more to the parlement for assistance. The magistrates were initially
reluctant to become embroiled in the dispute. It was the failure of the
crown to act that created a mood of frustration and ultimately
anger. Moderate voices fell silent and the vacuum was filled by a
small but highly effective Jansenist party. There were no more than
twenty Jansenists in the parlement, but they included talented and
hard-working young magistrates such as Chauvelin, Lambert
and L'Averdy. They denounced cases of refused sacraments and urged
the parlement to use its right to hear appeals against the decisions
of the ecclesiastical courts. Between March 1752 and May 1753 alone
twenty-two such cases from six different dioceses were investigated,
and relations between the parlement and the episcopate became
ever more strained. With both sides determined to uphold their
corporate dignity, it proved impossible to isolate either Beaumont
or his Jansenist opponents.

Within less than a decade of Fleury's death, the fragile peace in the
church had been shattered. When confronted by the sacraments crisis, Louis XV had tried desperately to avoid treading on clerical toes
and had pursued the will-o'-the-wisp of a 'third way' that could unite
moderates against the fanatics on both sides. As failure brought
frustration, the king questioned the loyalty of those he termed 'the
republicans' in the parlement. The crisis came to a head in May 1753
when he refused to receive the so-called 'grand remonstrances' that
combined a denunciation of the refusal of the sacraments with a
forceful reassertion of the parlement's role as guardian of the fundamental laws. In response, the magistrates went on strike before being
exiled by their angry monarch.

[2] E. J. F. Barbier, *Chronique de la régence et du règne de Louis XV, 1718–1763* (8 vols., Paris, 1857–8), v. 226.

Unfortunately for Louis XV, the parlement was exiled without anyone giving serious consideration to what might be put in its place, causing grumbling from Parisians about a government incapable of providing either 'bread or justice'. No less damaging was the effect on the provincial parlements which began to agitate on behalf of the exiles. Finally, the judges themselves, especially the Jansenists, spent their enforced leisure time studying French history and refining their constitutional arguments. They were ably assisted by the lawyers, most notably Le Paige, who published the highly influential *Lettres historiques* during the crisis. Revising arguments last seen during the Fronde and the religious wars of the sixteenth century, he argued that the parlement was the direct descendant of the national assemblies held by the Frankish kings. His work also contained the seeds of what, after 1755, became known as the 'union of classes', the theory that together the parlements formed the one and indivisible parlement of France. These ideas had their roots in some of the most troubled years in French history and their re-emergence during the peaceful reign of an adult king underlines the damage caused by *Unigenitus*.

Exiling the parlement of Paris was therefore counter-productive. Negotiations for a recall began almost immediately, but, with both sides convinced that they were the injured party, more than a year elapsed before the magistrates were recalled. For once, Louis XV took the initiative, revealing his sadly under-utilized talent for government by personally drafting a new law of silence. Registered by the parlement in September 1754, it invited the magistrates to prevent disturbance of the religious peace which they took to mean the refusal of the sacraments. Louis XV demonstrated his new-found determination by exiling Beaumont, while simultaneously petitioning Benedict XIV for an encyclical clarifying the status of *Unigenitus*.

It might therefore be assumed that the law of silence marked a turning point in Louis XV's treatment of the parlement. Unfortunately his policy had all the consistency of blancmange. In October 1755, the king backed a half-baked scheme of chancellor Lamoignon and the minister of war, count d'Argenson, to bolster the powers of the grand council. It was a deliberate challenge to the authority of the parlement which responded in November 1755 with some of the boldest remonstrances ever written. Explicitly using the language of the union of classes, the Parisian magistrates not only rallied the provincial parlements, but even dared to invite the princes and the peers to join them in the defence of the fundamental laws. The affair was typical of government under Louis XV. Without planning or foresight, the government had picked an unnecessary fight with the parlement which then defended itself with forceful constitutional arguments. The government backed down in April 1756, but the king soon paid the price for his error. War was declared against Great Britain in June, and when called upon to register a second twentieth to pay for the conflict the parlement resisted tenaciously. A bed of justice was needed to impose the law, and ominously for the king the provincial parlements picked up the gauntlet, more than matching the resistance of the Parisians.

To make matters worse, the hardline bishops had continued to order refusals of the sacraments despite having been exiled by the king. Louis XV pinned his hopes on the pope, whose encyclical, *Ex Omnibus*, appeared in the autumn of 1756. A moderate document, it restricted the refusal of the sacraments to notorious sinners. It is easy to imagine the anger of the king when a Jansenist magistrate persuaded the parlement that the encyclical should be lacerated and burnt by the public executioner. Such an extreme response was a clear indication that the senior magistrates had lost control. Indeed they probably encouraged the king to resort to harsh measures. On 10 December 1756 a law based on the encyclical together with a disciplinary edict was imposed at a bed of justice. That night the overwhelming majority of the magistrates resigned. Needless to say, the government had no contingency plan to fall back on. Instead it dug itself into a deeper hole by exiling sixteen supposed ringleaders of the opposition in January 1757. It was all to no avail. At war and in dire need of the parlement to bolster credit, the king reversed his policy in September of that year. Cases of refused sacraments continued until the end of the reign, but the parlement was in future allowed to pursue those responsible. The magistrates had triumphed and the heat generated by the *Unigenitus* controversy finally began to cool.

A decade of conflict had taken the shine off public perceptions of Louis XV. Ministers and policies came and went with alarming regularity and they inspired neither confidence nor respect from the kingdom's elites. No less disturbing was the loss of public esteem for the king, who became the butt of popular insults, placards, and graffiti—some of it regicidal in tone. Yet despite the disenchantment, France was still not prepared for the shock of 5 January 1757. Amidst the turmoil of the political crisis provoked by the bed of justice of the previous December, Damiens, a deranged domestic servant, tried to assassinate the king. Louis XV only received a minor wound and his life was never in danger. It was, nevertheless, a rude awakening for the kingdom, conjuring up folk memories of civil war and briefly fanning the embers of affection for Louis the well-beloved. The king himself was plunged into melancholy, lying listlessly in his bed even when encouraged to leave it by his surgeons. When told that his wound was not serious he replied, 'it is more than you think, because it goes to the heart'.[3]

The diplomatic revolution

The peace of Aix-la-Chapelle failed to resolve the underlying causes of conflict between France and Great Britain in North America. To protect their thinly populated possessions, the French authorities began to construct a line of fortifications connected by regular patrols. Skirmishes between rival forces were an almost inevitable result, most famously in 1754 when a group of colonists led by George Washington killed an unarmed French officer as he approached to negotiate. Louis XV genuinely wished to avoid war. All the pacific sentiments in the world were not, however, going to halt the British. They sent an army under general Braddock to attack the French forts in 1755, and ordered their navy to block French reinforcements reaching Canada. The belligerent intentions of perfidious Albion were illustrated by the affair of the *Alcide* and the *Lys*. The two French warships were seized after coming under fire within seconds of being informed by British officers that the two nations were at peace! Satisfaction was, however, obtained against Braddock. In a perfectly executed ambush, French troops destroyed the enemy army, slaying the British general in the process.

It was not until June 1756 that Louis XV officially declared war on Britain. Responsibility for the conflict lay in London, but with Europe at peace there was every reason to believe that France could hold her

---

[3] L. Dussieux and E. Soulié (eds.), *Mémoires du duc de Luynes sur la cour de Louis XV, 1735–1758* (17 vols., Paris, 1860–5), xvi. 282.

own overseas. Confirmation of the theory was apparently provided by marshal de Richelieu's brilliant victory at Mahon, which saw the capture of strategically important Menorca. The British admiral Byng, who failed to relieve his compatriots, was court martialled and shot, as Voltaire cuttingly observed, 'to encourage the others'. Hopes were high that the British government would suffer a similar fate. It was not to be. Instead a war that had begun so promisingly would finish in defeat, thanks, in large measure, to the diplomatic revolution.

If the peace of Aix-la-Chapelle resembled no more than a truce in North America, much the same could be said of its effects in central Europe. Maria Theresa was determined to recapture Silesia and together with her chancellor, Kaunitz, had conceived a daring strategy. They proposed nothing less than a complete realignment of the diplomatic constellation by allying with France against Prussia. The not unreasonable assumption behind their thinking was that the two great continental powers would easily crush the upstart Frederick II. What persuaded Louis XV to accept the Austrian embrace was the duplicity of the Prussian king, who, without warning, abandoned his former ally by signing the treaty of Westminster with Britain in January 1756. Understandably piqued, Louis XV agreed to a defensive alliance with Vienna in May. The French public was astounded. Few could understand why the king had allied himself to the Habsburgs, the sworn enemies of France since the time of cardinal de Richelieu.

Yet with war against Britain certain, Louis XV clearly believed that the alliance would guarantee peace in Europe. Who would dare to attack such a militarily formidable coalition? The king's error was to overlook the intensity of Austrian ambitions to reclaim Silesia. Kaunitz wanted war, and was busily seeking to add Russia to a grand alliance against Frederick II. The Prussian king was not easily duped, and, disastrously for Louis XV, he decided that attack was the best form of defence. His forces marched into Saxony in August 1756, unleashing the Seven Years War in the process. Within just four months of signing a treaty that he believed would preserve peace, Louis XV faced the nightmare of fighting a world war on two fronts, obliged to pay for the naval and colonial conflict against Britain, while simultaneously sending armies and subsidies into Germany.

The Seven Years War

Initially the war went well for France, and Richelieu followed up his triumph in Menorca by defeating the British in Hanover. With the great Saxe dead, successful generals were at a premium, but Richelieu soon fell foul of Court intrigue and was relieved of his command. His fate was typical of French military appointments during the war, which depended on connections at Versailles rather than experience in the field. Never was the truth of this maxim revealed more clearly than on 5 November 1757. A French army, commanded by the prince de Soubise, a particularly close crony of the king and Mme de Pompadour, was routed by Frederick II's much smaller force at Rosbach. French armies had been defeated many times before, but Rosbach was different. With nearly 10,000 killed, wounded, or taken prisoner, as against only 500 official Prussian casualties, it was humiliation on a grand scale. For the first time since 1643, when the Great Condé broke the Spanish veterans at Rocroi, France was no longer the continent's foremost military power.

Nor would the shame of Rosbach be easily avenged. The demoralized French suffered further defeats at Krefeld (1758) and Minden (1759) and were a pale shadow of the force led so gallantly by Saxe. Frederick II, on the other hand, withstood the onslaught of France's allies, Austria and Russia, displaying a combination of military genius and luck which earned him the title 'great'. When peace was signed in Germany in 1763, Silesia was definitively his. Tellingly, Frederick II was a hero in France!

Praise of the Prussian king was a thinly disguised rebuke for Louis XV, who made no repeat of his campaigns of the 1740s. His only sorties were into the forests of Versailles where, his critics alleged, 'he made war on stags'. To the pain of defeat, Louis XV added the shame of dishonour. With the connivance of Mme de Pompadour, the king spent even more time in the company of a string of young mistresses housed in the *parc aux cerfs*. It was conduct becoming of an aristocratic rake, not 'his most Christian majesty', and, in official pronouncements, the proud title of well-beloved rang increasingly hollow.

Defeat in Germany was accompanied by spectacular losses overseas.

Once the British had recovered from their early setbacks, they were able to capitalize upon their naval superiority and France's distractions in Europe. The French coast was blockaded and in the major sea battles of Lagos and Quiberon (1759) Louis XV's fleet was destroyed. Starved of reinforcements and supplies, French forces in Canada were gradually overwhelmed. One by one, the Ohio forts, Louisbourg, and Cape Breton fell and in 1759 Quebec was taken. It spelled the end for New France because in 1763, unlike 1748, there would be no territorial gains in Europe to barter for losses overseas. Nor was North America the end of this tale of woe. The nascent French empire in India was lost, and possessions in West Africa and the Caribbean seized. When peace came in 1763, it closed one of the most disastrous chapters in French military history.

The parlements: the enemy within?

Wars, especially unsuccessful ones, are notoriously expensive. By 1763, the French national debt stood at some 2,200 million *livres*, a figure comparable to that of 1715. Massive borrowing had been accompanied by a sharp rise in taxation. A second twentieth had been levied in 1756 and a third in 1760, while the capitation had been doubled in 1760. Indirect taxes had also proliferated, and, with no glorious feats of arms to ease the burden, it had become increasingly difficult to persuade the parlements to register fiscal edicts. Opposition in Paris had fanned out to the provinces with the parlements of Besançon, Dijon, Rennes, and Rouen amongst the more vociferous. Radical remonstrances, judicial strikes, and the exile of judges became commonplace. Self-interest played a part in motivating their opposition. Yet, despite their faults, the parlements also sought to articulate public grievances and probably saved the government from more damaging unrest in the process.

Louis XV was frequently angered by the resistance of the parlements. The failure of hardline policies in 1753 and 1756 had, however, taught him the virtue of caution. He was therefore willing to allow cardinal de Bernis, author of the recall of the parlement of Paris in September 1757, to pursue more conciliatory tactics. He worked closely with the parlement, dispensing patronage to its members and seeking to defuse potential disputes before they became public crises in a manner reminiscent of Fleury. His disgrace in October 1758 produced many glum faces on the benches of the parlement, although any despair was premature. His replacement, the duke de Choiseul, shared the same general principles and until his fall in 1770 the Parisian magistrates enjoyed a complex relationship with the government that, at times, bordered on partnership.

Choiseul was an aristocratic freethinker whose skilful diplomacy secured better terms for the king at the peace of 1763 than he had the right to expect. In addition to preserving the Austrian alliance, he forged a solid Bourbon 'family compact' with Spain and oversaw the conquest of Corsica in 1769. The duke also turned his energy and talents towards the reconstruction of French military power with the aim of fighting a war of revenge against Britain. Under his guidance, much-needed military reform was begun and the navy was rebuilt, making possible the triumphs of the war of American Independence. To achieve his goals he needed money, and the duke concluded that more would be forthcoming from a policy of cooperation with the parlements. The most dramatic illustration of his approach was provided by the fate of the Jesuits. With the covert backing of Choiseul, who was anxious to court the fiercely anti-Jesuit Charles III of Spain, the Jansenist party in the parlement of Paris orchestrated a campaign that resulted in the expulsion of the religious order from France. The devout party at Court, led by the dauphin, and the clerical establishment was horrified. Yet it was noticeable that from April 1761, when the Jansenist magistrate Chauvelin first denounced the Jesuits, until the end of the Seven Years War, the parlement made no more remonstrances to the king.

Peace, as we have seen, brought a huge financial hangover. The finance minister, Bertin, was obliged to maintain high rates of taxation which he threatened to make more onerous by ordering a land survey designed to ensure that the twentieth was levied accurately. Howls of protest from the parlements indicated that he had struck a privileged nerve. Resistance was particularly fierce in Rouen, Toulouse, and Grenoble where there were attempts to arrest the military commanders bearing Bertin's orders. With its popularity and credit in tatters, the government capitulated and Louis XV transferred Bertin to other duties. Choiseul, aided and abetted by Pompadour, chose his replacement, the Parisian magistrate, L'Averdy.

The duke took a certain cynical delight in placing a parlementaire in charge of the treasury, but it was an intelligent tactic. L'Averdy brought integrity and goodwill to the office and quickly defused the crisis with the parlements. Although the land survey was abandoned, his ministry was more than just a capitulation to vested interests. He sought to reform the *taille*, reduce interest rates, and to work closely with the parlement. He did not solve the financial crisis, but the presence of a man universally recognized for his probity did revive confidence in the crown. L'Averdy was also prepared to listen to new ideas. In 1764, he was responsible for the first steps towards freeing the grain trade, a move that liberal economists hoped would stimulate notoriously backward French agriculture. No less daring was his reform of municipal government where venality was abolished in favour of elected officials. These measures pointed in the direction of the reforms of both the next reign and the Revolution, but as so often before they proved vulnerable once their author fell from office. L'Averdy was disgraced in 1768, and within four years his policies had been reversed. For reform measures to reach fruition required governmental stability, and that Louis XV was unable to provide.

The Brittany affair

L'Averdy's appointment had been accompanied by that of René de Maupeou as keeper of the seals and his son René-Nicolas as first president of the parlement of Paris. Such a combination suggested that misunderstandings and conflicts with the magistrates would be a thing of the past. What wrecked these calculations was the refusal of the provincial parlements to do as they were told. The parlement of Rennes was amongst the most turbulent, becoming locked in a bitter controversy with the local military commander, the duke d'Aiguillon, about both taxation and local administration. In the summer of 1765, the magistrates pushed their resistance to the limit by resigning. Urged on by d'Aiguillon the government struck back, establishing a new parlement manned by his supporters and clients.

What turned a provincial crisis into one of the most damaging political scandals in French history was the arrest of d'Aiguillon's sworn enemy, the distinguished Breton magistrate and minor *philosophe*, La Chalotais. During the summer of 1765, the secretary of state, Saint-Florentin, who was d'Aiguillon's uncle, received a series of anonymous notes insulting the king. The minister claimed to recognize the writing of La Chalotais, who was arrested and imprisoned. Over the next twelve months, he was subjected to what can be best described as a thoroughly incompetent show trial. Worse still, when the case against him collapsed he was sent into exile, where he remained until Louis XV's death.

La Chalotais might well be described as Louis XV's Fouquet, the subject of a vindictive punishment out of keeping with the king's normally mild character. It may be, however, that the possible involvement of La Chalotais in an intrigue over letters written by a former royal mistress was what outraged the king. Yet by 1765, it was no longer possible to lock away a national figure on the basis of royal whim, and the La Chalotais affair became a *cause célèbre* which split French elites in much the same way as the Dreyfus case would do more than a century later. Incensed by the government's flouting of basic legal principles, the parlement of Paris, seconded by the provincial courts, condemned royal policy in a flood of remonstrances. For the timorous, it seemed as if the union of classes had finally become a reality, and it determined the king to attend the parlement on 3 March 1766 to issue a stinging rebuke. In majestic tones he restated the basic principles of his own absolute authority, and no history of eighteenth-century France is complete without a reference to what contemporaries called the 'flagellation' of the parlement. In political terms, however, it was a one-day wonder. The parlements were not silenced and the case against La Chalotais collapsed. Nor did the remodelled parlement of Rennes survive. Its old members returned in triumph in 1769 within months of d'Aiguillon resigning from his post as military commander.

What stopped the Brittany affair from being just another failed attempt to weaken the parlements was the exile of La Chalotais. His colleagues refused to be silenced and blamed d'Aiguillon for his harsh treatment. The duke was a haughty and authoritarian man, convinced that he had followed the king's instructions to the letter. Determined to be publicly exonerated, he demanded satisfaction from the parlement of Paris, sitting as the court of peers. His decision would spark one revolution and prepare the ground for a second.

Maupeou's revolution

D'Aiguillon's willingness to stand trial derived, in part, from his growing political credit. His burning ambition was to replace Choiseul in the ministry and the bitter rivalry between the two men and their factions was the principal preoccupation of Versailles. In the struggle for the king's ear, d'Aiguillon and his uncle, Richelieu, adopted a classic strategy. They employed the charms of a beautiful courtesan to capture the credit and affection of the king. The ruse worked admirably and she was installed at Versailles in March 1769 with the title of Mme du Barry. Remarkably the devout party welcomed her arrival on the basis that God 'permits one evil to cure a greater one',[4] meaning the ministry of Choiseul. They blamed him for the expulsion of the Jesuits and for royal weakness relative to the parlements. Yet d'Aiguillon and his allies would be disappointed. Du Barry lacked Pompadour's wit and ambition and her political influence was slight.

Choiseul had no sooner weathered one storm than he was confronted by another. In 1768, Maupeou the younger replaced his father as chancellor. Ambitious and tactless, he was soon at war with Choiseul, who scored a spectacular own goal by allowing his rival to choose a new finance minister in December 1769. The chancellor recruited Terray, a long-time ally in the parlement of Paris. No less ruthless than his benefactor, Terray surmounted a severe financial and economic crisis in February and March 1770 by implementing a partial bankruptcy. Opposition was muted because informed opinion realized that he had little choice. In justifying his policies to Louis XV, however, he took every opportunity to criticize the excessive military spending of Choiseul.

When d'Aiguillon's trial began in March 1770, therefore, both the Court and the ministry were riven by personal and factional feuds. Both Maupeou and Choiseul stood to gain if his reputation was tarnished and they almost certainly encouraged the parlement with that aim. Fearing conviction, d'Aiguillon used his influence with Louis XV to halt the trial in June and to issue letters patent clearing

---

[4] Quoted in Duc de Castries, *La du Barry* (Paris, 1986), 73.

his name. As chancellor it was Maupeou who had to justify the sudden change of policy, and he was accused of acting arbitrarily. Despite a lifetime spent in the parlement and the prestige of his office, the chancellor had few friends amongst his former colleagues. Nor was he temperamentally inclined to compromise. Instead he sought to bully the magistrates into submission. When harsh words failed, he resorted to authoritarian methods, holding a bed of justice in December 1770 to impose a disciplinary edict that combined the rhetoric of the flagellation speech with restrictions on the parlement's rights of remonstrance. The magistrates refused to be intimidated and began a judicial strike. Many hoped that their resistance would topple the chancellor, but his position was strengthened by the disgrace of Choiseul on 24 December. He had incurred the king's wrath for risking war with Britain in defence of Spanish claims to the Falkland Islands. With the treasury bare, war would have been suicidal and Louis XV was spurred into action. Choiseul was dismissed and anxious letters were despatched to Madrid calming the bellicose Charles III.

With Choiseul gone, the devout party was in the ascendant and d'Aiguillon's appointment to the ministry imminent. Hated by the magistrates and isolated at court, Maupeou had little room for manœuvre. It came as no surprise when the magistrates were exiled on 20 January 1771, but the resemblance to previous crises ended there.

Maupeou was an accidental revolutionary, but he was also a dynamic and resourceful one. The parlement of Paris was remodelled and venality abolished, although new magistrates were still appointed to their posts for life. Henceforth they were to be paid a salary, replacing the much criticized system of *épices* whereby judges received payments directly from litigants. The vast jurisdiction of the parlement was reduced and new courts created in towns such as Lyon, Poitiers, and Clermont Ferrand making justice more accessible to the people. The magistrates were still allowed to make remonstrances, albeit with the restrictions imposed in December 1770. When the provincial parlements protested, they too felt the heavy hand of the chancellor, who by the end of 1771 had effected what contemporaries christened 'Maupeou's revolution'.

Despite their enlightened veneer, the reforms of 1771 were hugely unpopular. For a generation weaned on Montesquieu's *Spirit of the*

Laws, the parlements were the intermediary powers which formed a barrier separating French monarchy from despotism. Maupeou was thus cast as the Turkish grand vizier, trampling French laws and liberties. Until his death in 1774, however, Louis XV supported the work of the chancellor. His actions should not be interpreted as a belated conversion to enlightened absolutism. The revolution of 1771 was the result of a particularly virulent case of Court and ministerial infighting, the sort of squabbling that had undermined French government since the death of Fleury. As so often before, the king had allowed a minister to take harsh measures against the magistrates and in Maupeou had found a man capable of making them stick. Yet the chancellor and his reforms were never secure because an elderly royal leopard could not change his spots. There was always the possibility that a fresh upheaval at Court or a new political crisis would engulf the chancellor. Indeed in 1774 d'Aiguillon, by now sitting in Choiseul's office as minister of war and foreign affairs, was plotting to overthrow Maupeou and recall the parlements. Nor was the public mood improved by the actions of Terray, who profited from the emasculation of the parlements to make the twentieth permanent and to collect other taxes more rigorously. By May 1774, royal finances were healthier than at any point for a generation, but the monarchy had rarely been more unpopular.

Conclusion

In May 1774, the still physically robust Louis XV contracted smallpox. Within a few days he was dead and like his great-grandfather before him was buried in haste to avoid unseemly celebrations. Yet the passing of the years would not bring nostalgia for a 'golden age' of Louis the well-beloved. Despite possessing many of the qualities needed to govern, the king had reigned but never ruled. Drift, discord, and instability were the hallmarks of his government and often gifted ministers spent more time attacking each other than addressing the problems of state. Louis XV had also lost the affection of his subjects. This was more than just the result of his scandalous private behaviour. Shy and ill at ease in the company of strangers, he found it impossible to project a positive image of monarchy. During his reign,

Paris acquired many of the magnificent buildings and squares that adorn it today. French literature and art flourished and, although it was only dimly perceived by contemporaries, the kingdom enjoyed sustained economic and population growth. The tragedy of Louis XV was that he failed to associate himself with this positive picture. Instead, after 1748 he locked himself away in his royal palaces, venturing only rarely to Paris and never to the provinces. Cut off from the public, Louis XV drained the well of affection for his person and encouraged the often exaggerated rumours about his conduct. The words of one disgruntled subject offer a sad epitaph for a reign of wasted opportunities:[5]

Ami des propos libertins,	You liked lewd talk,
Buveur fameux et roi célèbre	You loved your drink.
Par la chasse et par les catins:	A famous king—in hunting pink.
Voilà ton oraison funèbre.	Notorious in your taste for tarts:
	Obituarists need all their arts.

[5] Mouffle d'Angerville, *The Private Life of Louis XV Annotated and Amplified by Quotations from Original and Unpublished Documents* (London, 1924). Lines translated by William Doyle.

8

Politics: Louis XVI

Munro Price

The reign in context

'We were walking on a carpet of flowers; we did not see the abyss beneath'.[1] The count de Ségur's famous description of the last years of the old regime has informed views of the reign of Louis XVI ever since. More than any other reign in European history, that of Louis XVI has been distorted by contemporaries and historians writing with hindsight. The period 1774–88 has been consistently seen as a mere prelude to the Revolution, evoked with regret and nostalgia by right-wing historical tradition, and dismissed by that of the left as the last gasp of a dying and corrupt monarchy.

Perversely, the sheer political complexity of Louis XVI's reign up to 1789 has encouraged these simplifying myths to take hold. In the face of the apparent lack of a guiding hand in policy, and a bewilderingly rapid turnover of ministers (eleven finance ministers alone from the accession to the calling of the estates general) it has been easiest for the historian to resort to generalization. Yet if the politics of the reign are examined in more detail connecting threads of policy and personnel can be discerned. These give the period a coherence of its own. They also help to put the Revolution in perspective, as the consequence at least in part of conflicts, decisions, and mistakes made from 1774, and not, as Clemenceau put it, a bloc, monolithic and self-standing.

The decisive event that shaped Louis XVI's reign in fact took place three years before he ascended the throne. This was the *coup d'état*

[1] *Mémoires ou souvenirs et anecdotes, par M le comte de Ségur* (3 vols., Paris, 1824–6), i. 29.

of his grandfather Louis XV and chancellor Maupeou against the parlements. Although one of the new king's first major policy decisions was to reverse the effects of the coup, its memory never remained far from the political surface throughout the next thirteen years, and his reign until the Revolution is best seen as an unsuccessful attempt to grapple with its legacy. If absolute monarchy was defined as a political system in which legislation was concerted between crown and parlements in the absence of the estates general, then Maupeou's coup, like a seismic shift, gave the edifice a shock from which it never really recovered. Outwardly, it was patched up under the aegis of the king's informal first minister Maurepas in 1774, but in reality the damage had been done.

Until 1771, the standard constitutional orthodoxy had drawn a distinction between a well-tempered absolutism, where potential royal caprice was restrained by Christian morality and the existence of intermediary bodies, and despotism on the Russian or Ottoman model, where nothing stood between the ruler's whim and the lives and property of his subjects. The relative ease with which the 1771 coup was imposed (the old parlements were successfully broken and troops did not have to be used on a large scale to contain protest) revealed to the political nation that this traditional distinction was in large part a fiction. As a result, the consensus between crown and elites that was sustained by this fiction, and which was best expressed by a harmonious collaboration between ministry and magistracy, began to break up. Maupeou's actions threw most of Enlightened opinion, much of the second and third estates, and even a powerful section of the Court into overt opposition to royal policy. Inevitably, the nature and even the basis of absolute monarchy began to be called into question.

The major theme of Louis XVI's reign to 1789 is the series of different—and sometimes contradictory—political responses by the king and his government to the loss of confidence in the monarchy after 1771. The most lucid of the king's ministers (who were often those most influenced by the Enlightenment) realized that the recall of the old parlements in 1774 could only be a temporary solution to this problem. This was the starting point for a series of attempts to widen the basis of political and social support for the crown. The objective was to substitute for its problematic partnership with the privileged orders, epitomized by the link with the parlements, an appeal to a more broadly defined class of property owners. In their different ways and with differing emphasis, the provincial assemblies envisaged by Turgot and Calonne, and the provincial administrations set up by Necker, all aimed at this goal, bypassing the resistance of the traditional elite, admitting increasing numbers of non-noble proprietors into a political partnership with the crown while leaving the royal authority essentially intact.

The second theme of the reign concerns the obstacles this project encountered, which by 1789 had not only ruined its chances of success, but destroyed the absolute monarchy in the process. Paradoxically, one of these obstacles was the king himself, probably inclined at heart to some form of enlightened absolutism, but prevented by his own scruples as well as a truly paralysing psychological problem of indecision from carrying his policies through to their logical conclusion. Another was the entrenched rivalries between court factions stemming from Maupeou's coup, which did not disappear with the new reign but instead survived and adapted in the new climate and by the mid-1780s had succeeded in destroying ministerial unity. The political battle here was between traditional absolutists, often heavily influenced by traditional Catholicism, who had rallied to Maupeou, and aristocratic constitutionalists, both at Court and in the ministry. Enlightened absolutism was inimical to both; to the former because it was too enlightened, to the latter because it was too absolutist. Turgot, Necker, and Calonne were successively overwhelmed by these divisions, their failure compounded by their inability to make the transition from finance minister to first minister.

It would be unfair to paint an entirely negative picture of the reign of Louis XVI before the Revolution. In foreign policy, which was after all the traditional 'royal craft' (*métier du roi*) the remarkable collaboration between the king and his foreign minister Vergennes created a diplomacy significant for its respect for the European balance of power and its renunciation of annexationist aims. It also produced the one victorious war against Great Britain of the eighteenth century. At home, the remains of serfdom were eradicated on the royal domain by 1779, a series of rationalizing reforms were introduced in a number of provinces by able intendants, and in 1787, virtually with its last breath, the old regime finally made amends for the revocation of the edict of Nantes and granted French Protestants a civil status. Yet none of these positive aspects of the reign can obscure its central failure, which was above all the responsibility of the king and his ministers. This was their inability to carry through the policy they themselves initiated, albeit fifty years too late, of transforming France into an enlightened absolute monarchy.

The new reign

The divisive legacy Louis XV bequeathed to his grandson and successor was aptly symbolized by the scenes around his deathbed. As the old king's condition worsened, his soul became the subject of a macabre tug-of-war between the major Court factions that owed far more to politics than to religion. Those who supported the 'triumvirate', the ministry of Maupeou, Terray and d'Aiguillon, were well aware of the deep hostility the breaking of the parlements had aroused and feared for their political futures in the uncertain climate of a new reign. Their chief representative at the king's bedside was d'Aiguillon's uncle, the duke de Richelieu; their only hope of political survival, in the unlikely event of a royal recovery, lay in maintaining the primacy of their most important ally, Louis XV's mistress Mme du Barry, in the king's affections.

Ranged against the d'Aiguillon–Richelieu faction were all those who had suffered from its rise to power; opponents of Maupeou's *coup d'état*, associates of the disgraced foreign minister Choiseul, and allies of the *dauphine* Marie-Antoinette, who hated the Richelieus for a variety of personal and political reasons. As the king's life moved into the shadows, it was around the dubious figure of the mistress that the battle centred. If the last sacraments were adminstered, fear of impending hellfire would certainly induce Louis XV to send away du Barry, removing her from his side at a critical juncture and announcing to the court the end of the influence of the Richelieus and the triumvirate.

The ensuing black comedy is best left to the laconic pen of the baron de Besenval. When it became clear that the last rites could no longer be delayed, Richelieu struck a bargain with the royal confessor that the king's repentance would not be publicly communicated in a way that would necessitate Mme du Barry's immediate exile. Shortly afterwards, however, the confessor was bullied by the other side into changing his mind. Having heard Louis XV's final confession, he announced that the king repented his scandalous life and would not return to it in the future, 'whereupon the duke de Richelieu, loudly enough for everybody to hear, addressed to [him] the most shocking insult'.[2]

The character of the 20-year-old king who inherited this poisoned political and constitutional chalice was an enigma to contemporaries and has remained so since. Louis XVI has traditionally been portrayed as decent, stupid, and ineffectual, essentially a spectator of the major events of his reign. This view of the king was epitomized by Pétion's verdict on him during the Revolution: 'truly this mass of flesh is insensible'. In fact, the future king was intelligent and informed, excelling in mathematics, physics, and geography, fluent in Latin and—in a departure from tradition—English. His love of geography was to translate itself into an impressive command of maritime and naval policy, and his knowledge of English into an ambivalent fascination with France's greatest contemporary rival.

Louis XVI's problem was not intellectual, but psychological. At crucial moments during his reign he was afflicted with crippling attacks of indecision. Psychohistory would no doubt link this to the loss of both his parents before he was 13 (Louis XV, who had similar problems, lost virtually his entire family to smallpox before the age of 2). The result was obvious and the subject of much comment by contemporaries: 'getting the king to make a decision', his brother the count de Provence once cruelly observed, 'is like trying to hold two oiled billiard-balls together in the palm of one's hand'.[3] This trait worsened as the monarchy's problems intensified, and from 1787 spilled over into what today would probably be classified as clinical intermittent depression.

The king's private life was to have a profound influence on the structure of politics during his reign. In stark contrast to his two predecessors, he never took a mistress. The age of Maintenon, Pompadour, and du Barry, of royal favourites wielding political power, was not renewed. It might seem that the ending of a tradition which constantly subordinated policy to the personal passions of the monarch and the manœuvring of Court factions could only benefit

[2] Baron de Besenval, *Mémoires* (2 vols., Paris, 1821), i. 304.
[3] Cited in J. Hardman, *Louis XVI* (New Haven, 1993), 21.

the smooth running of government. Paradoxically, this was not to prove the case. Despite the deep initial suspicion with which her husband viewed her, the eventual birth of an heir in 1781 enabled Marie-Antoinette to acquire an increasing hold on his affection and confidence. From this point on she combined the emotional hold over the king normally reserved for a royal mistress with the permanence of a queen, forming an alternative focus of power to the monarch, and a formidable obstacle to any minister who was not her creature.

The failure of the traditional structures of Court and ministry to accommodate this new situation ensured that the role of the queen became a major source of discord throughout the reign. This tendency was accentuated by diplomatic and domestic political factors. Marie-Antoinette was a Habsburg, and thus from the moment of her arrival in France in 1770 the bugbear of the Richelieu–d'Aiguillon faction, which hated the Austrian alliance. Equally, her loyalty to Choiseul, the foreign minister who had arranged her marriage and was toppled soon afterwards by d'Aiguillon and Maupeou, inclined her to Choiseul's indulgent policy towards the parlements, tacit acceptance of his aristocratic and discreetly constitutionalist view of the monarchy, and hostility to the work of his bitter enemy Maupeou. None of this was calculated to improve the royal marriage. Much has been made of the seven-year non-consummation of the union as an explanation of the initial coldness between Louis XVI and his wife. More important was the Austrophobia inculcated into the king while dauphin by his governor, the duke de la Vauguyon. As Marie Antoinette ruefully admitted as late as 1784 to her brother Joseph II: 'The king's natural suspicions were reinforced by his governor even before our marriage. M. de la Vauguyon made him fear that his wife would try to dominate him, and his black heart took pleasure in frightening his pupil with every evil tale he could invent about the House of Austria'.[4]

All the major divisions in the French body politic since 1771— indeed since 1756—were reflected in the marriage of this truly odd couple. The king was taciturn, intelligent, indecisive, pious, basically anti-Austrian and jealous of his domestic authority—as dauphin he

---

[4] Letter of 22 September 1784. *Lettres de Marie Antoinette*, ed. M. de la Rocheterie and the marquis de Beaucourt (2 vols., Paris, 1895–6), ii. 43.

had heartily approved of Maupeou's *coup d'état*. The queen was Austrian, outgoing, not stupid but no intellectual, not particularly religious, and predisposed by her difficult debut at Versailles to favour a Court clique loyal to a former minister her husband hated and which detested Maupeou and his work. She was also powerful. Under the circumstances, it is hardly surprising that the reign frequently lacked political direction.

The system of Maurepas

Despite these deep structural flaws, up until 1781 much of royal policy was unified and coherent. This was the achievement of the informal first minister chosen by the king on his accession, the 73-year-old ex-minister of the navy, the count de Maurepas.

Minister for thirty-one years until his dismissal in 1749, Maurepas made no secret of his nostalgia for the halcyon days of the previous reign, under the political direction of cardinal de Fleury. His own position was overtly modelled on that of Fleury. He took no formal title or government department himself, but based his power on his right to sit in on the working session (*travail*) of each minister with the king and thus to coordinate policy. He became, as he himself impressionistically put it, the 'shadow meeting-point' (*ombre de point de réunion*) of the ministry. Until Maurepas's death in November 1781, this arrangement generally worked well. It had one other advantage; at a time when the young king was taking his first steps as a ruler, the Mentor, as Maurepas was generally known, provided a screen between him and the pullulating factions of Versailles. Above all, this meant shielding the king from his wife's pressure. Mercy-Argenteau, the Austrian ambassador, shrewdly observed that in France the power of first ministers was always exercised at the expense of the queen, and the subtle but implacable presence of Maurepas was another crucial reason why Marie-Antoinette's real influence on policy only really began after 1780.

If Maurepas's impact on the structure of politics at the accession of Louis XVI was beneficial, this is less true of its content. Fatally for the long-term prospects of the reign, the Mentor had no interest in constitutional innovation. He was, however, aware that something had to be done to end the political divisions caused by Maupeou's *coup*, a particular innovation of which he thoroughly disapproved. His own solution lay in a return to the past, to the political arrangement that had functioned well for at least part of Fleury's ministry, of a partnership between the crown and the sovereign courts in which the royal authority was preserved by skilful ministerial manipulation of the leading magistrates. Even with the supremely cynical and pragmatic Maurepas, there was a hint of ideology in this preference: 'here is my confession of faith,' he once remarked, 'no parlements, no monarchy'.[5]

To get the young king, who genuinely approved of Maupeou's actions, to accept this course of action required six months of respectful brainwashing. By November 1774 d'Aiguillon, Maupeou, and Terray had all been dismissed and the old parlements recalled, although on stricter conditions than before; if they broke these terms a plenary court could pronounce forfeiture and only one remonstrance could be made after a bed of justice. Yet even at the time doubts were raised within government about the wisdom of this policy. The strongest supporters of the recall were Maurepas himself and Maupeou's replacement as keeper of the seals, Miromesnil, himself a former first president of the parlement of Rouen. Vergennes, d'Aiguillon's successor as foreign minister and a former client of Maupeou, spoke out in the council in favour of his patron's work.

In a sense all these protagonists were wedded to the past, supporting one side or another in the crown–parlement equation that had always defined the absolute monarchy. The one minister who genuinely wished to escape from this dilemma, and place the royal authority on both wider and firmer foundations, was Terray's successor as controller-general, Turgot. In August 1775 he commissioned a remarkable document, the *Memoir on Municipalities*, which launched for the first time the notion of provincial assemblies as a potential alternative to the sovereign courts. Turgot envisaged a hierarchy of local assemblies, composed of property owners without distinction of rank, raising and administering royal taxation, particularly the single land tax that, as a physiocrat, he wished to see as the future basis of crown revenue. Yet these assemblies were to be purely consultative,

---

[5] *Mémoires secrets de J-M. Augeard, secrétaire des commandements de la reine Marie Antoinette* (Paris, 1866), 78.

and sufficiently small and diverse to pose no threat to the royal authority. Although the plan was never implemented, it represented the first systematic blueprint for France's transformation into an enlightened absolute monarchy.

Turgot did not stay in office long enough to realize his ambitious projects. By 1776 he had made an enemy of the queen through his clumsy intervention against one of her protégés in a complicated diplomatic incident. By this time, too, his own colleagues had begun to oppose him. Whatever their differing interpretations of the absolute monarchy, Maurepas, Miromesnil, and Vergennes all became increasingly suspicious of what they perceived as Turgot's plans to alter its very nature. The crunch came in early 1776, when Turgot drew up the 'six edicts', which in the best fashion of enlightened absolutism sought to rationalize aspects of royal administration and French society. Most controversial were the proposed reform of the *corvée*, which its opponents rightly saw as an attack on privilege, and of the Parisian guilds, which they also saw as undermining the corporate nature of established society. Miromesnil was particularly vehement in his denunciation of the edicts; nonetheless on 12 March 1776 they were registered at a bed of justice.

Turgot survived in office for just two months more. To the opposition of the queen and Miromesnil were soon added that of Vergennes, whose policy of intervening in Great Britain's dispute with its American colonies ran counter to Turgot's insistence on economies; of Maurepas, who suspected the controller-general of wishing to replace him as first minister; and even of the king himself, who famously remarked, 'M. Turgot wants to be me and I do not want him to be me'.[6] The collective ministerial sigh of relief when Turgot was dismissed on 12 May 1776 is epitomized in a letter of Vergennes to the ambassador to Vienna, Breteuil: 'I cannot pretend, Sir, that M. Turgot's dismissal is a bad thing . . . Full of metaphysical ideas, with the best will in the world he would have thrown us into a confusion from which it would have taken us years to extricate ourselves'.[7]

The first ministry of Jacques Necker, director-general of finance from 1777 to 1781 (as a Swiss Protestant he could not formally hold the

[6] Abbé de Véri, *Journal, 1774–1780*, ed. J. de Witte (2 vols., Paris, 1928–30), i. 447–8.

[7] Letter of 26 July 1776, Archives Breteuil, château de Breteuil, Yvelines, 1st series, 1776, *lettres diverses*.

office of controller-general) resumed many of the themes introduced by Turgot, although with some significant differences of emphasis. The immediate reason for Necker's appointment was the looming prospect of France entering the American War of Independence. Determined not to raise taxation or declare any form of bankruptcy given the precedent of the previous reign, the government's only other option was loans, which Necker with his banking background was highly equipped to provide.

According to plan, Necker's appointment did ensure that the American war was successfully financed, although the amount and the implications for the monarchy of the debt incurred were fiercely controversial at the time and have remained so among historians since. Yet Necker was determined not to be limited to the functions of a mere money-spinner. He had views of his own on the future of the monarchy, and these bear instructive comparison with those of Turgot. Like Turgot, Necker was committed to widening the basis of support for the crown, and to this end he actually set up two provincial administrations (his version of Turgot's planned provincial assemblies) in 1778, in Berry and Haute-Guyenne. Although their powers were sharply pruned by Necker's immediate successors, they remained in operation until the end of the old regime, and were clearly intended by their creator as an administrative (and perhaps ultimately constitutional) trial balloon.

That said, there were substantial differences between Necker's and Turgot's projects: 'this resembles my ideas on the municipalities as a windmill resembles the moon',[8] was Turgot's grumpy verdict on Necker's administrations. The bodies in Berry and Haute-Guyenne were nominated and co-opted rather than elected, contrary to Turgot's preference, and retained the distinction between the three estates, in contrast to his proposals for municipalities. Yet the third estate in Necker's administrations was doubled, and voting by head rather than by order instituted. Given that the Revolution eventually began with a dispute over precisely this issue in the estates general, this was a significant precedent.

Necker's second major innovation came in February 1781. This was the publication of the *Compte rendu* (balance sheet), the first public

[8] G. Schelle (ed.), *Oeuvres de Turgot et documents le concernant, avec biographie et notes* (5 vols., Paris, 1913–23), v. 163.

statement of royal revenue and expenditure in the monarchy's history. It did not endear Necker to his more conservative colleagues, accustomed to the tradition of secrecy in crown financial operations. The immediate cause of the director's downfall, however, was a clash over war finance, centring on what he saw as one of the major flaws of French government, the independence of individual ministers vis-à-vis the finance minister. With no developing doctrine of cabinet responsibility as in England, each minister was only reponsible for his actions to the king in his individual working session with the monarch, in which major sums could be assigned to him without any consultation with the minister of finance. Maurepas's practice of sitting in on each minister's session with the king provided some of the necessary control, but as war expenditure progressively mounted after 1778 and France's entry into the American war, the strains became too great for the ministry to bear.

Necker's aim was a coordinating role over all aspects of government finance, and he almost achieved it. In October 1780 he forced out the recalcitrant navy minister Sartine, and orchestrated his replacement by his friend the marquis de Castries. In May 1781, however, he went too far, and tabled a series of demands aimed at strengthening his position, including the status of minister of state. Maurepas rightly sensed in this an attempt to supplant him, and replied with a grudging counter-offer, calling Necker's bluff and forcing his resignation on 19 May.

The Genevan's departure was a final, if pyrrhic, victory for Maurepas. Weakened by illness and extreme age, he died on 21 November 1781. Appropriately for one who had striven so hard to recreate the political and diplomatic glories of the past, his deathbed was illuminated by one last ray from the *grand siècle*. In his final hours the news of Yorktown reached Versailles and Louis XVI sent the duke de Lauzun to Maurepas's apartments with the news. As Lauzun went through the lists of cannon, standards, prisoners taken, Maurepas could only mutter 'good, good' as each item was read to him. Courtier to the last, he apologized for his infirmity: 'I'm dying and I don't know whom I have the honour of addressing'.[9]

The resignation of Necker was a turning point of the reign. Although there were clear differences between himself and Turgot,

[9] 'Journal du maréchal de Castries', Archives de la Marine, Vincennes, Ms. 182/7964 1–2, 1, fos. 91–93.

both men had shared the essential aim of restoring the monarchy's fortunes through the involvement of a wider section of the political nation. In this sense, with modifications of his own, Necker did make a start at practising what Turgot had preached. Had the provincial administrations been extended, the monarchy would have taken a long step forward along the lines advocated by reforming ministers and the reform constituency. This might have led to the French form of enlightened absolutism that Turgot advocated and Necker claimed to espouse. Alternatively, the final result could have been a more constitutional monarchy brought about by the increasing appetite for participation in government that Necker's and Turgot's reforms themselves encouraged. Neither option was palatable to defenders of the traditional absolute monarchy. Vergennes had a point when he wrote secretly to Louis XVI begging him to dismiss Necker: 'your majesty finds himself in the situation he was in with M. Turgot, when he decided to speed him on his way: the same dangers and problems flow from the nature of their analogous systems'.[10]

Foreign policy and the American war

The foreign policy of the reign was dominated by two major themes: the search for a stable diplomatic equilibrium on the continent, and the pursuit of redress from England for the humiliations she had inflicted on France during the Seven Years War. Of course, the two aims were intimately linked. Since any war of revenge on England would be essentially maritime, no military entanglements on the continent could be permitted if France were to avoid the nightmare of a two-front conflict on land and on sea, as had happened during the Seven Years War.

Although Maurepas as informal first minister played an important role in shaping this foreign policy, its main architects were the king himself and his foreign minister from 1774 to 1787, Vergennes. Of all the ministers of the reign, Vergennes was probably the one to whom Louis XVI felt closest: pious, cautious, and monogamous like his master. Most important, Vergennes's diplomatic views

---

[10] J. L. Soulavie, *Mémoires historiques et politiques du règne de Louis XVI depuis son mariage jusqu'à sa mort* (6 vols., Paris, 1801), iv. 213.

dovetailed exactly with those of the king. Still deeply suspicious of the Habsburgs, both men aimed to return to the traditional Bourbon foreign policy as far as the Austrian alliance would allow. They also resurrected the old maxim of preserving the smaller northern and eastern European powers, particularly Sweden and the Ottoman empire, and viewed Russia's accelerating westward expansion with growing alarm. Significantly, these were also the principles of Louis XV's old secret diplomacy of which Vergennes had been a long-standing agent. With his ministry the unofficial diplomacy of Louis XV was finally integrated with the official diplomacy of his grandson. The burlesque of the 'king's secret' with its cast of princely intriguers, duped ministers, and transvestite spies, came to an end.

The most paradoxical feature of continental policy was an ingrained distrust of Austria despite the 1756 alliance and the king's own marriage to a Habsburg. On every occasion Austria asked for French support in her diplomatic ventures, especially over her attempts to exchange her possessions in the Low Countries for Bavaria in 1778–9 and 1784–5, and her dispute with Holland in 1784, she was refused. By the outbreak of the Revolution, the Franco-Austrian alliance existed only in name. Yet there was a consistency in the king's and his minister's attitude to Austria. The Habsburg alliance was useful, indeed vital, as a means of keeping the peace in Europe and enabling France to grapple with her main rival Great Britain. On the other hand, any attempts by Austria to embroil France in her continental quarrels on the pattern of the Seven Years War, or to expand on her own account, particularly in partnership with Russia at the expense of Turkey, were strenuously to be resisted. Finally, France's traditional influence in the Holy Roman Empire as defender of the smaller German states was to be preserved, even to the point of bolstering Austria's hereditary enemy Prussia. As the king pithily put it in 1778 to Vergennes: 'We have an alliance which links us closely to Austria, but this does not oblige us to share her ambitious and unjust plans. On the other hand we must maintain France's position in Germany . . . and as you put it so well the guarantee of the treaty of Westphalia is inherent in the French crown.'[11]

[11] Letter of 4 February 1778, in J. Hardman and M. Price (eds.), *Louis XVI and the Comte de Vergennes: Correspondence, 1774–1787* (Voltaire Foundation, Oxford, 1998), 256.

The most important diplomatic and military event of the reign was France's intervention in the American War of Independence on the side of the rebellious thirteen colonies. In a sense, it was inevitable that France should seek to profit from George III's dispute with his American subjects following the humiliation of the Seven Years War. Indeed, Vergennes argued that a lasting Anglo-French peace would only be possible once the peace of 1763 was overturned and a diplomatic equilibrium re-established between the two countries. Yet, paradoxically, the main justification deployed by king and minister for going to war was defensive rather than offensive. This was the fear (in reality groundless) that if France did not swiftly intervene in the conflict, there was a great danger that Britain and her colonies might reach a compromise solution and seal it by a joint attack on France. Whether Louis XVI and Vergennes actually believed this reasoning, or merely deployed it to mask their appetite for a simple war of revenge, remains a mystery.

The decision to enter the American war presents the irony of two cautious men galvanizing themselves through fear of the consequences of inaction into taking a massive political and military gamble. What is now clear from the king's correspondence with Vergennes is that once he had been convinced that intervention was necessary, it was the king who forced the pace. As a result, France entered the American war in the spring of 1778 alone, and without the participation of her Spanish ally whose fleet was regarded as of critical importance in helping to tip the maritime scales against England.

The naval strategy behind this gamble was that France, with her rapidly rearming fleet, would be able to knock the British out of the war in one campaign. Admiral d'Estaing's first expedition to America, however, failed to deliver, leaving Versailles hoist with its own petard. Spain did enter the war in April 1779, but her differing campaign priorities and grandiose war aims—Menorca, the Floridas, and especially Gibraltar—came close to nullifying the advantage to the French forces of her fifty ships of the line. When no decisive successes were scored in either 1779 or 1780, France seemed to be staring disaster in the face. Even after the victory of Yorktown (only achieved by refusing Spain's demand for a naval diversion in European waters), the prospect of continuing hostilities simply to enable Spain to realize her war aims was terrifying. It was clear that if the war dragged on beyond 1783 the monarchy's finances would collapse, which would probably entail some sort of political upheaval. It is quite possible that had Spain not moderated her demands in the nick of time to enable France to salvage peace with honour at the treaty of Paris, historians might now be dating the Revolution from 1783 and not 1789.

The end of the American war brought a peace dividend not in terms of territorial aggrandisement (that was not Louis XVI's and Vergennes's aim) but of prestige. It also brought a promising new alliance, that of the Dutch, who had been alienated from their traditional Britsh ally during the war. The Franco-Dutch alliance, signed in January 1785, held out the prospect not only of increased French influence on the continent, but also of the bases and resources of the Dutch East Indian empire if the struggle with Britain were to be resumed. Unfortunately, the success of the alliance was predicated on the success of the pro-French Patriot party in their incipient civil war against the pro-English and pro-Prussian stadholder. This last paradoxical gamble did not pay off; Vergennes died of overwork in February 1787 as it was becoming clear that the Patriots had overplayed their hand and were rushing to their doom. France's inability to aid the Patriots when a Prussian invasion that September restored the stadholder served notice to the rest of Europe that her domestic financial problems now precluded any active foreign policy.

The diplomatic history of the reign has a twofold significance. First, it shows Louis XVI in a very different light from the vacillating incompetent of tradition. Here above all the king was in his element, consulting closely with his minsters but almost always in control, implementing a conservative but entirely coherent foreign policy and taking a close interest in its details, particularly where they concerned maritime affairs. Secondly, the impact of foreign policy on domestic affairs in this period has been underestimated, most specifically in providing a motivation for the crown's last great effort at internal reform in 1787. The memory of the financial vicissitudes of the American war was probably a major factor in the decision of the king and his most trusted ministers to make this final effort to reform the royal finances, lessening dependence on the unreliable parlements through collaborating with yet another version of Turgot's provincial assemblies. In this respect, above all, the foreign policy of the reign cannot be viewed in isolation.

Finance, 1774–1787

The immediate cause of the fall of the absolute monarchy was a financial crisis; in August 1788 the crown found itself unable to raise further loans or to pay its creditors. Argument and polemic about the genesis of this collapse was intense at the time and has remained so among historians since. All the finance ministers of Louis XVI's reign, particularly Necker and Calonne, have had their detractors and partisans, who have attempted to portray their subject either as uniquely responsible for the deficit, or as the saviour of the monarchy if only he had been given the chance. Judging the actual records of these ministers is a peculiarly difficult task, since it involves working with the figures they themselves provided, figures which may have been accidentally or deliberately misleading. However, recent researches that have cross-checked the differences and similarities in these various accounts have arrived at a clearer picture of the financial history of the reign than ever before.

The monarchy under Louis XVI faced three major financial challenges: inequalities in the tax system, inefficiency and corruption in the treasury (or rather treasuries) that administered it, and the lack of a stable system of public credit. The main differences between finance ministers lay in the priority which they accorded to each of these problems, and the relative success or failure with which they grappled with them. Terray, whom Louis XVI inherited from his grandfather, had implemented a policy of financial rigour that was deeply unpopular at the time, but now seems to have been effective. Calculating the deficit on his entry to office as 60 million *livres* per annum, Terray both raised taxation through making the first twentieth permanent and extending the second, and ending some tax exemptions. He also abolished a number of venal offices in the crown's financial administration. His partial bankruptcy of 1770 temporarily damaged the monarchy's credit, but in the long term probably revived its borrowing ability through demonstrating that the crown was now committed to sound financial administration. By the time he was dismissed in August 1774, Terray had turned the deficit into a modest surplus of 18 million *livres*.

Terray's successor Turgot was constrained from the outset both by the recall of the parlements, which made recourse to some of his predecessor's more draconian methods henceforth impossible, and by his own principles as set out to the new king on 24 August 1774: 'No bankruptcy, no new taxes, no new loans, only savings'.[12] Turgot's achievements are difficult to judge since his period in office was so short. He did try to implement free trade measures to stimulate the economy, but when applied to the grain trade this provoked a peasant revolt in the form of the 'flour war', while his first attack on the corporate society embodied in the six edicts was bitterly resisted by the parlement of Paris. Turgot was, however, a responsible financial manager; if one adjusts his projected budgets for 1775 and 1776 to eliminate debt repayments, the figures for ordinary revenue and expenditure remained in surplus.

Of all the finance ministers of the reign, Necker has undoubtedly aroused the strongest passions. This is largely a result of his unprecedented and controversial policy of funding France's participation in the American war almost entirely through loans. The war cost France 1,066 million *livres*, of which 997 million came from loans, 530 million of which were raised during Necker's tenure of office. Necker's critics claim that the particular form of loan he favoured, the life-rent bearing annual interest of up to 10 per cent, was ruinous. Yet Necker's loans policy was only one part of his general financial strategy. His aim was to maintain the crown's ability to service its extraordinary war debt by economies in ordinary expenditure. Through a sustained assault on venality in the royal financial administration, which brought not only savings but also efficiency gains, Necker claimed to have done just that, paring 84.5 million *livres* off the ordinary accounts. This assertion is credible if one accepts that his own figures are indeed accurate. More solid testimony to Necker's success lies in the relative buoyancy of the crown's credit throughout the American war.

Necker's fall marked a clear shift in financial policy, implemented by his three successors Joly de Fleury, d'Ormesson, and Calonne. This reversed his assault on venality in the finances, while preparing the way for a radical reform of the tax system that would increase yield by eliminating exemptions. Thus Joly de Fleury recreated many of the venal financial offices abolished by Necker, and in 1782 persuaded

---

[12] Cited in L. Laugier, *Turgot ou le mythe des réformes* (Paris, 1979), 83.

the parlement of Paris to register a third twentieth as an emergency wartime measure. His most interesting innovation, however, was an administrative one. This was his attempt to break the financial independence of ministers by instituting a 'committee of finance' composed of the king, Vergennes, Miromesnil, and himself, which would hold all government departments to account. This predictably ran into fierce opposition from the high-spending service ministers Castries and Ségur, whose opposition contributed to Joly de Fleury's resignation in March 1783.

Yet the committee of finance had a further significance that has until recently been overlooked: it was also intended as an instrument of long-term tax reform. In January 1783 the minister outlined an agenda which included revision of the twentieth, the *taille*, the capitation and much of the system of indirect taxation. Admittedly, the first results of this plan were not impressive. He resigned before he could inaugurate it, and his successor d'Ormesson was brought down in November 1783 by the concerted resistance of the tax farmers when he attempted to implement the planned reform of indirect taxation. Yet even though d'Ormesson's successor Calonne abolished the committee on entering office, the proposals for tax reform he presented to the Assembly of Notables in 1787 owed much to the programme first elaborated by Joly de Fleury and his collaborators five years previously.

Calonne was initially concerned to re-establish investor confidence in the monarchy after the botched assault on the general farm. He did this both by confirming and improving the position of the venal financiers, and by what has been dubbed an early 'New Deal' policy, stimulating the French economy through public spending. While confidence certainly returned in the short term, the ultimate result of this strategy was static revenue and rising expenditure. The most recent estimate of the total of Calonne's borrowing is 651 million *livres*. Having reversed Terray's, Turgot's, and Necker's policy of economies, and added approximately 45 million *livres* of his own to the monarchy's annual interest payments, by 1787 the controller-general was no longer able to service the accumulated extraordinary debt from ordinary revenue. This was the origin of the celebrated deficit, which he himself estimated at 112 million *livres*, that he was forced to announce to the Assembly of Notables.

Calonne's solution to the deficit problem was a recast tax system administered by the crown in partnership with provincial assemblies. This concentration on rationalizing the tax system, however, fatally ignored the real Achilles heel of the royal finances. This was the failure, often noted by contemporaries, to establish a sound system of public credit. Focusing simply on the deficit and its causes ignores the fact that Great Britain's extraordinary debt after the American war was substantially greater than France's. Yet the British political system did not collapse as a result, whereas the French one did. The issue was less the size of the debt than how effectively it was serviced, and here the French weakness is very apparent.

In this critical area, the French monarchy's heavy reliance on native financiers who doubled as venal administrators and as lenders to the treasury had major disadvantages. The consequent blurring of the demarcation line between public and private finance not only encouraged corruption, but left the financiers themselves danger-ously exposed. They were merely wealthy individuals with no major corporate or international resources, and proved unable to sustain the increasing demands from the crown as the financial situation worsened. With truly destructive timing, this ramshackle credit system collapsed just as the Assembly of Notables opened; between January and June 1787 five of the crown's most important venal financiers went bankrupt. Coupled with the shocking revelation of the deficit, this disaster doomed both Calonne's programme and the political and financial system he represented. With some justification, the Notables could argue that France's real problem was less inequal-ities in taxation than the corruption and maladministration of the royal finances themselves. It was the crown's failure to reform its credit system that dealt the decisive blow to the absolute monarchy.

Politics, 1781–1787

The death of Maurepas marked the end of an era. With his demise, the guiding hand the ministry needed to tackle the financial and political problems of the peace was removed. Since 1780 the Mentor had been visibly failing. Tangible proof of this was his inability to prevent candidates backed by the queen, in the shape of the marquis de Castries and the marquis de Ségur, from entering government for the first time late that year. Henceforth the central political theme of the reign was the descent of the ministry into civil war as the queen and her *protégés* pressed home the attack on the remaining defenders of Maurepas's system that had denied them power for so long.

In response to these pressures, Vergennes made one major bid to fill the Mentor's shoes, assuming a role in financial policy himself and backing Joly de Fleury's creation of the committee of finance. It was no coincidence that the committee's main targets, the navy and war ministries, were also those controlled by the queen's allies Castries and Ségur. From February to November 1783 Vergennes was briefly a true first minister, his power buttressed by the king's confidence and Joly de Fleury's new institutional arrangements. That autumn, however, the collapse of the general farm reform combined with accusations of cupidity from his enemies not only ended Vergennes's dominance but almost drove him from office. From 1784 to 1787 there was no predominant minister.

The obvious candidate to step in and provide the necesssary unity was the king himself. Indeed, with the demise of Maurepas there were clear signs he was preparing to do so; Castries noted in his diary that the day after the Mentor's death Louis XVI summoned a ministerial committee 'at which he spoke more than usual, as one who was saying to himself, "I intend to reign." '[13] Unfortunately, the king, who had shown himself a capable ruler within the limits of the protective system Maurepas had constructed around him, proved unable to contain the surge of factional ambition triggered by its decline. This was encouraged by the queen, by now armed with a dauphin, and increasingly determined to make her presence felt. Louis XVI lent consistent support to the committee of finance, but was alarmed by the credit crisis of late 1783 and his confidence in Vergennes, his favourite minister, was dented by the allegations of the latter's dishonesty.

Over the next two years the ministry became increasingly divided. Vergennes and Miromesnil clung on to office, but at the price of ceding the initiative to their enemies. In 1784, however, they scored a notable coup by winning Calonne over to their side, yet this did nothing to help the government. The battle-lines were now drawn across the council table, with the foreign minister, keeper of the seals, and controller-general facing the ministers for war and marine and a new recruit, Breteuil, minister for the royal household.

The most damaging aspect of this ministerial split was its impact on the parlement of Paris. One of Maurepas's cardinal principles had been to ensure the restored parlement's docility by careful political management. All the crown's reserves of patronage were deployed to dispose its leaders, the so-called 'ministerial party', towards cooperation with the government. This arrangement began to falter with the appointment of Calonne, whom the leading magistrates viewed first with suspicion on account of his early reputation as a foe of the parlements, and then with mounting alarm on account of his increasingly prodigal loans policy. Calonne responded by encouraging an emerging group of malcontents in the parlement to challenge the authority of their senior colleagues. This placed Vergennes and Miromesnil, who were fully aware of the dangerous consequences of alienating the 'ministerial party', in an increasingly impossible position.

All these tensions came to a head in the famous diamond necklace affair. When in 1785 cardinal de Rohan, anxious to win the queen's favour, was duped by a gang of confidence-tricksters into acquiring a fabulously expensive necklace which he had been induced to think the queen would like, he was tried for fraud in the parlement. The government and the 'ministerial party' seemed prepared to see him condemned unjustly to save the debatable reputation of an unpopular queen, but this gave all those magistrates discontented with their lot the cause they had been waiting for. They were helped by the fact that the ministry itself was palpably divided over the issue. Vergennes and Calonne, for example, worked consistently for the cardinal, while Breteuil did everything in his power to secure Rohan's conviction. As a result, the 'ministerial party' failed to deliver the required verdict; amid tumultuous scenes the cardinal was acquitted, and the monarchy's vital relationship with the parlement lay in ruins.

Yet despite this humiliation the senior magistrates remained in place, prime among them the first president, d'Aligre, by now Calonne's irreconcilable enemy. With the deficit becoming unmanageable, the controller-general had begun to elaborate a radical plan for tax reform and general administrative rationalization as the only solution to difficulties to which he himself had contributed. Yet Calonne knew that the 'ministerial party' as currently constituted would never support such a sweeping reform. He made a final attempt to dislodge d'Aligre in August 1786. It was probably the failure of this manœuvre that decided him to seek approval for his programme not from the parlement, but from a specially convoked and thus presumably more docile Assembly of Notables.

Recourse to the Notables, however, was more than a short-term decision; it was a damning verdict on over a decade of ministerial policy. It was a recognition that Maurepas's fragile reconstruction of the traditional relationship between crown and magistrates had failed, that dramatic measures were now called for, and that at the eleventh hour alternative collaborators had to be conjured up to carry them through. The monarchy was entering uncharted waters.

The final crisis

Calonne's programme was radical but not original; it was, as he himself told the Notables, the product of the best minds within the king's service for over a century. It was also wholeheartedly endorsed by the king: 'I did not sleep last night, but it was for joy',[14] he remarked to Calonne the day after the convocation of the Notables was decided. Calonne's reform package thus offers the best guide to the new type of monarchy Louis XVI would have most liked to see emerge from the ruins of the old. It was very much a blueprint for an enlightened absolute monarchy rather than a constitutional one. Its centrepiece was a new land tax, replacing the twentieths, to be levied without fiscal exemptions, and administered by a fresh system of provincial assemblies. These owed far more to Turgot's planned assemblies than Necker's administrations; they were organized in a hierarchy of parish, district and provincial assemblies, were not divided by order, and were purely consultative. The abolition of internal customs barriers and the reform of indirect taxation were also proposed.

Unfortunately, Calonne fatally underestimated the Notables' potential for resistance. By the time the assembly opened on 22 February 1787, circumstances had already turned against him. The death of his ally Vergennes the week before was a stroke of fate, but his

---

[14] Cited in V. Cronin, *Louis and Antoinette* (London, 1974), 260.

failure effectively to pack the Notables with allies of the Court was an inexcusable human error. As it was, Calonne's revelation of the deficit caused consternation among his audience (which the official record tactfully rendered as 'diverse murmurs') and completely over-shadowed his positive proposals. To counter the threat to their privil-eged status embodied in the land tax, Calonne's opponents in the assembly found it easy to shift the focus of debate onto government financial maladministration, and accuse the controller-general of wishing to raise taxes at will in a despotic fashion. Nor was this argument entirely self-interested; many of the high nobility and clergy in the Notables were prepared to give up their exemptions, but felt that radical new taxation required greater representation than they could provide, and were baffled by the yawning gap between Calonne's deficit and the surplus described only six years earlier by Necker.

Faced with an alarming situation and equally alarming remedies, the Notables' easiest course was to make a scapegoat of the controller-general. Accused of incompetence, prodigality and worse, Calonne was hounded from office on Easter Sunday 1787. This treat-ment was harsh, since he had honestly if belatedly tried to reform the abuses at which he had earlier connived. Chamfort, a trenchant liter-ary observer, put it best: 'He was applauded when he lit the fire, and condemned when he sounded the alarm'.[15]

The monarchy was increasingly being outstripped by events. It had stepped outside its traditional structures, revealed its financial incompetence, and lost control of the extraordinary assembly it had summoned to rubber-stamp its reform proposals. As ripples spread from the surface of a pond, the crown's attempt to enlist public opinion in its cause by summoning the Notables simply magnified the demand for a wider and more effective national representation. The first significant calls for the convocation of the estates general as the only body with the authority to consent to further taxation were heard in July 1787; a year later they had become unstoppable.

The man called to preside over the agony of the monarchy was the archbishop of Toulouse, Loménie de Brienne, who became on 26 August 1787 the last prime minister of the old regime. Intelligent,

---

[15] S. N. R. Chamfort, *Maximes et pensées, caractères et anecdotes*, ed. P. Grosclaude (2 vols., Paris, 1953–4), ii. 121.

liberal, afflicted with eczema, and probably an atheist, Brienne was Marie-Antoinette's favourite politician, and his elevation marked the decisive conquest of the ministry by the queen's party. Conversely, his triumph broke the king. Calonne's proposals had been Louis XVI's as well, Brienne had led the attack on them in the Notables, and having to capitulate to this virtual leader of the opposition was more than the monarch could bear. Behind the king's increasing escape from his misfortunes in hunting and immoderate eating one senses the onset of a depression that was to render him periodically *hors de combat* for the rest of his life.

Although he was reviled at the time as a shallow opportunist, it is fairer to see Brienne as a pragmatic political operator who did what he could to retrieve an increasingly impossible situation. His first instinct was to use his initial credit to persuade the parlement to register a modified land tax, but the magistrates replied that only the estates general could concede such a measure. By November 1787, following France's humiliating failure to intervene in the Dutch crisis, a bargain appeared to have been struck guaranteeing the crown a final massive loan of 500 million *livres* in exchange for the abandonment of Calonne's programme and the promise of the estates general within five years. The plan was sound; if it now seemed unlikely that the estates general could be avoided (and Brienne, whose leanings were probably towards constitutional monarchy, may even have welcomed this), at least the crown had gained five years to put its own house in order and prepare for the event.

This delicate compromise, however, was blown apart by the mismanagement of the royal session called to register it on 19 November. For this occasion, the magistrates had been joined by the peers of the realm. It was expected that majority voting would be observed, and it is likely that had this been so, the royal measures would have passed. Yet Louis XVI, for reasons which still remain mysterious, decided instead to order registration on his own authority. As he did so, there was a shocked silence. The duke d'Orléans protested that this was illegal. Completely taken aback, the king rapped out some spectacularly ill-chosen words: 'It is legal because I wish it'. The participants' worst suspicions of the French monarchy's intrinsic despotism were confirmed, and they refused to recognize the forced registration.

Brienne's only remaining option was to imitate Maupeou and break the parlements, which he attempted on 8 May 1788 by confining them to purely judicial functions and transferring their political powers to a new, central plenary court. Yet this was not simply an act of 'despotism', since the plenary court was given significant powers. The promise to call the estates general before 1792 was also repeated. There is no reason to doubt the sincerity of this commitment, on which Brienne himself laid great stress in his posthumously published memoirs.

These subtleties were lost on public opinion. The immediate result of the May coup was an outburst of popular protest in support of the injured parlements. Troops had to be called in to quell riots at Rennes and Pau and in the famous 'day of tiles' at Grenoble, where the townspeople pelted the soldiers with bits of roofing from their houses. Ominously, the first signs of weakness in the armed forces now appeared, less in the case of the rank-and-file soldiers, who kept discipline even when ordered to fire into the crowds, than of their commanders. Here, the rigid military promotion system meant that at this critical juncture the government was forced to rely on senior officers of advanced years and impaired capacity. The aged and dying marshal de Biron showed himself an unreliable instrument of force in Paris, while at Grenoble the 86-year-old marshal de Vaux was immobilized by retention of urine.

What the disturbances did do was destroy what was left of the crown's credit. On 16 August, Brienne was forced to concede that the treasury was empty. On the 25th, having promised to call the estates general for 1 May 1789 in a desperate attempt to stave off his own fall, he resigned. The recall of Necker, the only royal servant who had retained some reputation in recent years, was a further step towards the fall of the regime. The first minister of finance, as he now became, had no policy for managing the fast-approaching meeting of the estates general. Most important of all, he gave no clear lead on the looming issue that in the summer of 1789 was to transform the crisis of the monarchy into a full-blown revolution, that of whether the estates when they met should vote by order or by head.

Significantly, the secret negotiations that brought Necker back into the ministry were handled not by Louis XVI, but by Marie-Antoinette and her closest adviser, the Austrian ambassador Mercy-Argenteau. Amazingly, it was not a minister sent by the king, but Mercy, on the orders of the queen, who went to Brienne to demand his resignation. The reason for these unprecedented actions was probably that depression had rendered the king incapable of action. Marie-Antoinette hinted as much to Mercy on 19 August. Commenting on the need to restrain Necker once he was back in government, she added that she did not feel capable of doing this, while 'the person above me is in no fit state'.[16] The disintegration of the monarchy was paralleled by the disintegration of the monarch.

The prime cause of the fall of the absolute monarchy was its failure to break free of the bonds of the social hierarchy and transform its basis of support. Turgot's and Necker's early attempts to do so were swiftly defeated. The most systematic effort of all, Calonne's programme of 1787, came too late, and had authoritarian overtones that rendered it easy prey to the fatal accusation of despotism. Ironically, the crown's blundering efforts to increase its resources by finding a more tractable political partner than the privileged orders ended with the resurrection of the one body that posed most dangers to the royal authority, the estates general. By September 1788, only one thing was clear: whatever the future held in store, the old regime was at an end.

---

[16] *Lettres de Marie Antoinette*, ii. 123.

Conclusion

William Doyle

In 1788, Maximilien Robespierre was a 30-year-old lawyer in sleepy provincial Arras, overeducated for his prospects, surviving on the occasional earnings of hopeless briefs and a petty part-time judgeship, reading Rousseau, and dreaming of utopia. Six years later, almost as much to his surprise as anyone's, he dominated the government of France, still dreaming, but now in a position to massacre anybody who did not share his dreams. The French Revolution would be the midwife of countless other life changes scarcely less astonishing. 'Political writers', Robespierre would later declare, '. . . had in no way foreseen this Revolution', much less any other sort. For the vacuum of power produced by the collapse of the old monarchy forced everybody who lived in France to rethink every aspect of their existence. The authority to which the French instinctively looked had suddenly disappeared, and they had to reconstruct their world from its very foundations.

That did not mean from nothing. The revolutionary generation brought to the upheavals confronting it minds stocked with ideas, attitudes, and reflexes moulded by education and experience when wholesale changes had been quite beyond expectation. As a member of the National Assembly wrote to a provincial friend in 1790: 'Today it is impossible, in rebuilding an edifice just demolished, not to employ some of the materials which made it up'.[1] And so, with one authority vanished, they cast about for another. They found it in the the Nation, soon to be invested with all the absolute sovereignty of the fallen monarchy. They used it to force through a range of rationalizing and humanitarian reforms which had become

[1] G. Debien (ed.), *Correspondance de Félix Faulcon* (2 vols., Poitiers, 1939–53), ii. 165.

commonplaces of public discussion since mid-century, but which had only been hesitantly tried, if at all, by kings and ministers only too conscious of the constraints upon them. And, with the world turned upside-down, many found the opportunity for wreaking revenge on their former enemies or oppressors irresistible. Thus lords, nobles, judges, priests, tax collectors, even in the end the king and queen themselves, all suffered to one degree or another for the authority they had wielded before 1789. Innumerable private quarrels were also resolved or transformed now that the old rules had changed. The one thing everybody agreed on was that all this had been unimaginable beforehand. Looked back upon from revolutionary times, the old regime, good or bad, seemed an age of immobility and changeless routine, when nothing of importance had happened, or could happen. One of the founding myths of the French Revolution was the myth of the *Ancien Régime.*

Nobody who has read the preceding pages of this book could accept this myth. France and the French underwent profound changes between the 1650s and 1788, even if they occurred less suddenly and spectacularly than over the subsequent generation. The population rose to unprecedented levels, the economy expanded vigorously (if unevenly), and an independent public opinion emerged which grew accustomed to making judgements about everything. By the 1780s the periodical press, virtually unknown when Louis XIV established the all-controlling template of absolute monarchy, had a readership of half a million. This in turn reflected shifts in the balance of society, as the recognized elites came to comprehend not just the nobility, but the whole community of educated property owners. What failed to change was the monarchy and its ambitions. Louis XVI, advised until a mere seven years before the collapse of his authority by a man who had first been a minister in 1718, never questioned until it was too late the nexus of nobility and corporate privilege upon which his mighty ancestor had consolidated his rule after the Fronde. Nor did he or his foreign minister Vergennes, preening themselves still as the guarantors of the peace of Westphalia, see France as entitled to anything less than the hegemonic European power that Louis XIV had thought his by right. The problem was, in a world where new powers and new sources of power were emerging to challenge French pretensions, how to marshal the kingdom's resources to sustain these claims. That the resources existed was shown by the way the revolutionaries and Napoleon were able over the subsequent generation to release them, and thereby dominate Europe in a way that even Louis XIV would have envied. Absolute monarchy could not manage it.

Ministers from Colbert to Choiseul recognized that part of the power of the 'modern Carthage' across the Channel depended on a worldwide empire; but they could never find enough resources to create a French one of comparable range and coherence. Vergennes's attempt, if not to recreate the empire shattered in 1763, at least to cripple its triumphant British rival, only hastened the monarchy's final bankruptcy. Meanwhile the army scarcely fired a shot in anger in Europe after the disasters of the Seven Years War, while continental rivals carved up Poland, picked at the shrinking shadow of the Ottoman empire, and squashed helpless French protégés in Holland. Even sustaining the appearance of military readiness strained budgets in a country where subjects considered themselves overtaxed, would not trust their money with a state bank, but regarded debt renunciation and even consolidation as a breach of public faith. The apparently painless success of the American war only reinforced resistance to innovations which seemed unnecessary. Meanwhile, attempts to boost taxable wealth by economic stimulation were limited by privileges and property rights purchased from previous kings, often several times over, and now indestructible unless compensation could be found. Policies that ostensibly cost nothing to introduce, such as free trade in grain, undermined the subject's faith in royal paternal benevolence. And although there were no institutions capable of stopping a determined monarch from overriding any resistance, no king wanted to appear a despot. It was accordingly essential to allow the parlements to obstruct and remonstrate, however much this educated the public in the rationale and techniques of disobedience.

The result was not inertia. It was paralysis. It was no longer possible to run an eighteenth century polity on seventeenth-century principles. And so, within seven years of the last great triumph of Bourbon arms at Yorktown (1781) the king of France found himself internationally scorned for his inability to help his Dutch friends, suspending payments to his creditors, recalling the Swiss conjuror Necker whose sleight of hand had already fatally deluded his subjects, and entrusting the kingdom's fate to the estates general, an institution that embodied no contemporary realities. The old monarchy's bankruptcy was as much intellectual and imaginative as financial. It would take new men, after a new start, to show the world how formidable in every sphere the French could still be.

Further reading

General

No single volume covers the whole of this period. A survey of most of it by a leading French authority is E. Le Roy Ladurie, *The Ancien Regime: A History of France, 1610–1774* (Oxford, 1996). The earlier part, and its essential background, is covered in R. Briggs, *Early Modern France, 1560–1715* (2nd edition, Oxford, 1998). Problems of overall interpretation are addressed in P. R. Campbell, *The Ancien Regime in France* (Oxford, 1988) and W. Doyle, *The Ancien Regime* (2nd edition, London, 2001). The most authoritative recent French treatment of the eighteenth century is D. Roche, *France in the Enlightenment* (Cambridge, Mass., 1998), while a much older but still very accessible introduction is J. Lough, *An Introduction to Eighteenth Century France* (London, 1960). International affairs are conveniently encapsulated in J. Black, *From Louis XIV to Napoleon: The Fate of a Great Power* (London, 1999).

The economy

Two works by great mid-century French masters have been translated into English: E. Le Roy Ladurie, *The Peasants of Languedoc* (Urbana, Ill., 1976) and P. Goubert, *The French Peasantry in the Seventeenth Century* (Cambridge, 1986). A challenging new interpretation of long-term agricultural history is P. T. Hoffman, *Growth in a Traditional Society: The French Countryside, 1450–1815* (Princeton, 1996), while a detailed example of the diversity of rural life is to be found in L. Vardi, *The Land and the Loom: Peasants and Profit in Northern France, 1680–1800* (Durham, NC, 1993). A long-term view of a classic industrial centre is taken by J. K. J. Thompson, *Clermont-de-Lodève, 1633–1789. Fluctuations in the Position of a Languedocian Cloth-Making Town* (Cambridge, 1982). Fruitful and authoritative comparisons between British and French economic growth are made by F. Crouzet, *Britain Ascendant: Comparative Studies in Franco-British Economic History* (Cambridge, 1990). A well-established starting point for studying policy-making is C. W. Cole, *Colbert and a Century of French Mercantilism* (2 vols., New York, 1939). Contemporary critiques of Colbertism can be followed in R. L. Meek, *The Economics of Physiocracy* (Glasgow, 1963). The misconceptions they fostered about the urban world of work are dispelled in M. Sonenscher, *Work and Wages: Natural Law, Politics, and the Eighteenth Century French Trades* (Cambridge, 1989). The organization of indirect tax collection is anatomized in G. T. Matthews, *The Royal General Farms in the Eighteenth Century* (New

York, 1958), while problems of direct taxation stand out from M. D. Kwass, *Privilege and the Politics of Taxation in Eighteenth Century France. Liberté, égalité, fiscalité* (Cambridge, 2000). The classic survey of the central organization of the royal finances remains J. F. Bosher, *French Finances, 1770–1795: From Business to Bureaucracy* (Cambridge, 1970), while a central question is reviewed afresh in E. N. White, 'Was there a solution to the ancien regime's financial dilemma?', *Journal of Economic History*, 49 (1989), 545–68.

Society

The lowest reaches of society are memorably surveyed by O. Hufton, *The Poor of Eighteenth Century France, 1750–1789* (Oxford, 1974). Perhaps the most accessible introduction to the peasantry, at least in the later part of the period, is in the earlier chapters of P. M. Jones, *The Peasantry in the French Revolution* (Cambridge, 1989). Peasant behaviour over the long term is shown by J. Dewald, *Pont-Saint-Pierre, 1389–1789: Lordship, Community and Capitalism in Early Modern France* (Berkeley, Calif., 1987) to be less brutish and routine-dominated than is often assumed. D. Roche, *The People of Paris: An Essay in Popular Culture in the Eighteenth Century* (Leamington Spa, 1987) is authoritative on the metropolitan populace, while the culture of working populations in general is the subject of W. H. Sewell, *Work and Revolution in France: The Language of Labour from the Old Regime to 1848* (Cambridge, 1980). C. C. Fairchilds, *Domestic Enemies. Servants and their Masters in Old Regime France* (Baltimore, 1984) brings out an often forgotten element in urban populations; and the social role of cities more generally is explored by the essays in P. Benedict (ed.), *Cities in Early Modern France* (London, 1989). A vigorous but contentious approach to social elites is G. Chaussinand-Nogaret, *The French Nobility in the Eighteenth Century. From Feudalism to Enlightenment* (Cambridge, 1985). The main way of entering their ranks is one of the subjects of W. Doyle, *Venality: The Sale of Offices in Eighteenth Century France* (Oxford, 1996). The workings of privilege in general are exemplified in G. Bossenga, *The Politics of Privilege. Old Regime and Revolution in Lille* (Cambridge, 1991). The intimacies of social life are explored in J. L. Flandrin, *Families in Former Times: Kinship, Household and Sexuality* (Cambridge, 1979) and A. Pardailhe'-Galabrun, *The Birth of Intimacy: Privacy and Domestic Life in Early Modern Paris* (Philadelphia, 1991).

Culture and religion

An enduringly important overview and interpretation of the development of European philosophy is E. Cassirer, *The Philosophy of the Enlightenment* (1932; Princeton, 1968). More emphasis on social and political theory, as well as the attack on religion, can be found in P. Gay, *The Enlightenment: An*

Interpretation (2 vols., New York, 1966). An influential analysis of how criticism of the old regime emerged from interaction between social developments and new forms of communication is J. Habermas, *The Structural Transformation of the Public Sphere. An Enquiry into a Category of Bourgeois Society* (1962; Cambridge, Mass., 1989). The earlier essays of a pioneer in the interaction of 'high' and 'low' Enlightenment are collected in R. Darnton, *The Literary Underground of the Old Regime* (Cambridge, Mass., 1982), while the importance of art criticism in the intellectual development of the period is the subject of T. Crow, *Painters and Public Life in Eighteenth Century Paris* (London, 1985). The importance of salons and the women who ran them is the subject of D. Goodman, *The Republic of Letters: A Cultural History of the French Enlightenment* (Ithaca, NY, 1994). A path-breaking French survey of half a century's work on the transformation of culture in the eighteenth century is R. Chartier, *The Cultural Origins of the French Revolution* (Durham, NC, 1989); while D. A. Bell, *The National and the Sacred: The Origins of Nationalism in Eighteenth Century France* (Cambridge, Mass., 2001) explores the transformation of national and patriotic sentiment, with an emphasis on their relation to the 'privatization' of religious belief. The contribution of religious heterodoxy, especially Jansenism, to the collapse of the old order is the subject of D. Van Kley, *The Religious Origins of the French Revolution* (New Haven, 1996), while a vast survey of institutional religious life in general is provided by J. McManners, *Church and Society in Eighteenth Century France* (2 vols., Oxford, 1998).

France overseas

The *Historical Atlas of Canada*, eds. C. Harris and L. Dechêne, vol. I (Toronto, 1987) contains innovative essays. Other valuable treatments are by D. Miquelon, *New France 1701–1744: 'A Supplement to Europe'* (Toronto, 1987) and A. Greer, *The People of New France* (Toronto, 1997). J. Demos, *The Unredeemed Captive: A Family Story from Early America* (New York, 1994) covers the interaction between Natives and colonists through a celebrated individual case. On the Caribbean, P. R. Boucher, *Cannibal Encounters. Europeans and Island Caribs, 1492–1763* (Baltimore, 1992) sets the scene, while C. Fick, *The Making of Haiti: The Saint-Domingue Revolution from Below* (Knoxville, 1990) both covers the most important French settlement and contains valuable chapters on colonial slavery in general. How the slave economy interacted with the metropolis is studied in R. L. Stein, *The French Sugar Business in the Eighteenth Century* (Baton Rouge, 1988). A characteristic approach to colonization is analysed in L. Blussé and F. Gaastra (eds.), *Companies and Trade. Essays on Overseas Trading Companies during the Ancien Regime* (Leiden, 1981), while their impact in the east can be studied in H. Furber, *Rival Empires of Trade in the Orient, 1600–1800* (Minneapolis, 1976).

The state and political culture

A maddeningly idiosyncratic but wide-ranging work of reference is R. Mousnier, *The Institutions of France under the Absolute Monarchy, 1589–1789* (2 vols., Chicago, 1979). A more up-to-date survey of the whole period is J. B. Collins, *The State in Early Modern France* (Cambridge, 1995), while essential background is clearly set out in D. Parker, *The Making of French Absolutism* (London, 1983). A remarkable collection of essays is K. M. Baker (ed.), *The French Revolution and the Creation of Modern Political Culture*, i: *The Political Culture of the Old Regime* (Oxford, 1987). Key institutions are surveyed by J. H. Shennan, *The Parlement of Paris* (London, 1968) and V. R. Gruder, *The Royal Provincial Intendants* (Ithaca, NY, 1968). New elements in eighteenth-century political culture are the subject of D. A. Bell, *Lawyers and Citizens: The Making of a Political Elite in Old Regime France* (New York, 1994), J. R. Censer, *The French Press in the Age of Enlightenment* (London, 1994) and S. Maza, *Private Lives and Public Affairs: The Causes Célèbres of Prerevolutionary France* (Berkeley, Calif., 1993). How the Maupeou Revolution changed everything is explained in D. Echeverria, *The Maupeou Revolution: A Study in the History of Libertarianism. France, 1770–1774* (Baton Rouge, La., 1985). While the political importance of public opinion is now widely acknowledged, its novelty remains contentious: see J. A. W. Gunn, *Queen of the World: Opinion in the Public Life of France from the Renaissance to the Revolution* (Oxford, 1995).

Politics: Louis XIV

A sound and reliable overview is D. J. Sturdy, *Louis XIV* (London, 1998). Perhaps the most accessible of many massive biographies is J. B. Wolf, *Louis XIV* (London, 1968). An uneven collection of essays providing a transatlantic update on the whole reign is P. Sonnino (ed.), *The Reign of Louis XIV* (London, 1990), while the military and diplomatic sides are surveyed in J. A. Lynn, *The Wars of Louis XIV* (London, 1999). R. Mettam, *Power and Faction in Louis XIV's France* (Oxford, 1988) shows how the king's power worked at the centre; a classic study of the periphery is W. H. Beik, *Absolutism and Society in Seventeenth Century France: State Power and Provincial Aristocracy in Langue-doc* (Cambridge, 1985). A superb analysis of a key crisis is P. Sonnino, *Louis XIV and the Origins of the Dutch War* (Cambridge, 1988). A key aspect of the royal style is anatomized by P. Burke, *The Fabrication of Louis XIV* (London, 1992). Of enduring value on a central episode and problem is W. C. Scoville, *The Persecution of the Huguenots and French Economic Development, 1680–1720* (Berkeley and Los Angeles, 1960). Other religious problems are covered in W. Doyle, *Jansenism* (London, 2000), while less overt opposition is brilliantly discussed in L. Rothkrug, *Opposition to Louis XIV: The Political and Social Origins of the French Enlightenment* (Princeton, 1965).

Politics: Louis XV

A readable introduction to the king's private life remains N. Mitford, *Madame de Pompadour* (London, 1954). On the regent, J. H. Shennan, *Philippe, Duke of Orleans: Regent of France, 1715–1723* (London, 1979) is reliable, as is A. Murphy, *John Law: Economic Theorist and Policy-Maker* (Oxford, 1997) on his most notorious collaborator. The ministry of Fleury is put into a wider context by P. R. Campbell, *Power and Politics in Old Regime France, 1720–1745* (London, 1996), while one of the most important problems with which he had to deal is the subject of B. R. Kreiser, *Miracles, Convulsions and Ecclesiastical Politics in Early Eighteenth Century France* (Princeton, 1978). Mid-century politics are best approached through J. Rogister, *Louis XV and the Parlement of Paris, 1737–1754* (Cambridge, 1995) and J. Swann, *Politics and the Parlement of Paris under Louis XV, 1754–1774* (Cambridge, 1995). The burden of international conflict is analysed in J. C. Riley, *The Seven Years' War and the Old Regime in France: The Economic and Financial Toll* (Princeton, 1996). Post-war problems are covered by D. Van Kley, *The Jansenists and the Expulsion of the Jesuits from France, 1757–1765* (New Haven, 1975), and S. L. Kaplan, *Bread, Politics and Political Economy in the Reign of Louis XV* (2 vols., The Hague, 1976). In the absence of a worthwhile book in English on Maupeou, see W. Doyle, 'The Parlements of France and the Breakdown of the Old Regime, 1774–1788', in the same author's *Officers, Nobles and Revolutionaries: Essays on Eighteenth Century France* (London, 1995), 1–47.

Politics: Louis XVI

Fortunately, the pre-revolutionary chapters of J. Hardman's *Louis XVI* (London, 1993) are the best. The same author's *French Politics, 1774–1789* (London, 1994) is also invaluable. There are good biographical studies of key ministers, including D. Dakin, *Turgot and the Ancien Regime in France* (London, 1939), R. D. Harris, *Necker, Reform Statesman of the Ancien Regime* (Berkeley, Calif., 1979), and M. Price, *Preserving the Monarchy. The Comte de Vergennes, 1774–1787* (Cambridge, 1995). Relations with the parlements are covered in B. Stone, *The French Parlements and the Crisis of the Old Regime* (Chapel Hill, N C, 1986), while foreign affairs are conveniently summarized in O. T. Murphy, *The Diplomatic Retreat of France and Public Opinion on the Eve of the French Revolution, 1783–89* (Washington, DC, 1998). The classic treatment of the regime's terminal crisis is J. Egret, *The French Prerevolution, 1787–1788* (Chicago, 1977), but it is put into a wider context by W. Doyle, *Origins of the French Revolution* (3rd edition, Oxford, 1999), and P. M. Jones, *Reform and Revolution in France: The Politics of Transition, 1774–1791* (Cambridge, 1995).

Chronology

1698–1700	Partition treaties on Spanish empire; Charles II of Spain dies
1699	First French settlement in Louisiana
1701–13	War of the Spanish Succession
1704	French defeat at Blenheim
1709–10	Economic crisis: 'the great winter', worst of the century
1709	Closure of Jansenist abbey of Port-Royal; indecisive battle of Malplaquet
1710	Introduction of tenth (*dixième*)
1711	French victory at Denain
1711–12	Most heirs to throne die; legitimation of royal bastards
1713	Peace of Utrecht: France loses peninsular Acadia and Newfoundland; bull *Unigenitus* promulgated
1715	Death of Louis XIV; accession of Louis XV; full right of remonstrance restored to parlements
1715–23	Regency of Philippe d'Orléans
1716	John Law establishes bank; chamber of justice
1717	Jansenist appeal against *Unigenitus*
1718	Abolition of conciliar government (*polysynodie*); New Orleans founded
1720	Louisbourg founded; collapse of Law's 'System'
1721	Montesquieu, *Persian Letters*
1723	Death of the regent d'Orléans
1726	*Livre tournois* stabilized; ministry of Fleury begins
1730	*Unigenitus* declared a law of church and state
1732	Convulsions of Saint-Médard
1733–8	War of the Polish Succession
1734	Voltaire, *Philosophical Letters*
1738	Forced labour on roads (*corvée*) introduced; Peace of Vienna: France guaranteed succession to Lorraine
1740	Poor harvest and floods
1740–8	War of the Austrian Succession
1743	Death of Fleury
1744	Louis XV's illness at Metz: proclaimed 'well-beloved'
1745	Victory of Fontenoy; presentation of Mme de Pompadour

1748	Peace of Aix-la-Chapelle; Montesquieu, *Spirit of the Laws*
1749	Establishment of twentieth (*vingtième*); refusal of sacraments to Jansenists
1751	*Encyclopédie* begins publication
1753–4	Exile of parlement of Paris
1754	Law of silence on religious disputes
1755	Hostilities in North America; deportation of Acadians
1756	Diplomatic revolution brings France and Austria into alliance
1756–63	Seven Years War
1757	(Jan.) Damiens stabs Louis XV; (Nov.) Prussians defeat French at Rosbach
1759	Fall of Quebec
1761	Attack on Jesuits in parlement of Paris begins
1762	Rousseau, *Social Contract*; *Emile*; Calas case in Toulouse
1763	Peace of Paris: loss of Canada
1764	Death of Pompadour; expulsion of Jesuits; first relaxation of restrictions on grain trade
1765	Brittany affair
1766	Lorraine becomes French on death of king-duke Stanislas; 'Flagellation' session in parlement of Paris
1767–70	Series of poor harvests followed by bread riots
1768	Annexation of Corsica
1770	Partial bankruptcy of Terray; future Louis XVI marries Marie-Antoinette of Austria
1771	Maupeou remodels the parlements
1774	Death of Louis XV; accession of Louis XVI; fall of Maupeou and Terray
1775	'Flour War'
1776	Fall of Turgot; military venality abolished
1778–83	French participation in American War of Independence
1778	Necker's 'provincial administrations'; death of Voltaire and Rousseau
1781	*Compte rendu* of Necker; resignation of Necker; death of Maurepas; Ségur ordinance requiring nobility of army officers; Franco-American victory at Yorktown
1783	Peace of Paris; committee of finance established; Calonne joins ministry

1785–6	Diamond necklace affair
1785	Beaumarchais's *Marriage of Figaro* first performed
1786	Commercial treaty with Great Britain; (20 Aug.) Calonne presents reform plans to Louis XVI
1787	(Feb.–May) Assembly of Notables; fall of Calonne; (Sept.) Prussians invade Holland; (Nov.) disastrous royal session in parlement of Paris
1788	(May) Lamoignon attempts reform of parlements; (13 July) harvest destroyed; (16 Aug.) payments from treasury suspended; fall of Brienne, recall of Necker

Maps

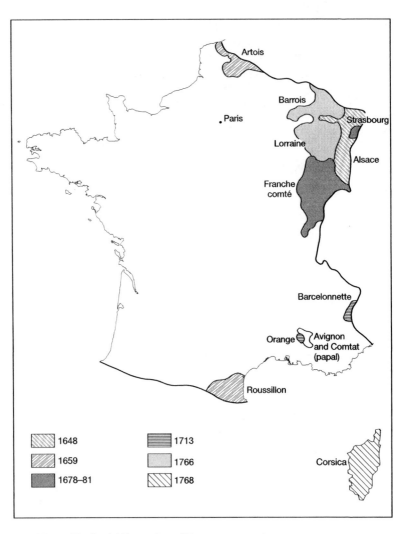

Map 1 Territorial Expansion of France, 1648–1678

Map 2 Administrative Divisions. Amended from J. Lough, *An Introduction to Eighteenth Century France* (London, 1960).

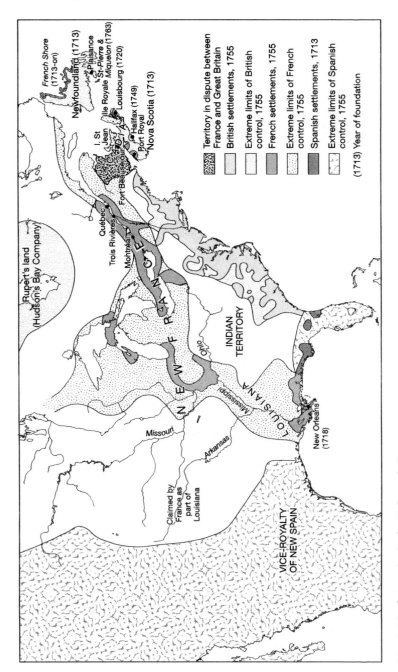

Map 3 North America in the Eighteenth Century

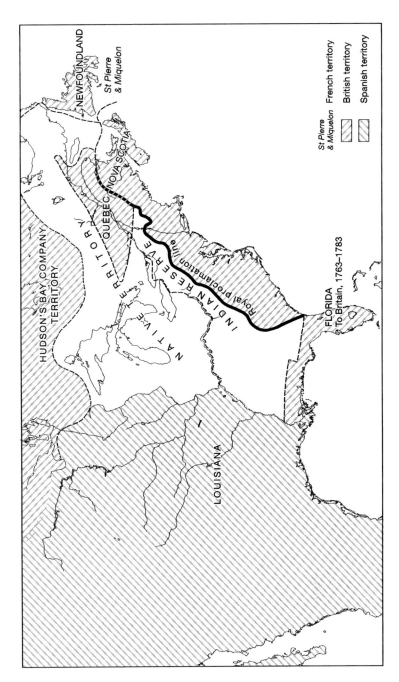

Map 4 North America after the Treaty of Paris, 1763

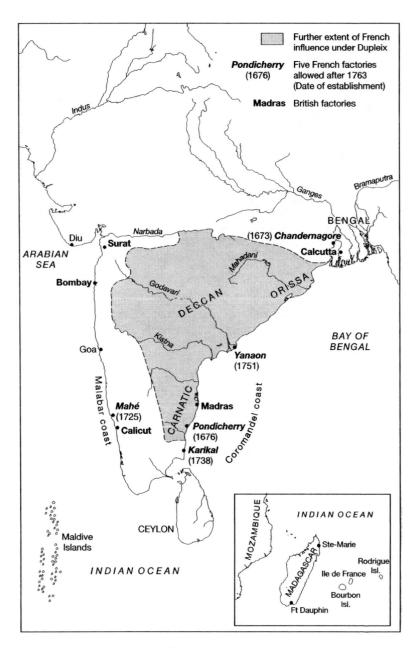

Map 5 India in the Age of Dupleix

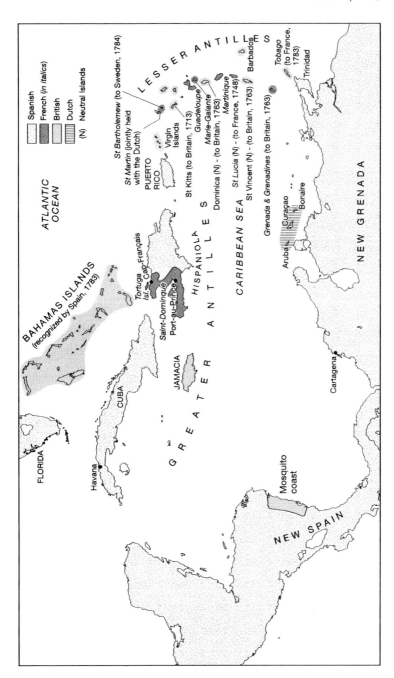

Map 6 The West Indies in the Eighteenth Century

Spanish

French (*in italics*)

British

Dutch

(N) Neutral Islands

ATLANTIC OCEAN

LESSER ANTILLES

St Bartholemew (to Sweden, 1784)

St Martin (jointly held with the Dutch)

PUERTO RICO

Virgin Islands

St Kitts (to Britain, 1713)

Guadeloupe

Marie-Galante

Martinique

Dominica (N) – (to Britain, 1763)

St Lucia (N) – (to France, 1748)

St Vincent (N) – (to Britain, 1763)

Barbados

Grenada & Grenadines (to Britain, 1763)

Tobago (to France, 1783)

Trinidad

CARIBBEAN SEA

Aruba

Curaçao

Bonaire

NEW GRENADA

Cartagena

BAHAMAS ISLANDS (recognized by Spain, 1783)

Tortuga Isl.

Cap-Français

Saint-Domingue

Port-au-Prince

HISPANIOLA

GREATER ANTILLES

JAMAICA

CUBA

FLORIDA

Havana

Mosquito coast

NEW SPAIN

Index